In Praise of *Our Black Year* by Maggie Anderson

"Our Black Year is a blistering, honest journal of the Andersons' efforts to buy black, and those efforts can only be described as Herculean. . . . A brisk call to action, offering clear-eyed perspective on how African Americans got to where they are today and what they can do to support black business owners. In Maggie Anderson's eyes, it's a moral imperative."—*BookPage*

"[A] dynamite subject . . . an effective probe into how African Americans spend so much money that flows so overwhelmingly out of their community."
—*Publishers Weekly*

"Any serious attempt to close the racial wealth gap and build Black American wealth must leverage the trillion dollars of buying power controlled by the Black American consumer. In *Our Black Year*, Maggie Anderson offers a clear, cogent, and intensely personal view of one family's journey to do just this. An important book that provides a path for others to follow."
—**Marc Morial, president and CEO, National Urban League**

"The Empowerment Experiment is a movement that the African American community needs to embrace. As African American entrepreneurs and consumers, we must have a better understanding of the business segments that offer the greatest economic opportunities. Maggie Anderson chronicles her own family's commitment to patronize only Black-owned businesses for a whole year in this phenomenal book."
—**Ron Busby Sr., president, U.S. Black Chamber, Inc.**

"All those charged with the responsibility of leading twenty-first-century organizations will learn valuable lessons by internalizing and acting on the conclusions laid out in *Our Black Year*. Bravo! We all now have something worth reading on this critical subject of supporting and thus growing Black businesses in America."—**George C. Fraser, author, *Success Runs in Our Race***

"Thank God for this level of commitment to our Black community. *Our Black Year* is an incredible documentation of what we all could do, if we just made up our minds to do it."
—**Cathy Hughes, founder/chairperson, Radio/TV One, Inc.**

Equality is entitled.
Empowerment is earned.

Our Black Year

One Family's Quest to
Buy Black in America's Racially
Divided Economy

Maggie Anderson

Founder of The Empowerment Experiment

with Ted Gregory

PublicAffairs
New York

PublicAffairs books are available at special discounts for bulk purchases in the U.S. by
corporations, institutions, and other organizations. For more information, please contact the
Special Markets Department at the Perseus Books Group, 2300 Chestnut Street, Suite 200,
Philadelphia, PA 19103, call (800) 810-4145, ext. 5000, or e-mail
special.markets@perseusbooks.com.

"The Empowerment Experiment: The Findings and Potential Impact on Black-Owned
Businesses" (© 2010 Dwetri Addy et al.) reprinted with permission of the study's authors.

Book Design by Brent Wilcox

The Library of Congress has cataloged the hardcover as follows:
Anderson, Maggie.
    Our black year : one family's quest to buy Black in America's racially divided economy /
Maggie Anderson with Ted Gregory.
        p.   cm.
    Includes bibliographical references and index.
    ISBN 978-1-61039-024-8 (hardcover : alk. paper) — ISBN 978-1-61039-025-5 (e-book)
1. African American business enterprises.   2. African Americans—Economic conditions.
3. Consumer behavior.   4. United States—Race relations.   I. Gregory, Ted.   II. Title.
    HD2358.5.U6A53 2012
    330.9730089'96073—dc23

                                                                                    2011040609

ISBN 978-1-61039-228-0 (paperback)
LSC-C
10 9 8 7 6

To Mima, for showing me how to love,
how to fight, and that oftentimes,
there is no difference.

Contents

Introduction

It all started with dinner.

In 2004 my husband, John, and I were celebrating our fifth wedding anniversary. That night we were the only Black people at Tru, a five-star restaurant in Chicago's ultra-exclusive Gold Coast neighborhood. Instead of enjoying the romance of the moment, though, I ruined it by bringing up the discouraging status of Blacks in America. Although we moved on to other topics, they all seemed to lead us back to how fortunate we were and how we should be doing more to help improve the situation—The Black Situation.

John, a highly educated financial planner, talked about how too few Blacks own businesses, and this has led directly to forlorn neighborhoods and a general hopelessness that ultimately results in crime, violence, drug abuse, lousy academic performance in miserable schools, teen pregnancy, and shattered families. Eliminate economic disparity and you start to make structural progress on all these intractable problems.

Don't get me wrong. Black people have made great progress in America. We fought for and achieved integration in housing and education, the right to vote, and equal employment opportunities. When we came together to elect the nation's first Black president, it sparked an awareness of our power. And yet there is no awesome American success story like that of Wal-Mart, Penney's, Hilton, Hershey, Sears, or McDonald's coming from a Black family because there is nothing in our culture, history, or experience that tells us we can do it. And it won't happen until we have a sense of pride in each other, like our Hispanic counterparts; until we believe in the possibility of intergenerational economic empowerment, like our Jewish friends; and until we make it our mission to become a successful group of entrepreneurs, like our Asian and Middle Eastern peers.

At the moment Blacks are a distant third to Asians and Hispanics in every measure of entrepreneurial progress, including success rates and revenue growth, even though just forty years ago we were first by a wide margin. Our neighborhoods had those grocery stores, dry cleaners, department stores, drugstores, and banks—all owned by local entrepreneurs. Now so many of our neighborhoods are run down that everyone has come to accept this as the norm. Black kids can go their whole lives without ever encountering a Black business owner.

These communities are starving to death because the money Blacks earn and spend—nearly $1 trillion of buying power—flows right out of those neighborhoods. Maybe you've heard the jokes about it, jokes along the lines of "Man, he was running away from the cops faster than a Black dollar out of the community!"

Only those people directly affected by these circumstances seemed to care—not people like us.

Okay, I thought. Maybe next time we'll go to a Black-owned restaurant for our anniversary. But what would that accomplish, aside from pacifying our guilt?

Anyway, who has the time to figure this out? We had our own great lives to build. John worked his way up from a middle-class Detroit neighborhood to Harvard and then earned an MBA at Northwestern. I grew up in drug-infested Liberty City, Miami, one of the poorest, most violent neighborhoods in America, and made it to Emory University, followed by the University of Chicago for a law degree and an MBA. We had achieved great success in corporate America—John as a financial adviser, me as a strategy consultant—but we hadn't completely lost our moral compasses. John is active in 100 Black Men, a national mentoring organization that enhances the educational and economic empowerment of the Black community. I had been active in the Rainbow PUSH Coalition of religious and social development organizations led by Rev. Jesse Jackson Sr. We were mentoring youth at our church, and we donated to the NAACP and the United Negro College Fund.

And, along with a lot of successful Blacks—especially those born in the mid-1970s and later, after the most explosive battles for civil rights had settled into a more nuanced tug-of-war or been ignored altogether— we had developed a dangerous sense of gratification, even entitlement, which is an awful state of mind. It renders you idle and robs you of the passion to make a difference. We'd played our part in allowing the Black community to be reduced to a massive consumer segment that every other group taps for their own benefit.

Black people say stuff like, "It's a shame how Black people think the White man's ice is colder." Then we get upset about how other groups— Italians, Jews, Arabs, Greeks, Asians, Hispanics—have, in effect, exploited the phenomenon. It's a staple of Black talk radio. Tune in and chances are you'll hear an angry exchange about how the Koreans took over the Black hair industry; or how so many major cosmetic, hair care, and toy companies have started Black product lines (Hallmark's Mahogany cards, Dove's "My Black is Beautiful" skin care, Mattel's Black Barbie) that millions of us support while quality, Black-owned firms like Carol's Daughter, Fashion Fair, and Kwanzaa Kidz struggle to stay alive; or how most poor, urban Blacks go years without seeing other races face to face, except for the shopkeepers and business owners who are draining money from Black neighborhoods.

It's called the Middle Man Minority issue.

Black filmmakers who depict life in the 'hood, like Spike Lee and John Singleton, always show it. The famous "D motherfucka', D!" scene in *Do the Right Thing* is a great example. Remember when the kid walks into a convenience store and engages in a hate-filled exchange with the two Asian owners over batteries? That scene—and the entire movie, really— was about the frustration Blacks endure because we don't own businesses in our communities. Not one Black business owner was depicted in a movie about a Black neighborhood. There were Hispanic-owned businesses, the Italian pizza joint, and the Asian convenience store. And there was racial tension that emerged because of it.

The film was highly acclaimed and provoked some great dialogue about race relations, but nobody mentioned the core issue: economics. No one talked about money leaving the community—a phenomenon called "leakage"—and that it's a critical reason why these communities are so battered.

Then there are popular Black comedies, such as *Friday*, *Booty Call*, and *Barber Shop*. Many scenes unfold in the convenience stores and beauty supply stores owned by Koreans and Indians. That fact barely registers with Blacks because it's part of our everyday experience that we've come to accept. In fact, a dollar circulates among banks, shopkeepers, and other businesses for nearly a month in Asian American communities before that money flows out of the neighborhood. In Jewish communities that neighborhood circulation is roughly twenty days, and in predominantly White Anglo-Saxon Protestant communities it is seventeen days. Want to know what it is in African American neighborhoods? Six hours.

Here are a few more disturbing numbers:

—Less than two cents of every dollar an African American spends in this country goes to Black-owned businesses.
—More than 11 percent of Whites and Asians own their own businesses, compared to only 7.5 percent of Latinos and 5.1 percent of Blacks.
—White-owned firms have average annual sales of $439,579. Black-owned firms? $74,018.
—In 1997 African Americans represented 13 percent of the population but owned only 3 percent of all US businesses, which generated 2 percent of the nation's business revenues.

The scenario is particularly galling when you consider that Blacks generally spend more on groceries, footwear, clothing, and shoes than the overall population and that Black teens in particular spend 20 percent more a month than the average US teen, especially on the categories of apparel, video game hardware, and PC software.

John and I came across statistics like this all the time. And just like us, lots of Black folks would wring their hands about it. But at the dozens of meetings we attended—including national conferences for organizations like the National Black MBA Association, the Rainbow PUSH Coalition, 100 Black Men, the NAACP, and National Urban League—no one was doing anything about it. Maybe, I thought, these problems were just unmanageable. Mainstream media only mentioned the dearth of Black business owners in passing. Universities seemed too bogged down or maybe frightened to offend benefactors; taking a stand was perhaps too dangerous, too militant.

John and I discussed these issues while we debated spending $60 for a celebratory lobster. But the irony wasn't lost on us. At the end of our meal, as we paid our $250 dinner bill, we realized we were part of the problem. That money could have done at least a little good in a struggling Black community. Maybe it could have helped a Black entrepreneur employ more people, mentor more children, and serve as a source of pride in his neighborhood. Maybe it could have contributed to the tax base and helped to improve underfunded schools or served to defray the cost of an at-risk youth program, the kind that helps discourage drug use and teen pregnancy and reduces the number of Black men in prison.

We realized something else, too, that so many others know deep in their hearts: Good intentions and spirited conversations won't cut it.

We had to act, and that action had to be distinctive, creative, and influential—something that would resonate with people who were feeling equally frustrated. We wanted to inspire, unite. We wanted to change things—or at least try.

But how? We were just one couple.

We thought about how we felt inferior when we'd go into a mass retailer and see nothing made by people like us, or the shame that would wash over us when walking through a Black neighborhood and the only functioning Black-owned businesses were a couple of chicken shacks, barber shops, and braid salons.

We were well aware of the statistic that, second to the government, Black entrepreneurs are, by far, the greatest employer of Black people.

And yet the African American unemployment rate is twice—and in some places, four and five times—the national average for Whites. Worse, we knew that and still never supported Black-owned businesses.

What we came up with was bold and simple. It was not starting a foundation promoting entrepreneurship or a program to show aspiring entrepreneurs how to get funding, or launching a Black business directory, or initiating a Facebook conversation, although we would end up doing some of these.

Rather, we would patronize African American–owned businesses exclusively for a few weeks and see what happened. We would "buy Black." We even came up with a name: "The Ebony Experiment."

The idea was beautiful in its clarity in that it focused on economic disparity, the core of all those other problems we had been talking about. Even if it were just for a short time, The Ebony Experiment would illuminate that disparity in a very personal way while highlighting the potential that exists in Black America. Best of all, we would be walking the walk, as they say—living our commitment.

I admit we got carried away that night, imagining how far something like this could go toward effecting real change. It was inspiring. It was heady. It was awesome.

And then life derailed it.

I got pregnant and we traded the yuppie condo near the University of Chicago for a split-level in Oak Park, a comfortable, slightly urban, fairly liberal, and racially diverse suburb on Chicago's western border. Ernest Hemingway was born and raised there, and Frank Lloyd Wright had lived there, designing twenty-five buildings in town.

Our first daughter, Cara, arrived in July 2005. Then came Cori in November 2006. We had a deck built, then the roof repaired. After spending $30,000 on remodeling the basement, we realized that would have been a plum gig for a Black contractor. The same thought popped into our heads a few months later after we bought a Cadillac at a dealer thirty-five miles away, just because it had the color we wanted right on the lot, when there was one—owned by a member of 100 Black Men and an active role model for at-risk Black youth—only ten miles from our door.

"So when are we going to start buying Black?" we would periodically ask each other. Despite our resolute response, the result was always the same: inaction.

Then came a rainy morning in June 2008. We scrambled to get the girls to day care as the torrential rains just kept coming. When the storm finally let up, I was late for work and hopped on the train into the city. Standing in one of the aisles was our old friend Nat, who I hadn't seen in years.

Nat's another Black professional like us, a lawyer. He's equally frustrated with the situation in the Black community and is trying to make a difference. Years ago we volunteered together at PUSH.

Maybe the rain brings out the more pensive person in all of us. Maybe not. But on the train we got beyond the small talk and began a discussion about problems plaguing African American communities. Nat finally asked me, *Well, what are you going to do?*

I mentioned our idea about "buying Black," and Nat wanted to hear more. We got off the train, and it turned out that we were headed to the same building. We walked and talked about The Ebony Experiment. His enthusiasm fed mine.

Before we said good-bye, he suggested John and I put the concept in writing. We could then pass it on to Nat's cousin Adrienne Samuels, a reporter at *Ebony* magazine, the iconic African American monthly that's been promoting uplifting images, news, and stories about the culture and community since 1945. She might be able to generate some media attention or maybe even set up a meeting with Linda Johnson Rice, chairman and CEO of Johnson Publishing, which publishes *Ebony* and *Jet* magazines.

That night John and I sat in bed and started outlining a plan. We would "buy Black" for ninety days—no, a year. We would save all our receipts and input our purchases into a spreadsheet to be analyzed later. We would enlist academics to monitor the potential of buying Black and use hard data to defy negative stereotypes about Black businesses. We would create a foundation, enlist a board of advisers, and set up a slick website. We would encourage others to join us. We would mount a media campaign. It would be part experiment, part social activism.

The major goal was to prove that average individuals could generate significant economic growth in the Black community if they committed to purchasing from Black-owned businesses. John and I—and Cara and Cori—couldn't do that alone. But our effort could shine a light on the issue and inspire the kind of examination that, in time, could make the point. It could—and, we hoped, would—inspire others to do the same.

And yet as much as we wanted to make the world think this was a natural and normal way to live, we knew it would be a challenging undertaking. But we were both well versed in creating and completing detailed projects, so we went to work on this one. I would end the consulting work I had been doing on a contract basis. That made John the sole breadwinner. We, as a family, would accommodate him so he could make as much money as possible. As for our specific roles in the project, John would be involved with major decisions, meetings, and media appearances. My job was to run the day-to-day operations: monitor and answer all e-mails, do interviews, maintain the website, find Black-owned businesses, research economic empowerment issues, and call on business owners, community leaders, and other VIPs to tell them about us and beg for help. In addition, I would drive the girls to and from day care, shop, cook, clean, and, in general, take care of the family.

The ground rules for our new lifestyle—and the lifestyle we hoped other African Americans would embrace—were simple: If we were going to make a purchase, we'd take a few minutes to do some research to see if we could get what we wanted from a Black-owned business. Or if we knew of a Black firm that offered the product or service, we would give them our business even if the company was a little out of the way or more expensive. We were going to be more proactive too. We would do research to find the Black-made products already available at mass retailers like Walgreens and Jewel, a prominent food-store chain in the Chicago area, and we would buy them. We would assess the recurring, everyday needs of the household and then see if a local or otherwise convenient Black business could fulfill them.

A week after my chance meeting with Nat, amid the flurry of planning, I met with Adrienne to talk about The Ebony Experiment. Like her cousin, she loved the idea and started the ball rolling. She talked about covering the story for the entire year and helped us refine the concept. She even offered to take it to the corporate folks to consider sponsorship.

———

In August of 2008 we got some jarring news from Atlanta, where my parents had been living, near my brother Eduardo and his family. My mother had been diagnosed with pancreatic cancer, which kills within a year 80 percent of the people diagnosed with the disease. The five-year survival rate is about 4 percent.

My mom, who I call Mima, the most powerful force for good in my life, had been given a death sentence at the moment I was embarking on what I saw as a life-changing experience and—if we were lucky—a powerful movement for all African Americans. Something she'd be so proud of. At first I was hesitant to tell her about our plans, but when I finally did, she loved the idea. I knew then that I couldn't back out, no matter what was going on with her health.

Also encouraging was the positive mood that seemed to be spreading across America at that time. Barack Obama—my favorite professor in law school, a fellow PUSH worker, and a member of my church—kept gaining ground in Democratic presidential primaries. After earning a surprise victory in the Iowa caucuses, he rolled through New Hampshire, Michigan, and Nevada, racking up win after win.

John and I marveled at how unified we were becoming as Black people. The barriers between the Black working, middle, and upper classes seemed to give way. Distances between Whites and Blacks—between all races and cultures—seemed to be narrowing as well. After Obama launched his presidential campaign in February 2007, our dreams about eradicating Black economic disenfranchisement seemed less preposterous.

We understood that we might take a little heat from folks who believed we were being racist. But is it racist for Blacks to support their own, just like other ethnic groups do? We believed that crime, unemployment, education, and housing would improve in Black neighborhoods if robust,

Black-owned businesses were there. Didn't that make buying Black key to a self-help solution that was beneficial to everyone?

Once we committed to The Ebony Experiment, everything changed. No more anguished conversations about the state of Black America—we were taking action. In the weeks that followed we kept bouncing ideas off each other, like we were starting a business, buying a new house, or planning an awesome party.

And then we elected our first Black president. Remember the rally in Grant Park? We were there that night. And yes, through our tears, we talked about The Ebony Experiment.

Mainstream America was in love with another smart Black couple from Chicago with two beautiful daughters. Folks like us were feeling triumphant, thinking about what equality really means. Whites were moved and encouraged, too—more prone to empathy and tolerance.

It was a perfect storm for a movement, and we were ready to be in the eye of that storm.

How hard could it be to start our experiment? After this one courageous move, public and well planned, the community would be sure to stand with us. The larger society would be watching too. Some of them might judge us, but for sure, enough would join in to ensure historic progress.

"This can be it," I remember telling John. "Can you imagine? What if it works?"

And John said, "It has to work. It just has to."

This was our moment, John and I thought.

But the news from Atlanta was dire. By Thanksgiving of 2008 Mima had undergone four months of chemotherapy. My mother was on life support in the Intensive Care Unit. She was totally unconscious. I left John and the girls in Chicago and went to Atlanta, where Papa, my two brothers, and I would spend what we thought would be Mima's last days together.

It was five weeks before The Ebony Experiment launch. John wanted us to postpone it, out of respect for my dad and me and in honor of Mima, but I wanted to press on, for precisely the same reasons. We had already hired a public relations firm to help us write the press release announcing the experiment and pitch the story to major media outlets. We'd also secured a website developer to design our site. In addition to that, we had invested our energy in trying to engage high-profile academics to help us conduct a study at minimum cost. We wanted to start building the directory of Black businesses we were finding. We were worried about funding, and much of my time was spent preparing presentations to land a key funding source.

But the website development was laborious. We had to write the content for all the sections, take the pictures, create and embed the video, design a logo, come up with a tagline. I remember whispering on the phone with the web team while my family met with doctors who were urging us to remove my mother from life support.

One day my dad talked with me about The Ebony Experiment. He knew I felt torn, so he told me that Mima would want me to go on with it. Still, I was overwhelmed and conflicted. But I started to look on this project as a fight, just as Mima was fighting, and just as she had always exhorted me to fight against injustice.

"Lucha M'iha," Mima would tell me. "Lucha!" Fight, my daughter.

And fight I did.

Somehow, Mima pulled through those grim days after Thanksgiving. She rallied, and the doctors let her out of the hospital right before Christmas. She would not walk, eat, or use the bathroom for the next few months. But she was home.

A few weeks after her release, John and I sat on a couch in our website developer's studio. We were reading from the cue cards I'd written for our website introduction. We were spending close to $5,000 on this venture, and it hadn't even started yet.

"Welcome to The Ebony Experiment," John said into the camera.

Then I jumped in and talked about our "typical Black family making a not-so-typical commitment. We publicly pledge to support exclusively Black businesses and professionals for an entire year."

John—Mr. Harvard economics degree—talked about the almost 2.5 million Black households in the United States with six-figure incomes, about how "Black businesses create Black jobs."

"If a few of us make a little sacrifice next year," he said, "we could infuse millions into struggling Black households and communities."

"And we can say that *we* did it," I said, "not some government program.

"Since the presidential election, all we do is talk about what's next," I continued. "In my house, this is what's next. Are you so busy living the dream that you have given up fighting for the dream?"

"Just be a part of this experiment," John added, "this movement, in any way you can."

Our yearlong odyssey of empowerment was about to begin. We had no idea what we were getting into.

Chapter 1

"You Have a Blessed Day"

January 2, 2009

The closer we got to J's Fresh Meats, the more my stomach hurt. It wasn't supposed to be like this.

When John and I came up with the idea for this adventure—officially launched with this shopping trip to Chicago's bombed-out West Side—we hadn't envisioned J's Fresh Meats. The store looked like a cement shack, more suited for staging some sort of illicit activity than buying groceries. Located about a mile east of our home in Oak Park, J's was in Austin, a neighborhood on the far western border of Chicago. One of the densest areas of the city, it is also one of the Blackest—91 percent—and has been plagued for years by illegal drug trafficking, street gang mayhem, and some of the highest murder rates in the city.

Initially Austin was a desirable, suburban-like neighborhood that attracted German, Scandinavian, Irish, Italian, and, later, Greek families who were looking to escape from the grittier parts of town. Well served by streetcars and Chicago's subway system—a mostly aboveground network known as the "L," for elevated—Austin experienced explosive growth during the first few decades of the twentieth century. The population was entirely White until the 1960s, until Blacks started moving to nearby neighborhoods, followed by sleazy real estate agents exploiting the fears of Austin's White residents, sparking "White flight" and racial strife. Then came the riots, fires, and looting on April 5, 1968, the day after Martin Luther King's assassination in Memphis. Within forty-eight hours an estimated 11 people had been killed, 162 buildings had been destroyed by fire, and 350 people had been arrested for looting. Bulldozers cleared away most of the charred ruins.

Four decades after the riots, on a crystal-bright winter morning, we rolled through, our two toddlers snug in their car seats. The neighborhood looked battered and dangerous, like it had never really recovered. We'd lived in the Chicago area for fifteen years and had been to Austin once or twice. That was plenty. Austin, like much of the West Side, is "Boyz n the Hood," whereas Oak Park is Norman Rockwell.

When we crossed Austin Boulevard, the border between Oak Park and Chicago, concrete and dilapidated structures with boarded-up windows replaced the lush lawns and tall trees of our suburb. The smiling folks sporting iPods and North Face gear while jogging or dog walking had disappeared. In their stead were tattooed toughs wearing castoffs from the Salvation Army and hanging around the bus shelters that were swathed in graffiti. Drunks stood outside the check-cashing joint on Austin and Chicago Avenue. The antique shops, yoga studios, and coffee and craft shops had become beeper and cell phone supply stores, liquor stores, funeral parlors, and pawn shops. There was nothing warm and inviting about this place. The area felt lifeless, filthy, and hopeless. Beer bottles and garbage were everywhere, even embedded in the snow.

It was a bit scary, but it made me sad too. This is the image most of the country has of Black America. And I wanted America to see the real reasons why the West Side looked like this and the people there suffer the way they do. Still, I wanted to cover my girls' eyes, spin the Trailblazer around, and blast out of there.

When we pulled up to the curb in front of J's, I thought, *What the hell are we doing here?*

"You get out," I told John. "I'm not taking Cara and Cori outside of the car. Look at those guys just standing there."

A cluster of unsavory types—they could have been bums, drug dealers, gang bangers, or maybe all three—loitered around the doorway.

These kinds of characters are fixtures in poor neighborhoods everywhere, but at least in other areas they're a little more discreet. On the West Side, they were brazen. These dudes had unkempt hair, dirty faces, and bloodshot eyes. They wore casual gear, looked tattered and grubby, and were clearly not going to work anywhere. They weren't talking or shopping; they were just standing around—because that's what drug dealers, pimps, and lookouts do.

They are part of the symbiotic relationship that keeps the impoverished, high-crime neighborhoods of America operational. The folks who are unemployed, depressed, listless, and frustrated know where they can get drugs—either to cope or to resell—because these guys are always there. Desperate store owners need the foot traffic, so they let the criminal activity persist right outside their door because it will bring customers into the store. This is why, in large part, those stores stock alcohol, candy, soda, and other junk food as well as basic dry goods and personal or household products. No one really *shops* at J's; instead, they stop in and buy on impulse. And J's can thank the shaggy street "entrepreneurs" out front, an unofficial marketing team, for the incremental uptick in sales.

Sitting at the curb in our truck, I was the intruder disturbing this delicate balance. The shady characters stared at me, as they did at everybody else, as if I was a threat or prey. I tried to disarm them with a smile. Then I turned to my husband.

"John," I said, "I'm not going out there."

After a moment, I exhaled. I knew I had to get out. This was the launch, however unglamorous, of The Project. It wouldn't work too well if I chickened out before it even started. After talking it over we decided that I'd go in alone and John would stay with the girls in the Trailblazer, engine idling, ready for a quick getaway. I gave John a slightly resigned, slightly fearful look and then stared straight ahead as I tried to channel my Liberty City mind-set. Then I pulled on the door handle, stepped on the sidewalk, and moved right by those punks, ignoring their stares.

Two weeks before the launch we researched business directories and collected phone numbers of organizations and individuals who could help us find Black-owned businesses. We also created two lists. One consisted of products (aside from food) that we would need immediately and throughout the year, the kind of stuff I had always bought at the Wal-Mart down the street: pull-up diapers, deodorant, toilet paper. The second list included the few businesses we would need during the early days of the experiment, such as fast-food restaurants, gas stations, a dry cleaner, a refrigerator repairman—our refrigerator was acting up—a grocery store, and a drugstore. Although fast food was not a staple of our family diet, we assumed we'd be eating at Burger King and McDonald's, as they both had impressive track records for franchisee diversity, and we were reasonably sure there were several Black-owned branches near us. In some cases we even tried to plot where these businesses were so we could fit them into our everyday routine as easily as possible. We were optimistic and naive enough to believe we could find what we needed, including restaurants near Oak Park and Oak Brook, the suburb where John worked.

We were trying to be as prepared as possible, but we didn't want to develop an extensive directory of products and businesses because we wanted to experience some uncertainty. The Ebony Experiment was supposed to be an adventure as well as an educational experiment, which included documenting the actual search for Black-owned businesses. Apart from supporting fantastic entrepreneurs, we were going to show that finding them is not so hard.

By the time of the launch we'd met with folks at the Chicago chapter of the National Urban League, a global civil rights organization that focuses on African American progress in business, education, and social programs through economic empowerment. They had given us the names of some Black businesses and entrepreneurs with whom they had been working, including Covenant Bank, located five miles from our home; Quench, a chain of healthy fast-food restaurants; a couple of Popeye's; some general contractors located near Oak Park; and Kimbark Liquor Store in Hyde Park, on the South Side.

When I called J's during one of my informal, prelaunch scouting missions, the woman who answered the phone had that stereotypical slurred speech I call the sleepy mumbles. I'm not trying to be mean here; I know Black folks use an informal style of banter when talking among ourselves. I can talk that way too. But in professional settings I choose not to. And I've come to expect that anyone who owns a business would try to speak as professionally as possible. Although I could barely understand what the woman at J's was saying, I launched into my brief, perky speech anyway.

"Hi, my name is Maggie Anderson," I'd said, "and we're trying to support Black businesses this year. Could you tell me whether you're Black owned?"

"Yeah, well, I'm Black," she said.

"Are you the owner?"

"Yeah."

"Okay. Thank you."

I wrote down the address of J's Fresh Meats, searched for food stores nearby, and found a second place, Mario's Butcher Shop. It was in the middle of a Black neighborhood, and based on that alone, I thought it might be Black-owned.

J's was Black-owned, for sure, but it was not what I would consider a grocery store. Inside, the space, about forty feet long, was cramped, dirty, and a little foreboding, sort of like the way it feels to walk into an abandoned building. Two more unsavory characters lurked in the aisles; one leaned against a dust-caked ATM machine while the other stood in the middle of the floor. Neither was shopping. They stared at me, looking angry. As I passed I could feel their eyes following me. I kept moving, looking at the goods. Almost nothing here was worth buying. There were no price tags on anything, and there was no meat—fresh or otherwise—at J's Fresh Meats. It had those flip-top freezers, where I could see some ice cream, a few burritos, and frozen pizzas—convenience store crap, basically. In the refrigerator case were sugary drinks, juices, and not much else, not even milk.

I was surprised that being inside J's could trigger that much anxiety in me. Growing up in Liberty City, I'd seen dumps like this on every thoroughfare. The Cuban-owned corner store and the Dominican-owned

7-Eleven always had canned goods, cleaning supplies, junk food, frozen junk food, cheap dried spices, soda, and, most of the time, alcohol. We also had a Jewish-owned liquor store and an Eastern European—owned decrepit grocery mart in the strip mall at the corner. All of those places were where the prostitutes handled their business.

The funny thing was that no Jews lived in our neighborhood, and almost no Europeans. In fact, all the shop owners in our part of town were something other than African American. Beyond draining money from the neighborhood, this was a source of racial tension, exacerbated by the fact that the merchants were openly condescending.

When we wanted real food, we got on the bus and headed to the White or gentrifying neighborhoods with full-service grocery stores stocked with produce, meat, fish, dry goods, fresh bread, and household products. My neighborhood was lucky in that respect: At least we had buses to take us there. Plenty of predominantly Black neighborhoods don't.

The depressing lineup of products on the store shelves in my old neighborhood and in J's is a common component of all food deserts—usually urban, poor neighborhoods with no decent food stores. Mainstream, full-service grocery stores traditionally want to have little to do with predominantly Black neighborhoods. Reasons vary, but the conventional wisdom is that those neighborhoods lack spending power and are dangerous, and that acquiring land is challenging, as is demolishing buildings and site cleanup. Local politics and opposition to commercial development can also play a role.

Regardless, the condition is a prevalent one. In 2008, for example, a report compiled by the New York City Department of City Planning found that "three million New Yorkers live in neighborhoods with high need for grocery stores and supermarkets." Minorities predominantly inhabit those neighborhoods, including Central and East Harlem as well as the South Bronx. According to the report, "Food dollars are likely being spent by residents in high need areas at discount and convenience stores whose line of food products is limited, of poor quality, and generally more expensive than the same products sold at supermarkets. . . .

These stores do not generally carry produce and meat at affordable prices or at all."

A 2004 report published in the *American Journal of Public Health* told a similar story. Researchers examined the availability of healthy foods in the minority neighborhood of East Harlem versus a neighboring slice of the city, the predominantly White and affluent Upper East Side, and found that "overall 18 percent of East Harlem stores stocked recommended foods compared with 58 percent of stores in the Upper East Side." The report also concluded, "East Harlem residents have many more undesirable stores [defined as those having less than one item from five healthy food and beverage groups identified by researchers] than do their affluent neighbors on the Upper East Side." These disparities may contribute to diabetes in East Harlem, something that the 2008 report also suggested.

After perusing the merchandise at J's, I thought, *Just get something and get out of here.* I grabbed a bag of potato chips, a few other packages of junk food, and diapers. When I got to the cash register, positioned on one of those glass counters with candy inside, I noticed that the clerk, presumably the woman I spoke with on the phone a few days earlier, was petite, tiny even. Her uncombed hair was pulled back in a rubber band. She was a little darker than me, with a small, pretty face, marred somewhat by acne, and she was young, maybe twenty-six.

She was standing on a milk crate. Out of the corner of my eye I caught something moving near its base and looked down to see a pair of unkempt kids—maybe eight and eighteen months old, probably hers—playing on the filthy floor. I also noticed—because it is my habit to look whenever I see a young Black woman who appears to be a mother—that she was not wearing a wedding ring. I glanced back at the woman and asked if she accepted plastic, which she did. This was unusual, as we would later discover. Businesses in Black communities that accept debit and/or credit cards are as rare as a beat cop strolling down the sidewalk.

As soon as the words "Do you accept credit or debit?" came out of my mouth, I noticed something else that became commonplace in establishments like J's: When the employees or owners realize you're a Black person who doesn't speak with the neighborhood inflection—who isn't

from around there—they treat you like the president. Everything
changes: They light up, smile, call you ma'am, and thank you emphatically, just as emphatically as they say, "Have a blessed day."

I wanted to tell her, "Look, I'm not so different from you. I grew up
in the hood. I shopped at places like this all the time."

—————

My parents, Cuban émigrés, arrived on these shores in 1967 with two
young sons and the clothes on their backs—literally. Mima had sold her
wedding ring to pay for their boat ride to Miami. Four years later I was
born. My father, who is bronze-skinned, drove a Coca-Cola delivery truck.
My mother, quite fair-skinned and with long, dark hair, peeled shrimp
and cleaned fish in a seafood factory. In Cuba their relationship was no
big deal. Here, they were a mixed-race couple, which they found be-
musing. In 1979 our predominantly Black neighborhood erupted in race
riots after an all-White, male jury acquitted five White police officers of
the beating death of a Black motorcyclist. Everyone wanted to know: Are
you Black or Cuban? Translation: Are you one of them or one of us?

Incensed by the racism toward Blacks from Cubans, my parents sided
with the Blacks. Soon they were explaining to us that we were Black too.
"Don't let people tell you you're Cuban or you're Latino," my dad would
say in broken English. "You're Black. You hear me? You're from Africa. Be
proud that your race is Black."

My mother reinforced that message on our walks to school. She'd say
that being from Cuba did not make us any less Black than my friends in
Liberty City or those in Jackson, Mississippi. Mima always taught me
that Black is beautiful, that I was from Africa—just like other Black people here—and that we spoke Spanish because our ancestors' slave ship
dropped them off at a different stop in the triangular slave trade.

This shift in my heritage was curious and, some might argue, arbi-
trary, but one I embraced without question.

Mima and Papa were deeply invested in all three of their children,
and it paid dividends. I became the first Black child to make it to the
state spelling bee and was bused to one of the best high schools in the

area, where I became president of the honor society, editor of the school paper, and prom queen. I ended up at Emory University in Atlanta, studied political science, dreamed of becoming a US senator, and immediately got involved in political campaigns.

But in my pursuit of all that, I drifted away from Liberty City, physically and psychologically.

John's story was similar to mine in that respect. Raised in Detroit, he attended a Jesuit-run, all-boys college prep school and ended up at Harvard. On his application he refused to mention his basketball prowess to ensure he was accepted based purely on his academic record.

John and I would often discuss how we had gotten away from the masses in our choices of food, places we liked to visit, books we read, and TV shows and movies we watched. Nobody enjoyed *Seinfeld* more than we did, and I'm guessing that it's not a huge hit on the West Side. We would notice that disconnect as we spent more time in our suburb, at the office, or when we were the only "chocolate chips" at a four-star restaurant and everyone treated us so nicely. We'd joke about whether they'd act that way if we looked like Lil Wayne.

For the most part the examination of the "class clash" in the Black community is, among members of the Black upper class, limited conveniently and comfortably to a rather benign discussion. Our educational and professional accomplishments have taken us to the higher echelons of American society. We can sample what John and I as well as some of our Black friends call "White Life," a phrase we soften to "The American Dream" when we're in mixed-race company.

We spend more and more time with educated, professional Whites, middle- and upper-middle-class folks who tend to be more progressive and less bigoted, but sometimes they are still very clueless. We are the affable, token Blacks at the dinner party, barbecue, or office party that just fifteen years ago was all White. That status can make us almost celebrities at these gatherings. People flock to us, asking about our backgrounds, where we live, even why my hair is "different" from most African American women's hair. (White folks never say "not kinky" or "more Black." They say, "Wow, your hair is so thin!")

At some point they tell us every detail about the lovely Black couple who attends their church or lives in their neighborhood. They want to introduce us. The logic goes something like this: They're nice Black people. The Andersons are nice Black people. Nice Black people will like each other. And if both husbands play basketball, as I'm sure they must, well, we're working up the Black friendship of a lifetime.

They try very hard and are well intentioned, and we appreciate it—really. But something starts to grate. Chris Rock jokes about it in his 2009 stand-up routine, *Kill the Messenger*.

> I will give you an example of how race affects my life. I live in a place called Alpine, New Jersey. My house costs millions of dollars. . . . In my neighborhood, there are four Black people. Hundreds of houses, four Black people. Who are these Black people? Well, there's me, Mary J. Blige, Jay-Z and Eddie Murphy. . . . [M]e, I'm a decent comedian. I'm a'ight. [applause] Mary J. Blige, one of the greatest R&B singers to ever walk the Earth. Jay-Z, one of the greatest rappers to ever live. Eddie Murphy, one of the funniest actors to ever, ever do it. Do you know what the White man who lives next door to me does for a living? He's a fucking dentist! He ain't the best dentist in the world . . . he ain't going to the dental hall of fame . . . he don't get plaques for getting rid of plaque. He's just a yank-your-tooth-out dentist. See, the Black man gotta fly to get to somethin' the White man can walk to.

In other words, we have to make it to the top 1 percent of the Black population in terms of wealth, education, and professional status just to earn such a welcome into the average, White, middle-class experience. John and I frequently discuss this issue with other Black professionals. Invariably, someone says, "With most White people, except maybe for the rednecks, it's not about race anymore. It's about class. They'd probably invite *us* to dinner before they'd invite some other White couple who works in a factory."

Then someone says, "Yeah, but they still don't want John marrying their daughter!"

And we all break out laughing. Oh, aren't we something. How nice it is that we've accomplished so much and went about it honestly, despite the obstacles our skin color and our country's history imposed. Doesn't this make us different, special, entitled? Haven't we earned our exemption from the misery that most everyone else in our community endures? *Being wonderful is so great.*

Of course, that is only part of the story. The more relevant and painful part involves tensions within the African American community, and we don't discuss these as often because, although the Johns and Maggies of this country socialize with their White counterparts, they *never* spend time with the lower classes in the Black community. That gap is widening. It's an issue discussed by various intellectuals, sociologists, and writers, the most prominent perhaps being the distinguished academic and author William Julius Wilson, who served as a social and public policy adviser to President Bill Clinton.

Professor Wilson started talking about the importance of class differences in Black America at least as far back as the late 1970s. In his groundbreaking book *The Declining Significance of Race*, he points out that political, social, and economic changes from about 1950 to the end of the century did away with barriers that restricted economic success to all Blacks. But those barriers have remained for the Black underclass, making life much tougher on them. In addition, Wilson contends that technological advances in the last couple of decades have exacerbated the problem.

"I think that the disadvantaged Blacks have really been hard hit by changes in the economy," Professor Wilson said in a 1997 interview on PBS. "The computer revolution, changes in scale-based technology, the internationalization of economic activity had combined to decrease the demand for low-skilled workers . . . the gap between low-scale and higher scale workers is widening. Because of historic racism, there are a disproportionate number of Blacks in the low-scale, poorly educated category, and they are falling further and further behind."

That day at J's Fresh Meats, we had unknowingly thrust ourselves into this more delicate part of the story: the widening chasm between the Black underclass and upwardly mobile Blacks. We realized that this experiment was not just about what we could teach an economically estranged and racially divided America; this journey would also teach us about our privileged roles as upper-class Blacks.

As in every group, social stratification exists in the Black community. But our common history, the solidarity it fostered, and the culture we had created together always helped us to overcome those differences. For the most part, tensions among the classes did not exist. The lower-class Blacks believed in and admired the upper-class Blacks, and vice versa. Regardless of our socioeconomic status, we all had a vested interest in the struggle for freedom and equality.

Collectively, we fought to ensure that some of us would be successful, a theory that W. E. B. Du Bois delineated in 1903, known as "The Talented Tenth." Essentially, Du Bois believed all African Americans must push for the most talented to succeed. "Negroes must first of all deal with the Talented Tenth," he wrote. "It is the problem of developing the best of this race that they may guide the mass away from the contamination and death of the worst, in their own and other races."

His vision was to develop Black men and women primarily through higher education. These exceptional few—teachers, doctors, lawyers, or engineers—would then become leaders in the community. It was a strategy dependent on the desire of those in the upper class to leverage their power and prosperity to help the underclass rather than improve their own individual standing.

"Education and work are the levers to uplift a people," he explained. "Work alone will not do it unless inspired by the right ideals and guided by intelligence. Education must not simply teach work—it must teach Life. The Talented Tenth of the Negro race must be made leaders of thought and missionaries of culture among their people. No others can do this work and Negro colleges must train men for it. The Negro race, like all other races, is going to be saved by its exceptional men."

Beyond leading our race with their education, wealth, and access, those who'd "made it" would serve another purpose, Du Bois contended. They'd explode or dismantle the foundations of the racist paradigm—that Blacks were inferior.

The problem is that The Talented Tenth was an idea conceived at a time when political liberty was still an elusive goal. In the '40s, '50s, and '60s we were fighting for the right to vote, for equal opportunity in the workplace, and for school integration. As these dreams became realized and The Talented Tenth (TT) population increased, there was a blossoming of professional organizations, alumni associations, and social and neighborhood groups. These societies became increasingly popular, but they were less a means to enhance Black solidarity and more a way to allow the elite to interact with their own within White society. There are dozens of groups now, from Jack and Jill, The Links, and Mocha Moms to the National Black MBA Association and Black Ivy (for alumni of the Ivy League). The average TT seems to be involved in at least two.

These groups do good for the community. Indirectly. Some of these groups emphasize community service, promoting a scholarship fund, or offering a mentoring program. But actually working with the masses just isn't done anymore. It takes up time that could be better spent planning that trip to the Inkwell—the section of Martha's Vineyard where Black people congregate once a year—or getting your daughter ready for Cotillion or your sorority's annual Debutante Ball. Besides, the problems in the Black community seem intractable—unemployment, drug abuse, educational regression, crime, gangs, AIDS, recidivism, and family disintegration. We just want to get away from them. These groups and events facilitate that exodus in a way that makes us feel like we are not actually "selling out."

Like many in The Talented Tenth, we had carved out our own lifestyle, combining the comforts and pleasantries of "White Life" with the traditions of the African American community. That's what living in Oak Park and being a member of the Harvard Club and Trinity United Church of Christ meant. What it did not mean was spending any time in dilapidated places like the West Side, much less shopping there or having a real exchange with someone like the woman on the other side of the counter at J's Fresh Meats.

But there I was, credit card in hand. I didn't want to embarrass this woman because of our obvious, painful class distinction. I tried to, let's say, "blend in." I changed my tone, infused a little more Ebonics and Southern drawl into my small talk. Basically, I reverted back to how just about everyone in Liberty City talked when I lived there.

She made adjustments too. I was a guest, like anyone from Oak Park with advanced degrees from the University of Chicago would be, even a White person. I was much more that person than I was a *sistah*, a Black mother needing some groceries. Unlike during the civil rights era, when Blacks from diverse backgrounds felt as if they were in the same struggle, the only thing that stood out now was the unavoidable, awkward relationship of a poor, uneducated Black woman serving an upper-class, highly educated Black woman—two planets orbiting around each other. "You have a blessed day," she said, smiling, trying to bridge all that was between us with kindness. I thanked her and smiled back. I headed out the door, climbed back into the truck, and was a little overwhelmed with all that had converged in that stooped store.

How dare you run a business like this, I thought. Then I remembered those babies on the floor, and my heart broke.

The J's Fresh Meats lady was the stereotype we see caricatured in the news and in the movies, the one we whisper about when we see her in the Black restaurants in gentrifying areas of Chicago's Hyde Park, or the one we disdain when she dares to make her way to the malls, parks, and restaurants of our exclusive suburb.

We were wrong to judge her, but the certainty of our assessment assuaged our guilt. That was one of the perks of being in the Black bourgeoisie: We could utter the most prejudiced remarks about people like her—comments we would denigrate White folks for saying—because we are Black. When White folks look at her with pity or hate, they do so without knowing who she is or why her life has ended up this way. But we know. Many of us come from backgrounds similar to hers, and we have cousins and childhood friends like her. That is the difference.

But my education in urban food shopping was just beginning.

Our next stop was Mario's Butcher Shop, a few forlorn blocks away from J's. "We're the heart and soul of the West Side," claimed the big sign out front. It looked like an ideal place for the adventure portion of the experiment. More of a full-service grocery, with a parking lot, shopping carts, even Martin Luther King Jr.'s picture on a front window, Mario's advertised seven different types of chitlins on sale—black chitlins, green chitlins, sausage chitlins, cleaned chitlins, boxed chitlins, tub-o-chitlins, half-tub-o-chitlins. I thought, *Am I in some parody flick? Is Martin Lawrence going to come stomping out of the door in drag?*

But finding a full-service grocery store in a place like the West Side is a miracle, no matter what it may look like. Folks living in Austin buy food from convenience stores, gas stations, and liquor stores, or they take the bus or drive to Oak Park.

We were about to park when I noticed a woman pushing a shopping cart. I rolled down my window.

"Hi," I said, in my Perky Maggie tone, smiling. "I'm trying to find a Black-owned grocery store. Do you know if this place is Black-owned?"

"*Hell*, no," she said.

"But, I saw the Martin Luther King picture and all that. Are you sure? Should I just get out and ask?"

"You don't have to go and ask, honey. No way is this place Black-owned. It's owned by some Italians or some Greeks. You walk in, the whole family is working there. No *way* is this place Black-owned. There are *no* Black-owned grocery stores."

She treated us like we were insane for thinking it might be otherwise. I said, "Okay, well, thank you," and she loaded her bags into the trunk, got in her car, and pulled out.

We decided to go inside anyway, just to be sure. On the wall, past the photos of Jesse Jackson and Malcolm X, was a photo of a White guy and his family—the owners. But all the customers in the store were Black. We walked to the produce section and saw that it was dirty; all we found were bruised apples, near rotten bananas, and smelly potatoes in a cardboard box. We found an entire lane of greens, but they were wilted and gave off a stench. I saw mold and decided we weren't going to explore the meat section. We turned and walked out. We had had enough for one day.

We soon learned the ugly truth: There was only one Black-owned, full-service grocery store in the area, and that was Farmers Best Market, located on the South Side. We were really surprised. After all, Chicago isn't exactly Bennington, Vermont. It's the third largest metropolitan area in the country and has one of the largest populations of African Americans. More than nine million people live there, and nearly two million of those folks are non-Hispanic Blacks.

But the Windy City, perhaps the most American of all cities, turns out to be much like the rest of the country. African American–owned full-service grocery stores are rare.

They once were abundant. In the early decades of the twentieth century there were 6,339 African American–owned and/or –operated grocery stores in the United States. In fact, according to *The Encyclopedia of African-American Business*, "grocery stores were considered the largest category of Black-owned enterprises" in the 1930s. Prospects started changing for Black-owned grocers and many other Black retailers with the emergence of the civil rights movement. Basically, their numbers dwindled.

By the new millennium nineteen African American–owned grocery stores existed in the United States. One of those was Community Pride food market, a highly successful grocery chain based in Richmond, Virginia, that by 2004 had closed, reportedly after its supplier forced the enterprise into poor business deals and failed to provide the stores with satisfactory material for sale.

More recently, in 2010, a team of students from the Kellogg School of Management at Northwestern University conducted online research and uncovered only three African American–owned grocery stores in the entire United States. Of the three, the phone number for one in Southfield, Michigan, was incorrect; another establishment, the Bravo supermarket in Harlem, was actually Hispanic-owned. The only store they could confirm was Leon's Thriftway in Kansas City, Missouri, founded by Leon Stapleton in 1968, a time when there were other Black-owned groceries in that community. Since 1968, the rest of them have all closed.

Looking at the 2002 Census Economic Report, the Kellogg team found 9,016 Black-owned food and beverage retail businesses, a number they noted was misleading because it includes liquor retail and specialty food stores in addition to grocery stores. But that number—as unlikely as it is—still amounts to only 6 percent of all the 148,901 food and beverage stores in the United States.

"This is disheartening," the team wrote in its report, "considering Blacks comprise 13 percent of the US population in 2002," and that they tend to buy more groceries per capita than other demographic groups. "In order to reflect the percentage of Blacks within the US, nearly 10,341 additional Black-owned grocery stores need to be opened."

That didn't look like it was going to happen anytime soon.

The next day we packed the girls into the Trailblazer and pointed it east then south. Forty-five minutes, fourteen miles, and about fifteen grocery stores later, we pulled into the parking lot of the Black-owned grocery store we'd heard about, Farmers Best Market, located at 1424 W. 47th Street on Chicago's predominantly Black South Side. From the outside the place looked decent—more than decent. My little internal bird of hope began chirping.

When we walked inside I felt like Dorothy making her first trip to the Emerald City.

It was clean. It was bright. The produce was fresh. The selection of foods was wide. The employees were professional. And they came in different flavors—some Hispanic, some Black, some White. What we couldn't figure out was why the place was almost devoid of customers. But we didn't dwell on that; instead, we went on a shopping spree. The girls were giggling. John was smiling, impressed and encouraged, and I was immensely relieved and grateful. Was that harp music I heard floating through the aisles?

We loaded up our cart and headed to the register. The tab came to $350. I'm pretty sure I've never been so happy to pay such a large grocery bill. We were so pleased, in fact, with the entire experience that we asked the cute boy bagging our groceries if we could meet the owner. He walked to the back, and in a few minutes this normal-looking Black man appeared: clean-cut and wearing an ironed shirt. I *was* in the Emerald City, wasn't I?

"Nice to meet you," he said with a firm handshake. "I'm Karriem Beyah. This is my place."

"A pleasure," I said. I might have been glowing. "We're the Andersons, your new best customers."

When we told him why we were there, he responded enthusiastically. Within minutes Karriem was telling us about people we needed to meet and resources we should tap for our experiment. He mentioned he was best friends with the owners of WVON, a local, influential Black-owned radio station, and he suggested we might be able to get a weekly segment. He played with the girls, and by the time our groceries were in the trunk, he was Uncle Karriem, an authentic hero of African American self-help economics.

He had earned it. Born and raised in Chicago, Karriem and his family had done all their shopping at local, Black-owned stores on the South Side. His first job was working at his godfather's grocery, which is where Karriem learned the business and dreamed of becoming an owner.

After working as a meat packer and a truck driver for years, Karriem obtained a business degree from Chicago State University and then spent nineteen years at Dean Foods, the largest processor and distributor of dairy products in the United States. When he ended his career there, he was director of sales and marketing for North America and Mexico—the first African American to run that unit, which was the company's largest. He left to become an entrepreneur, establishing and then selling his own milk distribution company. Then he opened Farmers Best Market in June 2008. It is a place that promotes healthy lifestyles through sound diets, which includes quality produce. It also has forty minority employees, many of whom lived nearby. That cute bagger we met on our first visit? He was Karriem's son.

All that made Karriem courageous enough, but as we got to know him better, we found that he had an even wider vision. He created and ran a Chicago Public Schools program that gives tours of the international wholesale food market in Chicago where he bought produce. His idea was to inspire "at-risk youth"—the generic phrase for poor kids prone to getting in trouble—to pursue careers in professions lacking Black representation, such as produce specialists, merchandisers, and store owners. He wants to expose children to fields in which they could make money *and* make a difference in their communities. He is a member of the Rainbow PUSH Coalition's International Trade Bureau, Jesse Jackson's Black entrepreneurship development and advocacy arm focused on ensuring that minority- and women-owned businesses earned their fair share of government and corporate contracts, and he is an investor in development projects in underserved neighborhoods on Chicago's South Side as well as a regular voice for economic activism on WVON.

We couldn't believe our luck. Before we said goodbye John and I wanted to hoist Karriem on our shoulders and carry him around the store. We didn't, of course, but we did forge an immediate bond that would deepen into an enduring friendship. Driving away, with the aroma of all those delicious, healthy groceries filling our truck, I carried such hope. I couldn't help thinking about what a difference just one store could make. Imagine if an enterprise like Karriem's opened in the decimated neighborhood around J's Fresh Meats. So much good was possible, and we were going to show people the way to make it so.

Chapter 2

Canvassing the Community

IN THE FIRST FEW WEEKS OF OUR EXPERIMENT WE continued our search for Black-owned businesses. If a place was in a predominantly Black neighborhood on Chicago's West Side, like Garfield Park, Lawndale, or Austin, or in the predominantly Black western suburbs of Maywood or Bellwood, we'd check it out. Other Black parts of town exist, of course. The South Side is almost all Black, including the areas of Bronzeville, Englewood, Chatham, and Pullman, as are some far south suburbs, such as Harvey, South Holland, and Calumet City. But they are farther away and we wanted to start our search closer to home.

We also explored some areas that are more stable and economically vibrant, such as Hyde Park, around the University of Chicago, and the near West Side around the University of Illinois at Chicago. Other pockets of the city are experiencing economic revitalization too, such as South Shore, a South Side neighborhood on Lake Michigan, and South Loop, located south of the city's central business district, known as the Loop, but north of the South Side. However, many of the predominantly Black neighborhoods are still largely impoverished, crime stricken, and gutted, much like the West Side.

Our experiment was getting off to a slow start. We did move our finances to Black-owned Covenant Bank on the West Side and signed with Foscett's Communication & Alarm Co., an African American–owned home security system in Chicago. We bought gas cards from Black-owned stations forty and fifty miles away with the intention of redeeming them at non-Black stations situated closer to us. We started getting our meals at Black-owned McDonald's, where we'd also buy food cards to use at other outlets in the fast-food giant's chain. Black-owned Evans Cleaners, in Maywood, got our dry cleaning.

I wasn't all that surprised that finding Black-owned businesses selling cell phone contracts, property insurance policies, or utilities was hard, if not impossible. In fact, finding one of those would have shocked me, but we looked anyway. What did surprise me was that we had so much trouble locating Black-owned stores for essential household goods—things like toiletries, cosmetics, and over-the-counter drugs. I searched all the online Black business directories for Black-owned dollar stores, the kind of place where I thought we could buy most of that stuff. I was sure—with so many dollar stores in predominantly Black neighborhoods—I'd find one. But the message that would flash across my laptop screen was always the same: "no results found."

In my quest for a Black-owned dollar store I looked for Black Chambers of Commerce. I found the Illinois Black Chamber, but there was no Chicago chapter or any directories. I called numerous community development groups in Black areas—nearly every neighborhood has one—figuring they would at least know of Black businesses there. It was tough just finding the groups, many of which don't have websites. I uncovered a few helpful organizations, including Black Wall Street Chicago, which represented the once vibrant, now downtrodden 71st Street corridor in the heart of the South Side. In the end I called twenty-five listings for dollar stores in Black neighborhoods and found that all of their lines had been disconnected.

Still, I continued looking. I went through twelve phone directories, pulling out more dollar store listings. Then I went to the library and dug up phone books for the entire city of Chicago, the South and West Sides, as well as for the predominantly Black south and far south suburbs. I also looked over two different versions of the Chicago Black Pages, a well-known and highly regarded directory found in many local

Black-owned barber shops, braid salons, restaurants, and churches and community centers. I must have spent thirty hours going through all the listings and making calls. I found many stores that were owned by Hispanics or by folks of Middle-eastern descent, but none that were Black-owned. I was astonished. Sometimes, out of curiosity, I asked for the owners' names, which I'd then Google just to see where they lived. None of these proprietors resided in Black communities, even though their stores were there.

That really bothered us. We started to absorb two disturbing dynamics: First, nurturing economic empowerment in a struggling Black community was not as simple as spending more dollars in that community because Black people didn't own the businesses there. Second, the inability to retain desperately needed wealth in underserved Black areas was not simply a matter of Black consumers failing to keep money in the community but had just as much to do with outsiders siphoning away that wealth.

The worst part for me was the message these dynamics sent our children. If they could not witness and engage with local Black business owners and professionals, how were these Black youth supposed to make it? They needed positive role models, especially in neighborhoods where drug dealers and gang bangers were actively recruiting them.

I started to feel a little desperate, especially after we began to "canvass the community"—our phrase for an intense, boots-on-the-pavement search through the West Side and Maywood for Black businesses. We'd exhausted the strategy of looking for Black-sounding names in the phone book and online, and because we knew Black businesses had such short life spans, we thought there might be some new businesses out there that were not even listed. At the same time, we figured we'd find some hidden gems if we looked hard enough.

Even though the brutal Chicago winter dampened our enthusiasm for spending hours outside, we could still do our exploring while staying warm in our car. We made a concerted effort to check out Madison Street, Austin Boulevard, Chicago Avenue, Roosevelt Road, and Cicero Avenue—main arteries on the West Side. In Maywood we focused on the main streets of 1st, 5th, 9th, and 17th avenues as well as Madison Street, exploring a different thoroughfare each weekend.

Madison Street, the city's official north-south dividing line, is named for the fourth president of the United States, James Madison, and runs west more than twenty miles, with four breaks, from one of Chicago's jewels, Millennium Park, to the tony suburb of Glen Ellyn. In between it passes some of the most architecturally significant buildings and important landmarks in the city—the Carson, Pirie Scott & Co. building, Chase Tower, the Civic Opera House, and the city's two commuter rail stations—through Greek Town, next to the House That Michael Jordan Built (also known as the United Center) and the heart of Garfield Park, with its gilded dome and conservatory. A little more than three miles west, it reaches Oak Park.

In the early 1800s, before Chicago was incorporated, Madison was the town's southern boundary. By the middle of the century the corner of Madison and State Streets—to this day the center point of all numbered addresses in Chicago—became known as "the busiest corner of the world" and had the highest land values in the city. In the 1860s the West Side's population quadrupled, from 57,000 to 214,000, casting the street's—and the West Side's—fate as a congested, almost entirely working-class swath of the city. It pretty much stayed that way, with a mix of ethnic groups—Italians, Jews, Greeks, and Irish—occupying chunks of the West Side. Though never an affluent area, the West Side and Madison Street deteriorated as they were pounded by the Great Depression, World War II, the construction of the Eisenhower Expressway and public housing projects, and absentee landlords. In the 1950s Blacks who were crowded out of the near West Side and South Side began moving to the Garfield Park neighborhood, which is just east of Austin. As a result, racial tensions grew, culminating in the riots that erupted after King's assassination.

Although Madison remains the commercial lifeline of several neighborhoods on the West Side, stretches of the avenue are sketchy. In February we would find out just how sketchy.

The section we started driving regularly—from Oak Park through the West Side—became more congested the further east we ventured.

We witnessed more life than what we'd seen further west around J's, which was encouraging, but the blight and self-inflicted grime remained the same. In some ways the bustle was similar to that of Oak Park Avenue, one of our town's commercial stretches, but instead of Cosi's and the Gap, the area sported Divine Design Tattoos, a pawnshop, and a nail parlor.

In addition, Madison was a fairly fast-paced street, not conducive to our slow cruising. All the shops were small and looked remarkably similar, which made spotting a potential gem difficult. If I saw one more church, day care center, funeral home, or liquor store, I was going to scream. What we needed to locate were a Black-owned convenience store, clothing shop, minimart, bakery, and general merchandise outlet or shoe store. It was hard to believe that we couldn't find any. We started to blame ourselves because we hadn't actually set foot in very many of the establishments.

After a few failed attempts at drive-by cruising, we altered our approach in order to increase our chances. When we learned of a business on the West Side that looked to be Black-owned, the whole family would pile into the Trailblazer and head for it. On our way there we'd keep an eye open for places that looked like they might be Black-owned. Even if the store didn't seem to offer anything we wanted, as long as it looked safe, we'd walk in and ask about Black-owned businesses in the area. Except when the weather was too miserable or when one of the kids was sick, we went on these adventures almost every weekend during the first few months.

One of the first places we found was MacArthur's, a restaurant on Madison about one mile east of J's Fresh Meats. We pulled up on a blustery Saturday in February, and the large parking lot was packed. A big, lovely sign welcomed folks, and from the outside, it seemed like an Old Country Buffet–type place that specialized in southern cuisine.

Making our way to the front door, we encountered several friendly Black folks who commented on how adorable Cara and Cori were. As we waited for a table, we took in the smells and scene. It was pretty much what we had expected. The restaurant was set up like a cafeteria with a buffet line. The room's burgundy walls were adorned with pictures of African American historical figures along with some of MacArthur's more famous customers, including Robert Townsend, one of our favorite actors and producers; local hero and hip-hop phenom Kanye West; President Obama; and Mayor Richard Daley.

The place was nearly full, with booths and tables spread across an expansive area. The upholstery was worn in places, but the tables were clean and each sported a small glass vase with a plastic flower. Most everyone there was our age or older and working class; there were some families, but many folks were in uniforms. The employees, wearing MacArthur's tees and black Dockers, were smiling, moving fast, looking for tables to clean and customers in need. The space was a little tight, and I could see a few folks bump into others, softening the interaction with a squeeze on the waist or shoulder along with a "Sorry, baby."

It was no Winberie's—our favorite Oak Park eatery that presented gourmet fare, luxury décor, and the skinny, blonde, blue-eyed, Northwestern University English-major hostess—but it had something else: at least twenty Black employees.

An attractive, chocolate-skinned hostess greeted us and took Cara's hand.

"Y'all eating in, right?" she said. "Just gon' be the four of you?"

"Yes, please," I replied.

She looked down at Cara with a warm smile. "C'mon, pretty lady. Right this way."

We sat down at a table, and she told us to wait until the buffet line shrank. Meanwhile, she'd bring us some juice and coffee. When she returned, she said, "Why don't y'all leave Dad here, let him rest, while you get the food? You can take the girls up so they can see all the desserts we have today. You want some chocolate cake, sweetie?"

"But how am I gon' carry all the plates back?" Cara said.

"I'm going with you, girl," our hostess said. "C'mon."

We walked together. Our hostess was tall, thin, and wore huge hoop earrings and sported a short, curly Afro. I started to think that she could be a model. Affable Cori liked the young lady and took her hand. We ordered from the stations and the hostess stayed with us, explaining that they were out of pork chops. She suggested the baked fish. We got to the cash register and paid.

When we had a chance to talk, I asked whether there were any other Black businesses around. "Not a braid or barber salon," I said, "or a fast-food place. A real business, like a grocery store, a shoe store, or a dry cleaner."

She paused to think. Then she asked a coworker for confirmation and told us about Double Door, a dry cleaner on Chicago Avenue—another commercial thoroughfare that ran parallel to Madison about a mile north—and a bakery and a clothing store a couple blocks west on Madison. We must have missed those on our earlier expeditions. I thanked her and we left. Despite the lovely visit, we rarely returned to MacArthur's. As much as we loved its warm, family atmosphere, Cori is a little too energetic to sit in a restaurant for more than a couple minutes, which is why we hardly ever go out to eat as a family. The other snag is that I'm not crazy about soul food, the restaurant's specialty. It's a little too greasy for my tastes. But they make sweet potato pie, John's favorite, just the way he likes.

We got in the car and beelined back west on Madison toward Oak Park in search of the bakery, Laury's, because we desperately needed bagels. The whole family loved them. Before the experiment I'd buy a dozen at a time from the Great American Bagel store a block from our house. John would have one every day before work. On Sundays, when the rest of the family ate pancakes, I ate a toasted bagel with smoked salmon and capers.

The address the hostess gave us was just west of Austin Boulevard, which meant it was technically in Oak Park, in that transition area that represented our hopes for the West Side—a Black, working-class, teeming commercial district that might spread east through the ruins, eventually reaching all the way to the gleaming skyscrapers, four-star restaurants, and landscaped parks of downtown. This Saturday afternoon, around the intersection of Austin and Madison, we saw Black people doing what most people do on the weekends—running errands, grabbing a bite with friends, and shopping—not lurking, selling drugs, or hanging around, dirty and disheveled, begging for money.

On the Chicago side of Austin was a check-cashing spot, the Currency Exchange, that sold payday loans, money orders for nineteen cents, Lotto tickets, prepaid cell phones, and services for Western Union and utility bill payments, which you need when you don't have a bank account, good credit, or a credit card. You can't walk three blocks in most Black areas without seeing one, and I hated them. The were never Black owned, and were predatory lending havens. And they were hangout spots, like the liquor stores and minimarts, only here thugs and scam artists loitered because they knew the folks at the store had money in their pockets.

On the Oak Park side of Austin was an insurance agency and a dry cleaner, neither of which had Black people inside. In fact, both stores were empty. We'd checked out so many businesses in Oak Park and nearby that we were pretty sure neither was Black-owned, but John ran in to check anyway. We were right.

Parking spots were jammed, so I went alone into Laury's bakery. As I walked in I knew that I was not going to find bagels here. Just like the other Black-owned bakeries we called, they did not sell them. I guess they thought bagels weren't a staple of the African American diet. Laury's sold cakes, pies, and some pastries, and you could order a fancy birthday cake, but there were no bagels, scones, or muffins. Everything was beautifully displayed and the place was clean and pleasant, with cute, wrought-iron chairs surrounding a couple tables. I saw a young Black girl behind the counter, and I leaned toward her as I spoke.

"This bakery is Black-owned, right?" I asked.

"Nooooo," she said. "Why would you think that? I'm not the owner."

"Oh, I'm sorry. I'm looking for a Black bakery and somebody at MacArthur's told me you were Black-owned."

"Naaaww. A Chinese lady owns this place. She ain't never here, though. Usually it's just me. Maybe that's why they thought it was Black. She been owning it for at least five or six years."

I thanked her, left, and shook my head as I walked to the truck. John didn't have to ask what happened.

But we found a little hope and reprieve on the cold Friday before Valentine's Day. An online directory, myurbanevents.com, listed businesses and events catering to African Americans by area. There, on 71st Street in the South Shore neighborhood, was what looked to be a promising dollar store with a one-of-a-kind name: God First God Last God Always.

While the girls were in preschool, I took a drive. I was familiar with South Shore, one of the desirable Black enclaves among some pretty rough neighborhoods. An "old Black money" community, it had clean streets, safe parks, and it was situated right on Lake Michigan. Plenty of African American professionals lived there, including attorney turned US Congressman Jesse Jackson Jr. and his wife, Alderwoman Sandi Jackson. In fact, John and I had considered planting roots in South Shore instead of Oak Park. We didn't because the main thoroughfares outside the residential areas made us a little uncomfortable; there were too many liquor stores, currency exchanges, and shady characters lurking about looking for trouble.

The online directory said to keep an eye out for the green awning on 71st Street. I found it easily, pulled up to the curb, and parked. The windows were jammed with everything from basketballs to CD players. Sale signs and posters covered much of the glass. I opened the door and a chime sounded.

"God bless you," I heard a woman's voice say, but I couldn't see where she was. "Welcome! Welcome!"

The store was relatively large with at least six aisles. Directly in front of me were boxes filled with an odd assortment of inventory—canned goods and air fresheners caught my eye. It was what I like to call a busy mess—not dirty, just busy—and it gave the place character. Shopping carts were parked neatly to my right, and a huge stand of rain boots and other winter shoes were to my left.

The store was cold inside—really cold.

I started to maneuver around the boxes to find the source of that voice, and I came face-to-face with a woman dressed in overalls and layers of sweaters. Her graying hair was rolled tight in a bun. She had soft, almond-shaped eyes, wore no makeup, and was smiling.

And then she hugged me, tight.

"Praise God," she said. "Thank you, Jesus!"

I didn't know what to think. It was, by far, the warmest welcome I'd received at any retail establishment. So I just hugged her in return, waiting for her to say something. Then it hit me. She recognized me and was grateful I'd stopped in her store.

"Oh, baby, no. Thank you," I said. "I know it can't be easy keeping this place going."

She ignored the comment, pulled back, and sized me up.

"You're even prettier than your picture," she said.

This was too much.

"Oh, you mean that one from the *Sun Times*?"

"No, this one!" she exclaimed and pointed at the window behind the checkout counter. It was a snapshot from the home page of our website, a picture of John and me hugging and smiling. I couldn't believe it.

"We're so proud of you," she said. "This was the right way to do it—with a beautiful Black family, just like the Obamas."

That one got me blushing.

Michelle Powell introduced herself and showed me around the store, mentioning plans to get more space, add a refrigerated section, and open another store. Every idea was punctuated with a "praise God" or "Hallelujah."

I bought dishwashing liquid, tissues, an ice tray, and a few other items, and I was pleased to discover I could use my debit card. Michelle pleaded that I stay a little longer until her husband, David, arrived. We talked about our families—she also had an ailing mother—and I learned that she and her husband, both longtime South Shore residents, had married a few years earlier and had no children. After a few minutes David entered. He was about the same size as his wife and had a short beard, light green eyes, and a deep voice. He was wearing jeans and a sweater under a leather jacket and baseball cap. He walked toward me and we embraced.

"I knew you'd be here sooner or later," he said. He stepped over to Michelle and they kissed.

"Baby," he said to her, "please tell me you said something to Maggie about the heat."

Michelle shook her head. David turned to me a little sheepishly.

"We just can't afford to keep the heat on all day," he said. "It's keep it on or stay open, you know?"

A pang of sorrow jabbed at my heart. How many shop owners in Oak Park or on Chicago's Gold Coast were forced to make that choice?

"Well," I said after a couple seconds, "I'm glad you're open! I'm cold but I'm here!"

We laughed and they asked about our project, mostly to see how they could help. David told me about a barbershop on 79th Street that also sold men's athletic apparel, something that would interest John.

God First God Last became one of our regular haunts, a place where we could recharge our batteries and obtain what was on our shopping list. We fell in love with David and Michelle as well as with their ability to work merchandise miracles. The store's offerings always changed, which was part of the fun. I'd walk in and ask, "So what's new in here now?" and one of them would smile and lead me down a packed aisle to another discovery. One time it was Ebon-Aids, darker-colored bandages. Another time it was a huge shipment of girls' underwear. If I needed something— a scooter for my nephew, undershirts for John—they'd find it.

"Just let go and let God," Michelle would say.

The only drawback was that, given its location, God First God Last was usually the last stop on my South Side route, so I would be short on time when I arrived. Plus, we got to be such an efficient shopping machine that I'd e-mail our list to the Powells, they'd pull the items from their shelves, bag them, and have everything ready to go when I arrived. When I'd get home, I'd always find candy for the girls tossed in the bag. David and Michelle are real sweethearts who also told us about Black-owned stores in the area—a T-shirt shop, a health food and vitamin shop, a record store—and shared stories of those businesses that had closed, some of which outsiders reopened. The Powells came to our events, taped news clippings about us on their windows, and even started a collection by the cash register. In March of 2010 I came by and picked up $171 they'd raised for the foundation we created. I had never been so moved by a donation.

I wish every shopping day was as promising as that first trip to God First God Last. Unfortunately, many outings had mixed results, which is what happened on another Saturday in February. It began with a visit to Mahogany Graphics in the Austin neighborhood. Owned by William Darke, Mahogany was listed in the Chicago Black Pages I had picked up at Farmers Best—Karriem was on the cover—and we figured it would be our new Kinko's. We needed business cards and promotional materials, and Mahogany seemed like an ideal business to provide that service.

The store was on Madison a couple blocks east of J's and Mario's Butcher Shop. As we drove we saw that the cleanliness spillover from Oak Park lasted for about three blocks or so, right up through J's. After that, it was pure, unadulterated West Side, with lots of trash strewn about as well as a fair number of drug addicts, homeless men, hopeless women, and restless teens way too young to look so hardened.

The short stretch surrounding Mahogany Graphics was full of activity. Most of the storefronts were open for business, even if there were bars on the windows. Mahogany's sported a unique design: It was windowless. The front facade was steel, like a garage door.

Although the streetscape was uninviting, it wasn't scary—just grimy and teeming with urban life. Some folks in work clothes or uniforms were rushing along. Kids by the bus stop, about a dozen feet from Mahogany's front door, were chilling as they waited for the bus to come, wearing standard urban gear: droopy jeans, Timberland boots, oversized sweatshirts, and plain, dark skullcaps. All of them had backpacks and headphones.

Then my eyes fell on a young lady—a girl, really—who looked to be fifteen at the most, with two babies tucked warm and snug in a double stroller. She wore a turtleneck with a jersey over it, a fleece hoodie over that, and pants. No coat. The temperature outside must have been 20 degrees, and a light snow was blowing around. My mind started working.

"I hope those ain't her kids, John," I said.

"Baby, you know they are. Who else does that but someone who has no choice? Stop wishing for stuff, honey. Do something about it."

I went silent, thinking about that kid and her babies. John looked over, placed his hand on my knee.

"She'll be alright," he said. "Let's park and meet Mr. Darke."

Finding a spot was difficult. So as John circled back, I tried to inventory the business prospects nearby, hoping I would see a shoe store, hardware store, fishmonger, bakery, or anything with products for my children or house. No luck. We did see three fried or barbecued food shacks, two churches, two tax preparation franchises, and an African braid salon.

Right under the bright Mahogany Graphics sign, I saw an older gentleman locking the door. He was wearing a dark wool overcoat, dark Dockers, and a Kangol hat.

"Just let me out," I said.

After locking the door Mr. Darke stood there for a second, maybe to make sure he'd remembered everything. As I approached, I felt jittery. Explaining what we were doing wasn't always easy. Most people got it, but there were always some, especially from poor, tough neighborhoods like Austin, who clearly saw me as one of those condescending, missionary types who went to African villages to tame the savages.

I was also nervous because he looked busy and his age was a little intimidating. No doubt he'd acquired a certain amount of wisdom about human nature and had seen plenty of efforts like ours come and go without really changing a thing. I had run into opposition from older folks before, and it's daunting. Once I met a local politician at the South Shore Cultural Center, a Mecca of Chicago's Black community, where the most exclusive events are held. The politician was giving a speech during Black History Month about how badly we needed to unite for the sake of our children and bring back the spirit of the civil rights era. I was so moved that, when he finished, I fought my way through the crowd to tell him about our pledge. His response?

"That's nice," he said. "You're wasting your time, though."

That kind of cynicism hurts, but I understand it and I guess it was on my mind as I walked toward Mr. Darke that cold afternoon. He looked tired and frayed, but when he saw me, he smiled. Then I noticed he was looking right past me, at John and the girls, who had just arrived. Though he didn't say a word about it, I knew Mr. Darke was pleased to see a Black man with his kids.

John stuck out his hand.

"How you doing? I'm John Anderson, and this is my family. Do you have a second? Looks like you're headed out."

"Naw, naw," Mr. Darke said. "I'm fine. I have to make a run. I have a long day ahead of me."

"Well, we like to hear that!" I said.

I told him about The Ebony Experiment, and he loved it. He insisted we call him Bill. When I said we'd like to use his printing services, he gave me a brochure and started walking us to our car.

"Actually, Bill," I said, "we're going to walk around a bit, find some more awesome Black businesses like yours."

"Well, sweetie," he told me, laughing, "you'll freeze to death before you do that."

He must have seen my spirits sink because right away he pointed across the street to a place called Amos and Andy's.

"Look, you ain't gonna find a better piece of fried chicken than right over there," he said. "There you go. A Black business!"

Just as I said we'd walk over and get a takeout menu, he shouted to a teenager at the bus stop, who smiled and came over.

"Hi, Mr. Darke," he said. "What you need?"

"I want you to run into Amos's and see if they have any paper menus. I don't think they do. Bring me one. Y'hear?"

While we waited, I asked about a liquor store down the street and the dry cleaner a block away.

"Ain't no other Black-owned stores around here," he said. "I'm telling you. I would know. You might have better luck on the South Side."

Bill's teenage helper came back and informed us that there were no takeout menus. Too bad—I would have ordered in dinner from there. John took the girls back to the truck, leaving Bill and me to chat, mostly about his business. Before we said our goodbyes, he looked me in the eyes.

"Don't give up," he said.

That day Mahogany became our printer; it still produces our business cards and promotional materials, along with a couple Black-owned Minuteman Press franchises we found in Philadelphia and Atlanta.

Bill's encouragement notwithstanding, I climbed back into the Trailblazer more than a little disheartened. But the girls were up for another adventure, so we headed east. In the distance I could see signs from some familiar brands—McDonald's, Advanced Auto Parts, Athlete's Foot—and thought the chances were decent that we'd find a business owned by someone in the community.

Turns out the stores were in a strip mall next to a large car wash, Captain's Hand Car Wash. *Hmmm,* I thought, *that might be Black-owned.*

We pulled into the mall lot and parked amidst the swirling trash. The bass thumping from the car in the stall next to us—a tricked-out Cadillac Escalade with spinning, twenty-inch rims—was so loud the girls covered their ears. I was tempted to say something until I saw the three hundred–pound driver push himself out of his vehicle. I did, however, give him my best disapproving mommy scowl. He responded with a smile, showing off his platinum grille. He was wearing a fur coat and had a massive amount of jewelry dangling from his neck. All I could think was, *Does everyone have to look like a damn stereotype?*

"Successful business owner perhaps?" I whispered to John.

"Um, successful business*man,*" John said. "And we ain't buying what he sells."

Cara walked, holding John's hand, and I carried Cori. We went into the Athlete's Foot, the McDonald's, and the car wash; we found Black employees and asked whether the places were Black-owned. They all said no.

The strip mall was big, though, so we kept canvassing and hoping. We visited MK Cleaners; Whale Fish & Chicken; Joe's Barbecue Fish, Chicken and Ribs; a T-shirt store; and a flower shop—completely struck out.

I wanted to stop our search because I was mindful of the psychological impact this might be having on my daughters. Admittedly, they were probably too young to appreciate what our research was uncovering, but everyone—I mean *everyone*—we saw on the street and in the stores was Black, but not the store owners.

I told John I wanted the girls to stay in the car if we were going to continue looking farther east. He suggested we take turns getting out so we could avoid the hassle of pulling the girls from their car seats and then plopping them back in a few minutes later. With that, we left the mall, got back on Madison Street, and the first place we passed was Moo & Oink. Figures. Moo & Oink is a Chicago-based, White-owned chain of stores selling low-quality, high-priced meats. Due to its famous ads—with Black voiceovers and Black singers, airing only on Black-themed (but not Black-owned) radio stations—and the fact that the outlets are situated in the poor, Black areas of Chicago, most people think the company is Black-owned.

After the strip mall, the car wash, the McDonald's, six barber shops or braid salons, a huge church and a couple of small ones, we had traveled almost a mile, walking into any business that was not obviously Black-owned—like the barber shop—and was not a funeral parlor, community center, or church. Even though the ratio of boarded-up storefronts to open businesses continued to grow, we still found a flower shop; a couple dry cleaners; five or six food marts; two check-cashing spots; a bunch of bulletproof, take-out joints; a soul food restaurant; two beauty supply stores; a Laundromat; and four liquor stores. Actually, it was more like eight liquor stores because the food marts and minimarts hardly had any food but were well stocked with alcohol.

We went into every business along a four-block stretch on Madison between Laramie and just past Cicero. Not one was Black-owned except for the funeral parlors, two of the fast-food places, and all but one of the barber and braid shops. These West Side neighborhoods were all Black. The idea that a non-Black business owner resided here seemed highly unlikely. But, to test our assumption, we'd ask. And just like when we went hunting for a dollar store, we discovered that all of these business owners lived in places other than the West Side.

And the residents were not happy about it.

People complained to us about Moo & Oink, about how it was overpriced and that they'd never put a low-quality store like that on the affluent North Side, the predominantly White, wealthier part of town— the Chicago that people refer to when they describe how great the city is. Residents lamented that they had to go to "White parts of town" to find a Wal-Mart or other decent place to shop.

Next, the four of us paused by a minimart, looking inside while debating whether to enter. A guy a shade or two lighter than me and underdressed for the weather was leaning on a pole outside a Laundromat, maybe getting ready to have a smoke while waiting for his clothes to dry. His short Afro needed combing and trimming.

"Are y'all lost?" he asked.

"No," I said. I decided to take a direct approach. "We're just looking for Black-owned businesses. You wouldn't happen to know of any in the neighborhood, would you?"

He looked at me like an antenna had sprouted from the back of my head.

"Man, we don't own shit!" he said.

John explained what we were looking for. The guy nodded and then shook his head.

"Nothing like that around here," he said.

We started to leave. But before we could, a middle-aged woman with freshly done microbraids who had overheard our conversation chimed in.

"These damn A-Rabs come up in here and take our money," she said. "Then, they got the nerve to treat us like shit when we in their store."

We got back in the truck, with a collective pall spreading over us, and headed home.

How naive we were. We went into The Ebony Experiment to engage in self-help economics—the practice of buying from Black businesses to empower the struggling Black community economically. All we had to do, we blithely thought, was "buy Black."

But it wasn't so simple. How were we supposed to shop at Black-owned businesses when next to none exist? And for all its fine points,

Karriem's store had its drawbacks. Its location was inconvenient for those who don't live on the South Side. It didn't carry the breakfast cereals, Pop-Tarts, or cheese crackers my kids were addicted to, and John was dying without his bagels. I missed my sundried tomatoes, feta and boursin cheese, and ahi tuna. Sometimes the store did not have skim milk or specialty foods for kids. And we couldn't always depend on it for basic personal hygiene or cleaning products, like toothpaste, baby wash, bubble bath, deodorant soap, bathroom cleaner, or detergent and especially pull-ups—a problem I never had at my local Dominick's or Jewel.

These cold realities—that buying from businesses in Black neighborhoods doesn't necessarily work, that so few Black-owned businesses actually exist, and that even competitive Black-owned establishments have shortcomings—became clear in the early days of The Ebony Experiment. Uncovering the reasons why would take longer.

Chapter 3

Leakage

THE FORMAL TERM FOR WHAT'S HAPPENING IN BLACK neighborhoods is "leakage." I wasn't familiar with the word—except in the context of diapers and roofs—until days before we embarked on The Ebony Experiment, when I met with Gus Tucker, director of the Chicago Urban League's Entrepreneurship Center. I conveyed to him the details of a recent instance in which we'd been accused of being racist. He said that we needed to make people understand that the central concern in empowering struggling Black neighborhoods wasn't as simple as choosing to support Black businesses over non-Black ones. Rather, it was about stanching the rapid exit of dollars—and much needed economic power—from these communities.

His statement prompted me to do some research of my own. One of the first things I uncovered was a report from 2004 showing that for every $100 flowing into an average underserved Black community, about $95 leaves, either by being spent at local businesses owned by "outsiders" or at businesses outside the community. I read about the Black community in Tulsa, Oklahoma, located in the area known as Greenwood. At the beginning of the twentieth century, because of segregation, these residents had virtually no contact with the city's White community yet still generated vibrant wealth. In those days a dollar would remain in the community for up to three years before circulating elsewhere—as opposed to the few hours it now remains in a Black neighborhood.

Just as illuminating was a radio piece produced in 2009 by WBEZ-FM, Chicago's National Public Radio outlet, that examined retail leakage in thirty Chicago neighborhoods. Its findings: "Thirty neighborhoods have more than 50 percent retail leakage. Of those, 20 are on the South Side. Almost all are majority-Black neighborhoods. In 2007, residents in these neighborhoods spent a collective $3.8 billion outside of their own South Side communities."

And in a book about Anacostia, one of the poorest neighborhoods in Washington, DC, author Michael H. Shuman notes that in 1998 the total income of all households there was $370 million a year. Where were all those dollars going?

"Most of this money quickly departs in the hands of landlords, business owners, and bankers who live in more upscale parts of town," Shuman writes. "The principal affliction of poor communities in the United States is not the absence of money, but its systematic exit."

Like many Blacks aware of economic disparities between us and everyone else, John and I were familiar with the oft-cited statistic that only 5 percent of the money spent in Black communities stayed there. I thought I would need only a few minutes of online research to verify that number, but I soon realized that little information exists about the economy of Black neighborhoods. There is a flood of data about problems in the Black community related to health, education, crime, drugs, unemployment, and poverty, but there is nothing about the fact that outsiders own most of the thriving businesses in Black neighborhoods. I found a couple of universities that studied leakage but none that focused on neighborhoods with an abundance of minorities. I also found two articles—the most poignant was almost thirty years old—about how many businesses were owned by outsiders in the Black community. Entitled "From Other Shores—Recent Wave of Asian, Latin American and Caribbean Immigrants Is Stirring Fears of Displacement in the Black Community," *Black Enterprise* published the article in 1983.

I had always ascribed that 5 percent—such a low number—to our own psychosis, our negative perceptions about Black entrepreneurs, goods, and services. John and I believed that the inclination to *prove* our worth by shopping at "White" stores was both a heavily promoted sign of our advancement as well as a reaction to the lower-quality Black businesses. We didn't think that practice had anything to do with the shockingly low number of Black-owned businesses.

But what I found—what The Ebony Experiment taught us—is that leakage is even more insidious than that. A big part of what's going on is that immigrant groups and corporate America took advantage of the situation. A more jaded individual might even say they exploited it.

Most discouraging was our realization that even when a West Sider "buys local," he or she is contributing to leakage. And this led to another, more ominous conclusion: Things may never change for areas like the West Side. Leakage is perpetual there and in all places like it in America. The social epidemics accompanying this corrupted economy were likely immovable. The "outsiders" had established strongholds, and the local Blacks could not compete. Meanwhile, Whites were not going to relocate to places like the West Side, bringing mainstream retailers, grocers, and banks with them.

All this was depressing and perplexing. John and I started wondering who or what we were fighting for. How can we admonish Black people for not supporting Black businesses when hardly any Black businesses exist? How could we tell our people we have so much to be proud of when we are the only group failing to harness the American Dream? Should I join the militant groups who hate the Koreans for taking over the Black beauty supply industry, or join the marches on stores owned by outsiders who are openly racist, refuse to employ from the community, and overcharge their customers? How are we ever going to turn around these suffering communities?

And where does that leave folks on the West Side? Are they supposed to keep relying on government generosity and corporate munificence? Are they going to continue the generations of hopeless dependency?

Seeing the situation any other way was difficult. Cynicism and pessimism were spreading in me. The Ebony Experiment was starting to feel more like pushing a boulder uphill than leading a charge on horseback.

———

Despite J's Fresh Meats, Mario's Butcher Shop, and the other examples of commercial decay we saw in our travels through Black neighborhoods, that the Black community has economic might is undeniable. Here are a few statistics that might change the way folks think about Black consumers:

—African American buying power rose 166 percent in seventeen years, from $318 billion in 1990 to $845 billion in 2007.
—In 2002 advertisers spent $457.9 million to market to African Americans, including cable TV, Internet sites, and magazines. Four years later that spending jumped by nearly 73 percent to $791 million.
—US Census Bureau data show that the Black population of about forty million is growing 34 percent faster than the population as a whole and that the number of Black households making at least $75,000 has increased 47 percent since 2005. Those statistics suggest that not only is our population growth robust but a Black middle class is expanding as well.

Although we might be a consumer group to reckon with, we still haven't figured out how to flex those muscles. According to author Robert E. Weems Jr., professor of African American history at the University of Missouri, "Black consumers . . . have a history of being disrespected," with retailers in the first half of the twentieth century regularly treating us as "second-class" citizens while advertisers insulted and belittled us by using "a proliferation of products . . . that included such derogatory terms as 'mammy,' 'pickaninny,' 'coon,' and 'nigger.'"

African American buying power started to gain the attention of companies and advertisers with the Great Migration of 1916 to 1970, when nearly seven million southern Blacks moved to urban areas in the north searching for jobs, largely in war-related industries and other manufacturing.

By 1920 Black spending power was more than $3 billion, about a third of which was spent on goods and services that African American companies produced. Record companies and makers of hair care products were two of the first industries to pay attention to the burgeoning Black market. White- and Black-owned companies alike began advertising heavily in African American newspapers, with much of that advertising pedaling products like skin lighteners and lip reducers.

The National Negro Business League, formed by W. E. B. Du Bois and others in 1900, started a national survey of Black businesses in 1928 in cities across the country, and it showed that savvy, powerful, White-owned corporations were hiring Black managers, sales reps, and employees to take business away from Black companies. At the same time, African American consumers were making purchases to, as Professor Weems states it, "buy respect and dignity. Sophisticated market research and advertising campaigns have helped American corporations to continually profit from Blacks' lingering social and psychological hangups."

In the 1940s and '50s the Black migration to northern cities accelerated, and more White businesses made a concerted effort to reach the "Negro Market." Beyond hiring Black managers, sales reps, and other employees, as had been done in the 1930s, large companies started to get into the act in a bigger way by bringing on Blacks as "Negro market specialists," whom Professor Weems calls "the true African American pioneers in corporate America."

One of the most prominent Black researchers was David J. Sullivan, who, in the early and mid-1940s, authored several pieces on African American demographics and offered advice to companies trying to appeal to African American consumers. Many of his tips are cringe-worthy to today's readers, such as: don't exaggerate Blacks' physical traits, avoid using White people in blackface makeup, and don't depict Black women as "buxom, broad-faced, grinning mammies." Sullivan also discouraged the use of "nigger," "coon," "shine," "darky," and "Pickaninny" in advertising.

If there were ever a point in time when we could have demonstrated unity and pride—and do so as consumers—it should have been then. Though we fought to force White business owners to hire, sell to, and serve us, we did not assert that same kind of might when it came to how we were portrayed in their advertisements and how we were treated once we were in their establishments. Historically, the NAACP has led the struggle to ensure that the media did not perpetuate destructive stereotypes of Black people, but consumers were never called on to boycott these firms or, better yet, support our own companies. We let the political and community leaders handle it when the consumers actually had the power to change things.

By the mid-1940s African Americans' gross income was $10.3 billion, which was $1.5 billion more than the national income of Canada. Pepsi and Esso Standard Oil were taking active interests in the Black market. But perhaps the most powerful embodiment of White overtures to Black consumers wore the number 42 for the Brooklyn Dodgers. When Jackie Robinson broke the color barrier in Major League Baseball in 1947, followed by Satchel Paige a year later, the move "represented not only a source of pride for African Americans but a box-office bonanza" for Dodgers owner Branch Rickey, Professor Weems writes. Of course, those players moving to the major leagues also led others to do the same, which ultimately caused the downfall of the Negro Baseball League.

In the 1950s major corporations followed Pepsi and Esso in paying attention to African American consumers. The National Alliance of Market Developers, established in 1953, was created to provide professional training for African American pioneers in corporate America.

Most of these professionals staffed the marketing departments and were specifically recruited to target African American consumers. The NAMD's mission was to ensure that African American dollars were valued and to promote more inclusivity in marketing and advertising in general. Black consumers wanted to see more people like them in commercials as well as more products that reflected their preferences. They wanted to see the corporations making an effort to respect their culture and appreciate their support. Several extensive studies of Black consumers and the impact of their spending on the American economy were also published during that decade.

But although corporate America responded vigorously with new products, ads, and diversity strategies, the efforts did not bring increased supplier, vendor, or franchisee diversity. This corporate munificence failed to benefit Black businesses. The fact that McDonald's and General Motors had begun placing Black folks in their commercials was seen as a historic civil rights achievement. We responded with our loyalty and our money—leaving Black businesses behind. The effect of these "accomplishments" was to further siphon dollars from Black businesses and neighborhoods.

The turbulent 1960s then brought the more confrontational "Black Power" movement. Marketers responded by creating and promoting the "soul" market, which sometimes celebrated but often dishonored Black culture and customs by relying on caricatures. This presented a great opportunity for Black marketing, branding, and advertising professionals, who offered advice on how to portray Black people respectfully by forgoing the exaggerated Afros, high fives, and jive talking.

The Negro Handbook, produced by the Johnson Publishing Company in 1966, is another telling example of how marketing to African Americans helped drain the lifeblood from Black-owned businesses. The book was a universally accepted, credible tool for mainstream marketers, brand managers, and advertisers. Unfortunately, it also showed a clear disregard for African American–owned businesses. "The Negro consumer who was once the private property of the Negro owner and operator of hotels, restaurants, night clubs, and beauty and barber shops," the handbook states, "has turned with increasing alacrity to white establishments which offer, in many cases, extra services, luxury atmosphere, and a degree of glamour for the same dollar." That statement is little more than a polished, ad executive–friendly way of saying, "the White man's ice is colder."

Then came the 1970s, when major motion picture studios discovered that urban Black consumers were an untapped market that could help pull those companies out of a collective financial nosedive. They made a series of "blaxploitation" films, starting with 1971's *Sweet Sweetback's Baadasssss Song* and including *Shaft* and *Trouble Man*, to name a few, that were made relatively cheaply but reaped tens of millions of dollars for mostly White film companies from largely Black movie audiences. Those films glorified drug dealers, pimps, and other nefarious characters who were able "to stick it to the man." By the mid-1970s Black audiences became more discerning, but those movies had a powerful, lasting, and corrosive impact on the souls of African Americans. Conspicuous consumption and rogue independence, which conflicted with the solidarity and widespread hope that the civil rights movement engendered, were fundamental to "blaxploitation" films and were particularly volatile in a culture that was angry at its powerlessness.

At about the same time, corporations started focusing on the booming industries of beauty and personal care products, on which African Americans spent about $750 million in 1977. Competition with Black-owned corporations for that market and others—notably advertising and insurance—became fierce and not always honorable. In 1975 the Federal Trade Commission ordered Johnson Products, the Chicago-based maker of Black beauty and personal care products, to place a warning that its popular Ultra Sheen Permanent Crème Relaxer contained sodium hydroxide, an ingredient that could cause hair loss and damage to eyes and skin. The company complied, but the FTC waited nearly two years before ordering the White-owned Revlon Company, whose products also contained the potentially dangerous substance, to place similar warnings on their labels.

In addition, Black-owned advertising agencies, aside from seeing business decline from the slow economy of the 1970s, were suffering a talent drain to larger, White-owned, better-paying agencies—a trend that struck African American insurance companies, too. The smaller Black insurance companies relied heavily on "industrial insurance," which carried greater administrative costs that were passed on to the consumer, and their smaller size hampered them from offering more reasonably priced coverage that White-owned firms, with their economies of scale, could provide. Like many Black-owned businesses, African American insurance companies were also hurt by the perception that transferring one's business to a White-owned insurance carrier meant one was "moving up."

Professor Weems points out the broader, troubling consequences of the failing African American insurance industry. The number of what he calls "significant Black insurers" declined from forty-two in 1973 to four in 2006. That drop has probably expedited the erosion of urban Black neighborhoods. The reason: African American–owned insurance companies traditionally invest in their communities' real estate, whereas White-owned firms do not—another example of how Blacks contribute to the bottom line of White-owned corporations without the corporations returning the favor.

Then, the 1980s brought a sinister form of Black consumer exploitation. When market research indicated that urban Blacks were significant imbibers of alcohol, liquor companies intensified their advertising efforts in those neighborhoods, often with ads that linked a certain brand of liquor with sophistication, increased status, and sexual prowess, which, of course, preyed on Blacks' inferiority complex. Cigarette companies were close behind. Both engaged in heavy billboard advertising in urban areas, funneling millions of dollars into marketing while the government spent far less on educating African Americans on the dangers of alcohol and smoking. In 1986, for example, the amount spent on such programs was the downright paltry sum of $512,193. Many of these alcohol and tobacco companies were Black advertising agencies' biggest customers, donating millions of dollars to financially struggling, ethical Black organizations. Anheuser-Busch, for example, sponsored a telethon that supported the United Negro College Fund, and the brewer made large contributions to the National Urban League. The Joseph Coors Company, a target of protests for purportedly racist and anti-union practices, agreed to invest nearly $625 million between 1984 and 1989 with the NAACP, Operation PUSH, and other causes in African American and Hispanic communities.

This was a destructive one-two punch: A rising, more aware Black consumerism coupled with intensifying competition from White-owned corporations worked to funnel more money away from Black businesses and communities. It continued in the 1990s and exists to this day.

Larger companies targeted products and marketing specifically to the African American market. In 1991, for example, Maybelline launched its Shades of You line, while the Estée Lauder Company unveiled its Prescriptives All Skins. Both brands offered a vast array of makeup and related products for African American women, and they proved to be extremely successful. But they also dealt devastating blows to smaller ethnic cosmetic companies, such as Afram Cosmetics and Spectrum Cosmetics, two quality enterprises that had enjoyed exclusive reign over the Black female market before behemoth firms like L'Oreal and Estée Lauder decided to pay attention to it.

The same thing happened in the film industry. Blacks comprise roughly 13 percent of the population, but we account for 25 percent of film revenue. Although recent Black-oriented films have a broader appeal and offer a more nuanced treatment of Black life than those in the early 1970s, most of the profits from these films end up in Whites' bank accounts. The fact that, as of 1995, less than ten movie theaters in the United States were Black-owned is shocking.

More recently, as hip-hop has moved beyond the Black community and penetrated the culture at large, it has broadened African Americans' influence, particularly in advertising, TV, and film. The problem, according to Professor Weems, is that "hip hop artists have been used to manipulate young consumers, to 'play' young people."

As he explained at a 2010 meeting of the Association for the Study of African American Life and History, African Americans' "acute case of status anxiety . . . fed the quest for bling," a self-centered goal that erodes Blacks' historical, unified struggle.

"It is also worth noting," he told the gathering, "that since African Americans do not own, in significant numbers, large jewelry stores, luxury car dealerships, yacht dealerships, or designer fashion businesses . . .

the primary beneficiaries of the 'Ghetto Fabulous' phenomenon have been white businessmen."

That one of the main legacies of the civil rights era has been the demise of so many Black-owned businesses is ironic. In the 1960s and '70s integration finally gave us the opportunity to shop with other people, and we reveled in the chance to show that our money was just as green as everyone else's. We righteously flocked downtown and to the suburbs, spending our money at mass retailers like Walgreens, Sears, and Woolworth's instead of our local, Black-owned firms. Those mainstream retailers were happy to take our money and target us with advertising that used Black models, but they didn't actually care to build stores in our neighborhoods. The combination fed an economic crisis in Black communities, starving those local businesses to death, decimating neighborhoods, and opening the door for a steady incursion of business owners from outside the community. By the 1980s and 90s immigrant groups—willing to locate businesses in our tattered neighborhoods and leveraging the low rents and available space—set up minimarts and liquor stores, hunkering down for the long haul.

As our spending power was growing, we experienced the hard-fought triumphs of integration and inclusion. At the same time, our economic strength was, in effect, being stolen out from under us. Opportunity and freedom in the 1960s feel like racist exploitation in the 1990s and 2000s.

As Professor Weems points out,

> if one were to take a stroll through most urban black enclaves in America, one would be hard-pressed to see where increased African-American spending has improved the infrastructure and the ambiance of these neighborhoods. Black consumers . . . enhance the economic bases of these outside areas to the detriment of their own enclaves. This self-destructive tendency raises the question "Is the slow, but steady, destruction of urban black America (and its businesses) too steep a price to pay for unrestricted African-American consumerism?" For contemporary African Americans who would answer "yes," the future demands the development of strategies that will stimulate more

constructive economic activity within the black community. A truly free people possesses the power to produce, as well as to consume.

What we found on Madison Street and much of the West Side conformed to this analysis. As discouraging as it was, reading those words made me realize all the more how important Karriem's store—and our little adventure—was.

Chapter 4

A Dose of Reality

LOOKING BACK OVER OUR BLACK YEAR, WE LEARNED valuable if painful lessons, including the dismal state of African American businesses in the Chicago-land area—not to mention the rest of the country. Other lessons underscored how naive we had been when we began this venture. But in our defense, the exuberant reactions we received even before we began our experiment had fueled our dreams. No wonder our expectations were so over-the-top.

It started back in July of 2008, when we met with *Ebony* magazine's Adrienne Samuels, the cousin of our friend Nat. She was so enthusiastic that she even gave us pointers on how to make my abstract—the written articulation of our vision for The Ebony Experiment—more appealing to the higher-ups at Johnson Publications. Her response was encouraging. It indicated that we would probably receive decent coverage from one of the oldest, most respected Black media companies in the country.

But we also knew we were going to need some PBFs—Prominent Black Folks—to lend The Ebony Experiment credibility. With assistance from some celebrity endorsers, a couple high-profile academics, and the Black media, a campaign could take shape and keep growing. Inspired individuals would make and honor their pledges to "buy Black," and The Ebony Experiment would track the cumulative spending and monitor how that money was having an impact in underserved areas and on our overall economic empowerment. We thought EE would be a great way to show that Black people of all backgrounds could unite to rescue our community.

We had our plan, but it wouldn't work without celebrity endorsers and commitments from Black media to keep the movement in the public eye. If those friendly folks would open their checkbooks to fund the project, things would move along faster. Our strategy to find the PBFs was fairly simple. We made two lists: one consisting of people we knew or had access to, and a second, generated in large part by the first, of prominent players who might be fired up enough to throw some support, financial or otherwise, behind The Ebony Experiment. When we finalized our lists six months before we launched the experiment, we had about thirty names.

At the top of our list was Professor Steven Rogers, executive director of the Levy Institute for Entrepreneurship at Northwestern University's Kellogg Graduate School of Management. John was a former student in his Entrepreneurial Finance class. Students rated him the most popular professor for ten-plus years. John had told me how impressive and demanding Rogers was in class. Kellogg is one of the top business schools in the world, and Rogers, at the top of its entrepreneurial department, is an icon. A member of the Minority Business Hall of Fame and the only Black person on the board of directors for eminent businesses like SC Johnson Wax and SuperValu, he used his influence to be an advocate for Black business. The principle of self-help economics in the Black community—that Black people cannot make it until their businesses do—was one of his core beliefs.

I'd sent him our abstract of the project and arranged a meeting at his office. Maybe his early review of the material eased his mind. Maybe he saw from the outset the value in what we were planning. Whatever it was, he didn't give me the anticipated third degree when we met. Instead, he asked about my family, my upbringing and goals, my politics, how I met John. He told me about his life growing up on the South Side and spoke lovingly about his parents. The conversation was warm and engaging. And then he asked me a question that gave me pause.

"Maggie, are you free?" he said, in almost a whisper. He waited, letting the question sink in. "Because most people who come in here are not. I'm free. Cornel West is free because he criticized President Obama the other day. He is committed to truth, not ambitions."

He paused again and looked at me hard, but he was grinning.

"I think you are free," he said.

At that moment I knew we were kindred spirits, or something close to that. I think he understood how difficult following through on our pledge to buy Black would be and that making that pledge took guts and a certain liberation from the fears most of us have about shaking up the status quo.

Without making any promises, Rogers let me know that he was there for us. He instructed me to convert the abstract to a business document and PowerPoint presentation, to make it a more concise read for the busy VIPs we were trying to recruit, and to include a budget and sponsorship request. He said, with all sincerity, that I could call him when I needed something. I gave him a few names of people on our wish list, and he promised to contact them. He also warned me that although the academic community might find this experiment intriguing, the business world might feel threatened by it. That turned out to be prophetic.

With Rogers in our camp, we had street cred. But as much of an inspiration and confidence boost as it was to have him on our side, I also wanted to get Michael Eric Dyson involved. A professor of sociology at Georgetown University, he is the most prolific, eloquent, outspoken public intellectual and commentator on Black culture in the United States. He also happens to be my personal hero. I used to joke with John that I wanted to be Professor Dyson when I grew up.

We first met in 2002 when he was a professor at DePaul University and a columnist for the *Chicago Sun-Times*, and we became e-mail buddies. When Michael left Chicago for a teaching job at the University of Pennsylvania, we kept in touch. Now he was in DC, and I was in Chicago with the abstract on this project that people were getting fired up about. How to get Michael Eric Dyson—The Heroic Michael Eric Dyson—on Team Double E?

John and I took three hours to write a three-paragraph e-mail. The focus was primarily on the personal, although I did share our idea for The Ebony Experiment with Michael. In September of 2008 we talked more about it when we met at a café in Washington, DC, where John and I were attending the National Black MBA Convention. After I finished my spiel, Michael was speechless for about three seconds, which was something of a rarity in itself. Then he went off: about how Soledad O'Brien and Oprah would interview us; about the mainstream marketability (he was the first to see that) of the young, highly educated, suburban couple with the two adorable daughters—and how crucial such media exposure would be; about wanting to place the issues facing Black neighborhoods and our youth into the national dialogue. He was on a roll, and once Michael Dyson gets on a roll, there is no stopping him.

"You don't fit the militant, activist profile," he said. "It's perfect. You'll be media darlings. They're gonna' fall in love with you. And if they love you, they'll listen. Aaaw man, Mag, that American Dream stuff—that your parents and big brothers came here with nothing, became hardworking, productive American citizens. That's gold, man. That's just beautiful. John with those glasses, the girls with that frizzy hair all over the place, and you with that kind of ambiguous racial makeup thing going on. You guys are so cute and disarming. They just *might* listen. And that's all you need. Everything else is backed up by facts, history, and science. If you get them to actually *want* to talk about this, everything can change. This is *beautiful*."

We were surprised that our little project so excited someone of Michael's stature. That reaction strengthened our confidence. We started thinking we were onto something bigger than we had ever imagined. He warned me how busy he was going to be—he was working on a book about Barack Obama—but said that we could depend on him. And, like Rogers, he stayed true to his word. For the next few months I would text his assistant asking for small favors like calling VIPs in Black media. He always did what we asked. Both he and Steven Rogers agreed to be our executive advisers.

The inspirational encounter with Michael led us to think more about the "movement" component of our project. I started channeling my energies into a presentation we were going to make to solicit the assistance of a group of the most powerful, wealthiest Black corporate executives in Chicago—the Big Dogs of Black business and finance. Rogers knew the president and many of the members. I wanted to convey to them what Rogers felt—that The Ebony Experiment was going to be transformative: It would be the next phase of the civil rights movement—not just another street march, after-school program, or community meeting to stamp out violence. It was going to be a game changer because it was coming from within the community. It would show what we could do—*finally*.

Rogers had called the president on our behalf. A few weeks later, during a brief conversation in late October, the president asked how much we needed, and I told him our budget was $300,000. He said that was quite doable and, with the holidays looming, put us on the agenda for the organization's meeting in early January 2009. Just like that. John and I were stunned. We had Adrienne and *Ebony* magazine's presumed coverage, which would get Black people talking about the lack of Black businesses and self-help economics as a way to solve our problems. We had Rogers for credibility, overall executive advice, and help in finding sponsors. We had Michael Dyson, the leading Black scholar in America, poised to do anything for us, and we had a group of wealthy Black business owners willing to give us a few hundred thousand bucks without even hearing our pitch.

Next, we needed a competent researcher or, more likely, a team, to study in detail what we did that year—including how we would spend our money, where we would spend it, and what we could and couldn't find from Black-owned businesses. Just as critical was the extrapolation of that spending—what sort of impact would occur if Black folks spent "X" amount with African American–owned businesses. We could passionately articulate the issues we hoped the study would uncover, but we had no idea how to create, fund, or execute such an undertaking, which in our view was a key component of the project. Such a study would demonstrate through scientific analysis and actual data that buying Black was not a form of racism but rather was absolutely necessary and promoted a greater good.

We knew that major foundations, like the Ford Foundation or the Gates Foundation, spent millions conducting social research, so we figured the process was complicated. But we were sure it started with a couple of brilliant and committed academics. We had those in our friends Walidah and Michael Bennett. Walidah is a sociology professor; Michael is an economist and an expert in urban planning, development, and financing. Early on, they'd explained the basic steps: Create a research design and then shop it to corporations, universities, and foundations for funding. According to the Bennetts, with the right team those first steps could be done rather easily. And we had an awesome team.

These were the giddy days, when almost everyone we talked to about EE acted like we had just shown them the business plan for Google. Their reactions made us feel as if we were creating the next NAACP or setting in motion Barack Obama's presidential campaign. People were honored to help in exchange for the privilege of being part of the inner circle.

Then we met with the Bennetts to discuss the project. The soaring, nonstop jet to Black Nirvana started hitting turbulence. In retrospect, that was a healthy thing.

They were supportive and, as African Americans and academics, understood the need. But they were also realistic. First, they expressed concern about how the study would play out. Among other things, they asked us what we were going to prove—a question that, I'm embarrassed to say, somewhat stumped me at the time. I remember Walidah stating, "One family does not a study make."

Then Michael said one of the most discouraging things we'd heard since we'd started the planning process—and perhaps one of the most valuable statements as well.

"There is no way you are going to do this," he said, adding that never before had such a study on the potential economic impact of buying Black been tried. "This is going to be much harder than you think."

In the end Michael agreed to help us with the research design at no cost, which was very reassuring. Leading the study, however, would understandably come with a fee. We were grateful for the assistance. But I also remember feeling a little irritated, almost as if our friends lacked the vision to see how this endeavor was going to take on a life of its own. Now I know the reason I felt that irritation: The truth hurts.

About this time, in September and October 2008, we started sharing our idea with a wider circle of relatives and friends. It was easy to get people stirred up about the potential for large-scale economic empowerment, recycling our wealth, enhancing our neighborhoods, demanding more respect from big business for our consumer dollars, and reclaiming our community from folks who take our money and treat us with disrespect. It was much harder to inspire excitement about actually going into poor Black communities and patronizing struggling businesses. Our friends were far more enthusiastic about those larger, nobler concepts than about doing the grunt work to make them a reality. Some of them voiced a complaint that we would hear ad nauseam throughout the next year: *We've tried patronizing Black-owned businesses and they are awful.* We let that one go.

John's dad told us he was worried about our safety, which made me a little uptight. *Our safety? What's he talking about?* He explained his concern that people would view our experiment as racist. We had given that issue some thought and figured we could counter the contention by explaining that this was an academic exercise and no different from the practices of other ethnic groups. John's dad sighed and shook his head when I told him that, as if to say, *You poor thing. You just don't know what it is really like out there.*

Then came more sobering news from Michael Bennett. He would run the study for $120,000. *Wow.* After we got over the sticker shock, I reworked our budget to include that number. Our major expenses were paying for the study as well as hiring a public relations firm and a website developer. Other costs included travel fees for us and our advisers; a part-time staff person; a part-time documentarian who could capture the journey in video, pictures, and audio; a fund for professional services like legal, administrative, and accounting; and basic operational incidentals like a phone line, computer, the website, and office supplies. This experiment wasn't coming cheap, but we didn't want to do it on the cheap. This was a big idea, and big ideas often cost big bucks. But now we realized we were going to need big help too. The January pitch to the business owners was becoming even more important.

Aside from the Bennett's warnings, we received other signals we should have noticed. Back in September, I had sent a bunch of letters soliciting support—monetary or otherwise—from places like the National Association of Black Hotel Owners, Operators and Developers; the National Black Chamber of Commerce; the National Black MBA Association; the National Black McDonald's Operators Association; and my former colleagues at McDonald's, where I'd worked as a Corporate Strategy Manager and Strategic Communications Manager, a fancy title for speechwriter. None were responding. Meanwhile, another friend, Shawn Baldwin, a hot-shot broker with media exposure as well as Capital Management Group founder and CEO, had tried to set up a meeting for us with a few African American corporate heavyweights, but they all fell through.

Only in hindsight did we realize that these were indications of what Rogers had cautioned us about—that The Ebony Experiment might scare businesses. But I perceived these disappointments as speed bumps and kept pushing, telling myself that something would break our way if we just worked harder. And we still had the big pitch meeting. Despite the discouragement, I felt like an inventor with an awesome new product who had scored a big meeting with the venture capitalists. I revised the PowerPoint presentation, giving a healthy workout to my business school muscles, rehearsing with John and my brother Eduardo over and over.

At the time we were sufficiently guileless to think that these corporate types would help us based on the merits of the idea. Not until later did we realize that those relationships would be based almost entirely on cold—dare I say selfish—calculations.

By the last two months of 2008 The Ebony Experiment seemed to have legs. Cheryl Jackson at the *Chicago Sun-Times* interviewed us for a story, and we'd received indications that AOL's Black Voices, the largest Black-oriented social networking site, might be receptive. Missing in action, however, was *Ebony*, a foretelling sign.

The *Sun-Times* piece ran on December 20, which made us feel—finally—that The Ebony Experiment was the real deal. It was encouraging, validating, and a little scary. For the most part, the article focused on our personal story as a family trying to give back, and it indicated how difficult the experiment would be to carry out, given the lack of Black representation in so many industries. The best thing about the article was how it positioned The Ebony Experiment—not as an outlandish, militant, or groundless scheme but rather as a unique, credible, and potentially historic social exercise that would explore an important issue for all Americans. Reading the article and seeing pictures of our family made me realize that we couldn't turn back now, not even if we wanted to.

What brought me to tears, though, were the negative comments in response to the article, calling us racists and worse. For days I went through the responses posted to the online article—all twenty pages of them—deleting those using the N-word or some other offensive stereotype. Here's a sampling of what was left (reproduced here verbatim):

"annie84" wrote: *If she does this she would be considered a patriot. If I did this I would be considered a racist. Ok what if something happened to one of their kids and they had to go to the hospital??? And had to see a white/hispanic/indian/chinesse doctor??? Are you going to deny help from them???. . . . What about taxes? You pay taxes dont you??? Who does that go to??? You can't refuse that!*

Anderson Family you are no better then me and I am no better then you. Get over yourself!

A person with the moniker "suburbia" wrote: *what a joke that the sun-times put these racists in the paper*

YOU ARE NOT AFRICANS

you are americans with a sightly different pigment level then your countrymen maybe black businesses should start wearing a uniform like i dont know a sheet with a hood over your head

Our friends and family were feeling sorry for now-dispirited Maggie the Optimist, trying to cheer me up and prepare me for what might ensue as the project progressed.

During the anxious weeks leading up to the EE launch, John—keenly intuitive John—was the one who calmed my anxieties, mostly by using humor to keep us loose. He likened the inevitability and fear of EE's launch to a scene in the movie *Vacation*. You may remember it. Chevy Chase's character is standing at the edge of the pool and about to cheat on his wife by skinny-dipping with Christie Brinkley's character. Chevy, as dad Clark Griswold, rocks back and forth on his heels, slaps his hands together, and repeats, "This is crazy. This is crazy." John would do a dead-on impersonation of a Black Clark, and it cracked me up every time. It became a running joke.

We sent an e-mail blast to all our friends, announcing our pledge and linking to the *Sun-Times* article. I guess you could say the news went viral. We even got the attention of Ann Coulter's blog, where she compared The Ebony Experiment to Kwanzaa, arguing it was another useless project aimed at stirring up Black nationalists.

Steven Rogers had forwarded the *Sun-Times* story to Cheryle Jackson—no relation to the reporter. In addition to being the president of the Chicago Urban League, Cheryle had a show on WVON radio as well as *Next TV*, a local Fox show focusing on Black issues and featuring Black entrepreneurs. She loved the idea. Other promising leads emerged.

Despite the decidedly mixed reaction we were getting, I was upbeat and a little nervous, sort of like how I felt before starting law school. The night before we launched, the girls couldn't settle down. This wasn't excitement over our new venture; they were just being adorably squir-relly. We hadn't discussed the project with them yet, as we were planning on taking an eyedropper approach—telling them a little at a time, as needed. News of their grandmother's sickness was enough for them to digest for the time being. Besides, how much of this effort could we ex-pect two girls under the age of four to comprehend? They barely under-stood the concept of shopping. John and I couldn't sleep either, so we decided to surrender and bring the girls into our room. They lay between us and finally started dozing while John and I held hands across them and whispered through the night, giving voice to our dreams for The Ebony Experiment.

We thought all we had to do was get things going and, in time, everyone would join the movement. It was going to be so cool.

What was an exciting adventure in January was, by March, an ominous undertaking. Despite almost daily searches online and elsewhere, I hadn't found a single Black-owned drugstore or pharmacy, small department store, or retailer selling electronics, athletic gear or clothing, shoes, or toys for the girls. Sometimes I felt as if I were a religious ascetic, testing my faith by driving past all these lovely, overstocked stores on my way to a desert in search of diapers.

By this time we all needed new clothes and shoes as well as stuff for the house, like a new coffeemaker, car seat for Cara, picture frames, and linens. God First God Last, our miraculous household goods supplier, did not stock appliances, and although they had a couple frames, they were of very poor quality and not the right size. Later in the year they were able to scrounge up some sheets. And as much as I loved Farmers Best, shopping there wasn't the visit to the Emerald City Grocer that it appeared to be in January. The employees who gave the girls lollipops and helped me find the freshest meats and produce were lovable, but they had trouble getting specific items that I'd request.

We got used to going without most of those items—not that the girls and John stopped asking for them. But there were a few products, especially pull-ups, which were crucial to Anderson Family, Inc. At three and a half, Cara was potty trained and wore underpants in the day, but sometimes she slept in pull-ups. Cori, age two, was still transitioning from diapers to pull-ups. Before the experiment we had been making progress in this area. But we'd run out of pull-ups, and the situation got more aggravating at Farmers Best. I'd make the fourteen-mile trek on the staff's promise they'd stocked the item. Then I'd get there to find no pull-ups. I'd storm back to the car, muttering a few choice words to myself, and be forced to stop at the dump we called J's Fresh Meats—the only Black-owned place I'd found that sold diapers. Not pull-ups—diapers. As any mom can tell you, there's a difference.

Those days would just about break me. Every time Cara wet her bed unnecessarily or Cori cried because the diapers I forced her to wear were for babies, I cursed everybody. One of my regular targets was that group of wealthy business owners that months earlier had made very encouraging noises regarding funding. This was another painful lesson learned.

Because the holidays had pushed our meeting to January, we had had to bank—literally—on the over-the-top enthusiastic vibes I was getting from their president three months earlier. We had public relations people, a web designer, and the Bennetts already working with the promise of getting paid when the funding arrived in the early weeks of our venture. It sounds risky, I know. Hell, that looks downright foolhardy now. But that's how confident we were at the time.

We experienced a couple hiccups at the meeting, including only half of the executive committee members showing up. Karriem was there, though, to offer his perspective as one of the business owners who would benefit from their support of the project. The meeting was going fine until someone asked about marketing opportunities. *Marketing opportunities?* This was about funding a movement that would empower under-served Black neighborhoods. But if they wanted marketing rights, that was fine with us. I also offered product displays, interview mentions, a prominent spot on the website—whatever they wanted.

Karriem and I left feeling encouraged. A few days later the group's executive director informed John, Eduardo, and me that the executive committee endorsed the idea and was going to present the proposal to the full membership on January 26. After that, the president called. He talked at length about how the group is self-funded and struggles to survive solely on membership dues. He mentioned that they typically don't sponsor causes or events as a group; support of this kind was up to the individual members. So when he wanted to know what the members were going to get for their money I thought, *Didn't we cover this at the meeting?*

My bullshit meter started crackling, and it was dead-on accurate. They didn't give us any money. We'd extended ourselves; had counted on them based on their early, effusive response; and now they were pulling the proverbial rug out from under us. This group had been slated to be our primary funding source. Without it, our "movement" felt a little emaciated.

I moped around for a short time, wondering how the project would proceed without a sponsor. John said we should just focus on the experiment and not let their unwillingness to support us deter our resolve. We decided this fiasco was a test of our fortitude, the quintessential character-building experience.

"Oh well," Eduardo said. "Their loss. We'll show them. One day, they're gonna need us, and not the other way around. That's how big EE is gonna be."

Despite that one huge disappointment, in other ways we were getting a little bigger. Our efforts to garner attention from the mainstream media began paying dividends. In February Cheryle Jackson featured a lengthy segment about EE on her *Next TV* show, which prompted me to create a Facebook group so that folks could watch the video. On March 9 the *Chicago Tribune* ran a front-page story about The Ebony Experiment under the headline, "Oak Park Couple Travel Far and Wide on a Mission to Spend Their Money Only at Black-Owned Businesses." Up to that point we'd received a lot of media attention, but most of the mainstream press focused narrowly on our personal story without going into why we made the commitment. The *Tribune* piece—which ran on the front page of its sister paper, the *Los Angeles Times*, a day later—offered a balanced perspective and put our actions into a greater context. It included an interview with James Clingman, a University of Cincinnati instructor on Black entrepreneurship and a prolific writer on Black economics who also served as an EE executive adviser.

"Unfortunately," Clingman said in the piece, "many black people abandoned their own businesses and supported others, thinking that politics was the way out. Politics still will not get you anywhere unless you have an economic base. Quite frankly, I'd rather have more black businesses than black politicians."

The placement of the piece in a major newspaper helped draw other national mainstream media, like CNN and MSNBC, who called shortly after the *Tribune* story ran. The reporter who wrote the story—a White guy from the suburbs—made an impression on us, which is why, ultimately, his name ended up on the cover of this book.

What the piece didn't do was ease the ongoing charges of racism leveled against us. More than twenty-one hundred comments were posted to the *Tribune*'s online version of the story, and an additional one hundred–plus e-mails were sent directly to the paper. The vast majority was critical, contending that we were engaging in racism:

"How about a white business owner that has decided to hire whites only?" one man wrote. "These people should have their butts kicked instead of being written up as saints on a mission to fix the world. I'll see if I can't get some balance here by going to white owned stores only."

"If these nitwits want to remain divided by race for the remainder of their lives, fine," wrote another.

A third respondent stated, "Consider the next step in racial polarization—should the white plumber decide not to fix the Andersons' sink because they are African-American?"

We were getting used to these kinds of comments, though we were dumbfounded that a guy in Oregon started a Facebook group opposing The Ebony Experiment.

The silver lining here was that the number of comments posted to our website increased, which meant more people were learning about The Ebony Experiment. We started feeling that intoxicating momentum again.

In addition to all the turmoil our project stirred up, I was dealing with another commitment I'd made: overseeing Mima's care from six hundred miles away. At this point in March she was home on hospice care, about four months after doctors in the ICU had given her ninety days to live. We were feeling blessed that, technically, she was cancer-free, but we knew it could reemerge at any time. My dad, who had been totally dependent on Mima for domestic duties throughout their marriage, now, at age seventy-seven, had to become a full-time nurse, maid, and cook, and he gave it his most sincere effort.

He and I talked every day, sometimes more than that. If he felt like crying or talking, he called me. When Mima felt a little hot, Papa picked up the phone. When she cried, he called me. He'd tell me what she ate that day, the time and date of her next doctor's appointment, or what she mentioned in her most recent depression-induced rant. I kept track of every test, screened any potential caregivers, and conducted extensive research on pancreatic cancer. I'd make phone calls to nurses for different medications and to doctors' offices to make appointments or to complain about lengthy delays on X-ray results. I was spending at least twenty hours a week on tasks related to Mima's care. If there was pressing EE business, it would have to wait.

Then something strange and wondrous occurred: Mima started recovering. The hospice folks took the wheelchair back, then the hospital bed and then the walker. The nurses stopped coming. Feeling less depressed, she started eating solid food and gaining weight, and she was able to get herself to the bathroom. The doctors finally took her off hospice. She was sick but not dying. It was a joyous time.

I felt guilty that The Ebony Experiment took me away from my family, but it had a therapeutic effect, too. I needed a break, and everyone needed a break from me. Plus, I knew how proud it made Mima.

Nonetheless, I didn't talk directly about EE with the doctors and nurses I encountered. It was hard not to notice, though, that primarily White or Asian doctors cared for Mima. About a quarter of her care providers—aside from registered and advanced practice nurses and doctors—were Black, like the lab or x-ray techs, physical therapists, medical assistants, pain management administrators, and many of the clerical, housekeeping, and food-service staff as well as the folks who cleaned and fed her. Of the roughly twenty-five physicians who tended to her over the course of her battle with pancreatic cancer, three were Black—a gastrointestinal surgeon, a respiratory doctor, and an internist. But that was it—and this was in Atlanta, the Black capital of the United States.

Mima's fight made me think about what would happen if John or the girls got really sick during our year. Cara and Cori had a Black pediatrician already, but if one of them needed to go to a hospital, very little if any of the money we'd spend there would make its way to the Black community.

The idiot with the online name "annie84" came to mind, the one who'd suggested in a comment to the *Sun-Times* that we'd deny our daughters medical care if their doctors were not Black. Just to be clear, I'd never deny any loved one medical treatment based on the race of the health care provider. Besides, one of the points of this exercise was to document what products and services we could and could not find. For example, we didn't think we would find a Black-owned health insurance company, but we were not about to forgo health insurance for the year; it just meant we would look for a competent Black health insurance broker and then note the futile search in our study records.

Our experience with Mima's health care team prompted me to investigate the role Blacks play in the health care industry. I wasn't very surprised with what I discovered. For example, a study published in 2007 in the *Annals of Internal Medicine* found that African American doctors suffer from "racial fatigue" stemming from stress related to a promotion that didn't happen, the meager patient referrals they receive, or other kinds of racism—however nuanced—they experience. In general, Black physicians feel isolated, lack mentors, and are held to higher standards than White ones. This drives Black physicians from the profession.

The National Medical Association, which promotes "the collective interests of physicians and patients of African descent," published raw numbers of physicians by race and ethnicity from 2006. The total number of physicians in the United States was nearly 922,000. Of this number, only 32,452 were Black. That's less than one-third the number of Asian American physicians, and 13,000 below the number of Hispanic physicians. In its September 2007 edition *The Journal of the National Medical Association* discussed what would be an appropriate ratio of African American physicians to the overall population: 218 African American doctors per 100,000 people. According to the article, the current ratio is 73 per 100,000 people.

In a related finding, the Duke University School of Medicine's Sullivan Commission—a group of sixteen leaders in health, education, law, and business chaired by former US Health and Human Services Secretary Dr. Louis W. Sullivan—in 2004 reported minority representation lagging below acceptable levels throughout the health care industry.

"Together, African Americans, Hispanic Americans, and American Indians make up more than 25 percent of the U.S. population," the report states, "but only 9 percent of the nation's nurses, 6 percent of its physicians, and 5 percent of dentists." In addition, "minorities make up less than 10 percent of baccalaureate nursing faculties, 8.6 percent of dental school faculties, and only 4.2 percent of medical school faculties."

The impact of these disparities is clear: Minorities, specifically African Americans, receive much poorer health care in this country. Study after study confirms it, but perhaps none is more comprehensive than the annual National Healthcare Disparities Report, produced by the US Department of Health and Human Services in 2009, which showed that Blacks received worse care than Whites and had less access to health care, the quality of which is not improving.

Poorer health care results in productivity loss, absenteeism, higher health care costs, and, of course, death. Former US Surgeon General David Satcher's research suggests that access to quality health care for Blacks is key to saving the lives of more than eighty-three thousand African Americans every year.

Now, I understand that "buying Black" is not the answer to creating more Black doctors—the issues are too complex and too entrenched in centuries of racism for that to work. Still, I don't think that it's a stretch to say that buying Black would help open the doors of the medical profession to more African American students. Spending your dollars in the Black community leads to strengthening lives, families, schools, and neighborhoods. Stabilizing those entities would create a ripple effect, helping to keep more kids in school and giving them hope for brighter futures.

But all that takes a lot of work. Although we'd been at it for only a quarter of a year, it felt like a hell of a lot longer. The truth is that we were the latest in a long line of folks trying to make a difference in this way. Our predecessors didn't have an easy time, either.

Chapter 5

"A Mighty Economic
Power"

THROUGHOUT THE YEAR, AND PARTICULARLY IN THE
first six months, we'd get excited after hearing that a particular store was
Black-owned. Then I'd follow up with a call and receive the disappointing news that our information had been wrong. One Saturday in February, when I tracked down a lead for a dollar store in Maywood, I got a
pleasant surprise: The person answering the phone said an African American owned the place.

Armed with a huge list of items we needed, I put Cara into her car seat
and the two of us drove off. A few minutes later we pulled up to a large
store. As we walked its aisles, I noticed that all the employees had a professional demeanor—and were Black. Cara and I had fun, just a couple
of girls on a shopping expedition. We found so many little things for her
and Cori—coloring books, bath toys, candy, Dora the Explorer cups and
plates, arts and crafts supplies—that we filled our cart.

But I couldn't quell my skepticism—the place looked too nice. It was
so orderly and clean. Moreover, I felt that if an African American owned
a general store this well stocked and large, we would have heard about it
by now or finding it would have been easier for us. I hated myself for
thinking that the store couldn't be Black-owned, but the idea wouldn't go
away. I asked the cashier if I could speak to a manager.

"Keep your fingers crossed, honey," I muttered to Cara. She looked confused.

The manager, who was Black, came over and I asked whether the place was Black-owned.

He shook his head, and I felt that familiar sorrow seep into my stomach.

"No," he said. "I'm the manager. I run this place, but a White family owns it."

I explained that I'd called earlier and an employee told me the store was Black-owned. He looked a little perplexed and called over the employee who'd given me the wrong information. She apologized, saying she didn't think I was asking whether a Black person actually owned the store.

"It's a silly question anyway," she said.

Now I had a tough choice: Cheat and make it easy for us or honor our commitment and create an awkward scene in which my daughter would come unglued. I looked down at the full shopping cart and then over at Cara, who had this slightly hopeful, slightly uncertain expression on her face. And then I swung the cart back toward the aisles.

"We've got to put it all back, sweetie," I said. "I'm sorry."

"But mommy," Cara protested, "I like the Dora stuff. Mommy, please . . . "

She was tugging on the side of the cart.

"No, Cara," I said, and I started to explain but then stopped because doing so only would have confused and riled her more.

"Sweetie, mommy left her money at home," I lied. "I'm so silly. I can't believe it. I'm sorry, honey. I just don't have any money right now. Maybe we'll come back later."

That didn't help much. I did what I had to do—returned the items to their shelves and countered the whining with a mix of apologizing and stern talk.

After that episode and a few others, we gave up on the West Side and accepted that we were going to spend the bulk of our dollars at establishments in the South Loop, Bronzeville, and Hyde Park, three gentrifying, predominantly Black neighborhoods that celebrate their diversity. We had been spending a great deal of shopping time there anyway because Farmers Best and God First God Last were both on the South Side. But the fact that we lived so close to several struggling Black neighborhoods and had to bypass them to shop on the South Side was irksome. However, it made sense for Black entrepreneurs to set up shop there, as the areas almost buzzed with disposable income. Many of the Black-owned businesses were high-quality establishments run by proud, intelligent owners who wanted to employ Black people and show local kids a better path.

But, inevitably, people misconstrued our patronage of those Black-owned businesses as racist, which continued to confound us. Obviously, these name-callers didn't know their history. Like almost every other ethnic group does for its own, Blacks have a long tradition of advocating for their compatriots to support their community by buying Black.

The concept of buying Black might trace its formal introduction to the last day of summer, 1832, when Maria Stewart stood in front of an audience of Blacks and at least a few Whites—men and women—in Boston's Franklin Hall and confronted them about the already touchy issues of race and gender. In the process, that brave lady became something of a great-great-auntie to The Ebony Experiment.

"Daughters of Africa, awake!" she exhorted. "It is of no use for us to sit with our hands folded, hanging our heads. . . . Let us make a mighty effort and arise . . . and let us raise a fund ourselves. Do you ask, what can we do? Unite and build a store of your own. Fill one side with dry-goods and the other with groceries. Do you ask, where is the money? We have spent more than enough for nonsense to do what building we should want."

Stewart, a woman whose life would make a great movie—are you reading this, Oprah?—was quite possibly the first African American, male or female, to call publicly, if somewhat indirectly, on Blacks to support each other in business.

Now lost to the pages of history, this feisty woman, whom historian William Andrew called "the first Black feminist-abolitionist in America," was born in Hartford, Connecticut, in 1803 and orphaned at the age of five. She worked as a domestic, and at twenty-three she married "independent shipping agent" James Stewart. A veteran of the War of 1812, he was then forty-seven. The couple regularly attended the African Baptist Church on the north side of Beacon Hill, where their circle of friends included the activist David Walker, who became Maria's mentor.

Three devastating events would light the fire of righteousness in Maria. First was the death of her husband of three years from heart disease. While reeling from the loss, Stewart suffered another setback: Her husband's White business associates robbed her of his estate. Nine months later David Walker was found dead near the entrance to his business, likely a victim of consumption, although whispers of something more diabolical persisted.

Instead of crumbling in the aftermath of such trauma, Stewart got angry and inspired, writing opinion pieces, speaking publicly, and calling on Blacks to lift themselves up from their spiritual, educational, and economic depths—nearly a decade before "The Great Abolitionist" Frederick Douglass started public outcries against racial injustice. In fact, Stewart was the originator of themes that Douglass, Sojourner Truth, Frances Harper, and even W. E. B. Du Bois later gave broader exposure.

For her trouble, she was run out of Boston—partly by her own people—and spent the rest of her life teaching at the Williamsburg Colored School in New York, then later in Baltimore and Washington, DC. She died in 1879.

"It would take deep faith to find hope for African Americans in the political landscape of 1830s America," writes Cheryl R. Jorgensen-Earp, professor of communications at Lynchburg College, in her 2006 piece for the journal *Voices of Democracy*. "Stewart found signs pointing to the secular redemption of black America in the sacred text of the Bible and provided them as a guide for what she knew would be a perilous journey." Her faith "served a black nationalist vision of unity, struggle, and progress." She was, Jorgensen-Earp writes, a woman with a "distinctive voice and prescient vision."

Stewart may have been the first formal promoter of African American self-help economics, but the concept got its start well before she stepped up to the podium at Franklin Hall. In the early years of enslavement in North America, African slaves created secret burial societies—about which they kept quiet out of concern that their owners would perceive them as conspiracies—to help them accumulate money for an opulent funeral, which they believed would guarantee a successful afterlife. Those secret organizations led to the establishment of mutual aid societies, the first Black economic empowerment networks in the United States. These included the African Union Society, begun in 1780 in Newport, Rhode Island, and the Free African Society, founded in 1787 in Philadelphia.

Just one year after Stewart delivered her speech, the National Negro Convention, the first national organization of African Americans that opposed slavery and advocated for Black economic empowerment, issued a directive that "black businesspeople would only sell, and black consumers would only buy those products that had not been produced from slave labor."

The "free produce movement," organized with these goals in mind, began in the mid-1820s. An African American produce store owner in Philadelphia, Lydia White, received this vote of confidence from the Convention in 1833: "All who feel an interest in promoting the cause of universal freedom, is [sic] cheerfully recommended to her store." In 1841 the Female Trading Association, a New York grocery store cooperative run by one hundred African American women, sold grits, rice, soap, candles, brooms, and brushes, among other items. At least one newspaper, the *Colored American*, advocated for Blacks to support it because, as the newspaper stated, "We believe this is the first successful organized effort of this kind among the colored people of this city."

Twenty years later Martin Robison Delaney, a Pennsylvania newspaper publisher and physician, documented the growth of Black businesses prior to the Civil War in his book, *The Condition, Elevation, Emigration and Destiny of the Colored People of the United States*. Delaney was an ardent supporter of touting Black business success as a vindication of Black society that would enhance racial pride and keep money in Black communities. In his book Delaney uses the phrase "buy black" in a chapter entitled, "Our Elevation in the United States," in which he encourages antebellum Blacks to do just that. Without this, African American–purchased consumer goods "are the products of the white man, purchased by us from the white man, consequently our earnings and means, are all given to the white man."

After the Civil War the devastated South needed Blacks to rebuild it. African Americans worked as tradesmen and established construction companies, but their mutual aid societies also expanded into other cooperatives, including manufacturing, real estate, banking, and insurance, mainly in response to the lack of capital available to them. By the end of the 1800s Black leaders, including W. E. B. Du Bois, were speaking at African American conferences, where they would present strategies for Blacks to succeed in business. Those strategies included, as Du Bois stated, "the mass of the Negroes (who) must learn to patronize business enterprises conducted by their own race, even at some disadvantage." He also encouraged Black churches, schools, and newspapers to promote African American–owned businesses.

In addition to Du Bois, Booker T. Washington and Marcus Garvey became prominent leaders of the Black economic empowerment movement in the late 1800s and early 1900s. Washington, after witnessing African American rights recede in the post–Civil War South, emphasized industrial business development over political and civil rights for Blacks. His theory: "No race that has anything to contribute to the markets of the world is long in any degree ostracized." In 1900 he helped establish the first formal business advancement network for African Americans, the National Negro Business League (NNBL), which spawned other African American business and professional groups, including the National Negro Bankers Association, National Negro Insurance Association, National Association of Funeral Directors, National Negro Retail Merchants Association, even the National Bar Association. The birth of the NNBL ushered in what has been called "the Golden Age of Black Business."

Marcus Garvey established the Universal Negro Improvement Association (UNIA) in 1914 in his native Jamaica with the goal of boosting Blacks politically and economically all over the world. Two years later he came to Harlem and expanded the UNIA. In addition to advocating Black businesses, he lobbied for liberating Africa, promoting Black nationalism, and appreciating Black culture, in the process converting UNIA into one of the most powerful Black organizations in the world.

Groups were springing up all over the country to support fellow Blacks. In 1915, for example, the Atlanta Mutual Insurance Association organized a Boosters Club "to encourage Negroes to trade with one another, to buy groceries, take out insurance, buy medicine, and employ Negro professional men in every case where it can be done without inconvenience or inefficiency." By 1919 more than 140 chartered Negro Business Leagues were functioning in 30 states. In the 1920s these groups took their actions national, urging African Americans to "Buy Something From a Negro Merchant!" and promoting National Negro Trade Weeks. In the 1930s editors of the Chicago newspaper *Whip* established "Don't Buy Where You Can't Work" campaigns that caught on in other cities. In a July 1931 editorial appearing in *The Crisis* magazine, Du Bois wrote, "If we once make a religion of our determination to spend our meager income so far as possible only in such ways as will bring us employment consideration and opportunity, the possibilities before us are enormous. . . . A nation twice as large as Portugal, Holland, or Sweden is not powerless—is not merely a supplicant beggar for crumbs—it is a mighty economic power when it gets vision enough to use its strength."

This was an era of robust growth for Black cooperatives—individuals or businesses (agricultural, financial, or social) can pool their resources to exert stronger economic leverage than any one or two of those entities could alone. There was the Colored Merchants' Association, a chain of thirty-five Black grocery stores, established in 1928 in Montgomery, Alabama; the Florida Farmers' Cooperative; and the Tyrrell Credit Union, in Columbia, North Carolina. Churches operated cooperatives. Even

Black colleges had the Community Consumers Cooperative, founded at Georgia State College in 1934, and the People's Cooperative supermarket at the Tuskegee Institute. Du Bois's 1907 study, "Economic Co-operation among Negro Americans," details the extensive number of "cooperatively supported schools, mutual aid societies, hospitals and churches in the late nineteenth century." There were also seventy-five to a hundred homes for orphans and the elderly as well as forty hospitals, all supported by African Americans. This kind of cooperation, according to Du Bois, was a direct result of Whites' economic oppression of Blacks and centuries of extreme poverty for African Americans.

Whatever the reasons for its genesis, nobody would dispute the impact of that cooperation. Du Bois published a study in 1898 that reported only nineteen hundred "Negro-owned" businesses; in 1930 that number was seventy thousand. What's interesting about this explosion of enterprises is that it came with growing numbers of Blacks in white-collar jobs, many of which were in Black businesses. Imagine what might have occurred if the number of white-collar jobs continued to increase.

At about this time thriving Black business communities were emerging in midsize cities. Two of the more prominent were the "Black Wall Streets" of Durham, North Carolina, and Tulsa, Oklahoma. In Durham an assortment of Black businesses flourished on the south side of Parrish Street, including fifteen grocery stores, eight barbershops, seven meat and fish dealers, and two drugstores, not to mention doctors, lawyers, and other professionals as well as financing and insurance companies. Hell, I could have done 90 percent of my shopping without getting in a car—or buggy—if I lived near such a business district. White businesses occupied the north side of the street, and apparently the setup worked. "We have in Durham today the outstanding group of colored capitalists who have entered the second generation of business enterprise," sociologist E. F. Frazier wrote in 1923. "These men have mastered the technique of modern business and acquired the spirit of modern enterprise."

In his 1927 book *The Story of Durham, City of the New South*, historian William Kenneth Boyd attributed the success of Parrish Street to

Blacks who'd come to Durham after the Civil War, folks he described as "industrious and thrifty citizens" who "established a tradition of industry, reliability, and integrity." And here's one of his more intriguing observations: "A second factor in the progress of the Negro," Boyd wrote, "has been the policy of white people, a policy of tolerance and helpfulness."

The Tulsa story was similar, except on a larger scale. Greenwood Avenue was the main artery of the commercial district, which folks also called Greenwood. From the early 1900s until 1921 the number of Black-owned businesses grew to more than six hundred, including a Black-owned bus line, six real estate companies, wealthy oilmen, construction firms, and other entrepreneurs. African American attorneys and about fifteen Black doctors and surgeons also had offices on Tulsa's Black Wall Street. More than forty grocery stores and meat markets were there, as were thirty restaurants and four hotels. Several Black millionaires had businesses in Greenwood, six of whom owned private planes—at a time when there were only two airports in the entire state.

Urban renewal in the 1960s destroyed Durham's Black Wall Street. This "renewal" brought construction of the East-West Expressway—now known as the Durham Freeway—through the neighborhood, killing hundreds of Black-owned businesses and displacing thousands of residents.

The demise of Tulsa's Black Wall Street came in a cauldron of racial violence. It started with the arrest of a young Black shoeshine man, Dick Rowland, on dubious charges that he'd raped a White woman. While he sat in the courthouse jail on May 31, 1921, an angry mob of Whites gathered outside with the plan to lynch him. Armed Blacks intervened, and a scuffle ensued. A gunshot was fired, and a race riot ignited.

A total of thirty-five square blocks was destroyed in about fourteen hours of rioting. That event was "the worst civil disturbance since the Civil War," according to an Oklahoma state commission's 2001 report on the riot. Historian John Sibley Butler set the number of dead at more than fifty, and "over 1,000 homes and businesses lay in ruins. Thousands of occupations were lost."

There is so much to mourn about these catastrophes. Think of the enduring value those businesses would have provided for countless families as well as all the dreams that nurtured those businesses that were lost to subsequent generations.

When the Great Depression arrived in 1929, Blacks suffered more than other groups did. About one-quarter of African Americans were on relief in 1935, a figure that looks comparable to the overall unemployment rate of 25 percent, although the percentage of Blacks receiving assistance was much higher in certain cities—up to 81 percent in Norfolk, Virginia, and nearly 66 percent in Atlanta. At the same time, from 1929 to 1939, retail sales among Black businesses declined nearly 30 percent, while the national aggregate retail sales drop was only 13 percent.

In the aftermath of the Depression and, later, with Black soldiers returning home from World War II, a growing, politically active Black middle class emerged. Occasional waves of discontent over economic mistreatment and human rights violations flared, like the 1955–56 Montgomery Bus Boycott, organized after Blacks suffered humiliating treatment in the city's public bus system. That protest gave Blacks an increasing sense of power, leading them to patronize local, Black-owned businesses. In 1955–57 Blacks in Mississippi boycotted a chain of stores that the families of the murderers of African American Emmett Till operated, a move that led to the demise of the family's business.

Throughout this period, as in others, African American leaders were trying to rally the people to use the power of their dollars. In a 1957 book by Black economic empowerment advocate William K. Bell, *15 Million Negroes and 15 Billion Dollars*, he states, "15 MILLION NEGROES cannot be kept from gaining economic power if they determine to keep within the race a certain portion of that 15 BILLION DOLLARS that is running daily through their fingers, as water does over a dam. . . . There is GREAT POWER in 15 BILLION DOLLARS!"

Other boycotts occurred. In Nashville, starting in late 1959, Black leaders and students waged sit-ins at diners across the city. About six months later, stung by a drop of about 20 percent in business, six department stores began serving African Americans, who then broke racial barriers in movie theaters, workplaces, hotels, and other public services.

That kind of action was the backbone of the civil rights movement, of course, as it was used in Tallahassee, Savannah, New Orleans, and elsewhere. One of the most successful boycotts was the Southern Christian Leadership Conference's Operation Breadbasket in Atlanta and Chicago in 1966 and 1967. Employing a strategy known as "selective patronage," Breadbasket called on Black ministers and their churches to pressure companies to employ a reasonable percentage of Blacks in businesses that sold primarily to the Black community. Armed with employment figures for those companies, the ministers would attempt to "negotiate a more equitable employment practice." If they couldn't reach a solution, the ministers would encourage their parishioners to boycott certain products. In Atlanta Operation Breadbasket created jobs for African Americans that accounted for an additional $25 million a year going to Black neighborhoods. In Chicago, in just fifteen months, Breadbasket brought about two thousand jobs, worth about $15 million.

In fact, it was economics, or at least the unacceptable treatment of Black consumers, that "sparked the civil rights protests of the mid-twentieth century," writes Professor Robert E. Weems Jr. in *Desegregating the Dollar.* In his view the Civil Rights Act of 1964, "in large part, appeared to be the culmination of years of sustained black consumer economic retribution."

But not everything that emerged from that historic struggle was positive; it's a little more complicated than the black-and-white newsreels we see on the History Channel. As previously mentioned, the civil rights movement clearly had a deteriorative effect on Black-owned businesses. We traded progress in politics and human rights for economic stability, which is where the Black Power movement comes into play—a well-meaning concept of the 1960s that fizzled. From my perch, Black Power is not much more than a catchy, ambiguous phrase rooted in those secret societies that emerged soon after slavery was established on this continent in the 1600s.

Black Power leaders did agree on a few general tenets, such as Blacks should be included in national political and economic decision making and should work to help all Blacks achieve success. They stressed business ownership and set the goal of pushing their agenda until Blacks obtained "a stake in the American capitalist system commensurate with their 12 percent of the American population," writes John T. McCartney, professor of comparative politics and Black political thought at Lafayette College, in the *Encyclopedia of African American Business History*. These admirable concepts were distilled from the work of Booker T. Washington and Marcus Garvey.

The problem is that the leaders could never agree on how to generate that economic growth. Some contended that skills training and equal opportunity for jobs were key. Others favored the accumulation of Black capital to spark African American industrialization. A third argument was that Black capital, even if amassed, wasn't enough to lift up African Americans economically. That thinking was widely accepted among political leaders, including President Richard Nixon, who established efforts to direct capital toward African American business ventures. But the federal government and the business establishment failed to fund the initiatives, so they faded.

In 1969 the total number of Black-owned businesses in the United States was 163,000, which accounted for 0.25 percent of all businesses in the country. By the late 1990s that number had grown to 620,912, or 3.5 percent of all businesses—a figure hardly commensurate with the nearly 13 percent of Americans who were Black.

More conventional forms of Black Power that were products of the civil rights movement included Affirmative Action and its cousin, minority business set-aside programs. Established by the federal government in 1972, Affirmative Action, via the Equal Employment Opportunity Act, created a system by which employers were strongly encouraged to hire and promote minorities. Affirmative Action has been successful to a point, but it remains a divisive effort that's been challenged no fewer than five times in the US Supreme Court, which has sometimes contradicted earlier rulings.

In addition, research in 1979 showed that an inordinately high percentage of Black executives were placed in personnel positions responsible for implementing Affirmative Action, jobs that are typically outside of the strategic power centers in corporations and are traditionally the hardest hit in economic declines.

Minority business set-asides, the program that originated in the 1977 Public Works Employment Act and calls for awarding a portion of government contracts to minority firms, is nearly as contentious. Research suggests that "efforts to assist minority businesses in obtaining contracts with state, local, and government bodies often help to increase minority employment," according to University of Minnesota professor Samuel L. Myers Jr., who studies racial inequality and public policy. But other data show that there are less expensive ways to help minority businesses, including subsidizing start-up capital—a huge issue for Black businesses— by waiving bonding and insurance requirements and reaching out "*to local enterprises in communities with large minority populations.*" Isn't buying Black a way to do just that—*without* spending taxpayers' money? Another problem with minority set-aside programs is that a large chunk of the business they offer is based on federal procurement or sales to minority communities, both of which can be very unstable.

Any discussion of the civil rights era must include the heroic, iconic Dr. King. It seems that virtually every civil rights action from the late 1950s through the 1960s—even after his death—emerged from or was connected to his work in some way. To properly characterize King's efforts in a few sentences is impossible, but his legacy in the arena of Black economic empowerment is unclear.

In short, Dr. King saw Black businesses as very limited in their power to change the economic plight of African Americans, and he held a slightly conflicting view of how Blacks could get ahead economically. On the one hand, he believed that creating more jobs for Blacks and growing a larger consumer bloc of African Americans would help them make economic gains. At the same time, he saw capitalism as exploitive and "denounced American capitalism and the futility of utilizing black businesses as the base for black economic empowerment . . . for anything beyond serving as icons of resourcefulness," according to Professor Juliet E. K. Walker, a member of our Executive Advisory team and the author of several books on African American business. "Rather than pushing for the expansion of black business," she writes, "it appears that King preferred that blacks march to the doors of white corporate America and demand employment."

Dr. Walker believes that Dr. King's view of human rights was changing as conditions evolved. At the time of his death he thought that Blacks would achieve economic empowerment by gaining jobs and using their consumer muscle.

The main goals of the civil rights movement, in Dr. Walker's words, "were to secure civil and political rights," which were accomplished—technically, at least—by 1965. But African Americans were still disproportionately poor, and when government and Black American rights organizations began looking at ways to solve that complex problem, Dr. King "was seeing the Black American economic picture within the context of the negative aspects of global capitalism."

Dr. Walker points to this excerpt from Dr. King's speech to the Southern Christian Leadership Conference in August 1967: "We must ask the question, 'Why are there forty million poor people in America?' And, when you begin to ask that question, you are raising questions about the economic system, about a broader distribution of wealth. When you ask that question, you begin to question the capitalistic economy."

"Here was a man," Dr. Walker says, "moving from denouncing segregation, racism and discrimination on a national level to [denouncing] segregation, racism and discrimination in the economic system on a global level. It's not that Dr. King didn't believe black business was important to the black community. It was that black business would not be enough to salvage the economic plight of blacks. Had he lived longer, he would have formulated more specific goals to achieve black economic parity."

I certainly can appreciate Dr. King's perspective, though I do wonder what he'd say now. Yes, Blacks made gains in the 1970s, '80s and '90s. We can vote. We go to the same schools as Whites, eat in the same restaurants, shop in the same stores. Yet it feels like Blacks are still stuck so far behind Whites and other races—in some ways we've lost ground. Why?

I think it comes down to economic strength, the kind that comes not from a government program—we've had plenty of those—but from creating it ourselves through discipline, smarts, and resourcefulness. And by building and patronizing our own businesses.

After Affirmative Action, minority business set-asides, and the failure of what Professor Walker calls a "communal economic effort" known as "black capitalism" of the 1960s and '70s, efforts to "buy Black" seemed to make a comeback in 1985, when Tony Brown, television producer, author, and Black business promoter, launched the "Buy Freedom" campaign that called for African Americans to spend half their money on Black businesses. His national public affairs TV show, *Tony Brown's Journal*, also pushes Black economic nationalism.

Efforts to "buy Black"—many of which are profit-oriented—are ongoing. Apart from the various Black business directories—some of which you can find through organizations listed in the back of this book—a handful of successful ventures promoting Black-owned businesses exist. These include Black Business Network, a mostly online community of nearly thirty thousand Black consumers who want to support African American–owned businesses, and iZania, started by a former IBM executive, whose goal is to enable members "to leverage Internet connectivity to achieve positive outcomes for the Virtual Black Community." Another is Recycling Black Dollars, a community-based nonprofit that has done a great deal to help the Watts and Compton communities in Los Angeles. The Black Shopping Channel is a for-profit company founded by Cleveland Gary, former Los Angeles Rams and Miami Dolphins running back, with the goal of marketing small- and medium-sized Black-owned businesses on TV, among other places. Additionally, there are a number of national organizations focused on directing business to minority—but not solely Black-owned—companies. Among the most noteworthy is the National Minority Supplier Development Council, which in 2010 coordinated $100.5 billion in purchases from minority-owned businesses.

There are organizations that promote the creation and support of our own products and industries, without outside assistance and instead of supporting businesses owned by other groups. The Harvest Institute, created by famed activist and author Dr. Claud Anderson, is based on the principle "that Blacks must aggregate, pool their resources, and build independent communities before allying with competing groups," and promotes this strategy as a way to build a community that is self-sustaining.

What all this history highlights is that we have immense buying power. Just smartly spending even a few dollars on quality Black-owned businesses would accomplish so much. That's one conclusion of a study that Northwestern University's Kellogg School of Management conducted. We enlisted their assistance via Steven Rogers after the group of wealthy business owners bailed on us. In another example of his commitment and generosity, Rogers lined up Thane Gautier, a recent Kellogg grad and Graduate Fellow of the Levy Entrepreneurship Center, to set up a team of students to conduct the study, which Thane managed even though we couldn't pay for it.

One piece of data the group uncovered was that the buying power of African Americans was estimated at about $913 billion in 2008, which is equal to the spending power of the sixteenth largest country in the world, Indonesia, below that of Canada and Turkey, and above Australia and Poland. The $1.2 trillion projection of US Black buying power in 2013 would make African American buying power equal to that of Canada. Of course, back in the 1940s African American buying power was much greater than Canada's. I'm not sure what that says about the economic growth of Canadians and African Americans, but I think you can conclude that conditions need to improve for African Americans.

Although finding actual data on how much African Americans spend on Black-owned businesses is difficult, the Kellogg analysis placed the figure between 2 to 5 percent, which would bring "only pennies on the Black dollar" to the Black community. Two percent of $913 billion spent with Black-owned businesses yields $18.3 billion. Five percent brings about $46 billion. What's left is $894 to $867 billion.

You're about to get a lesson in the value of pennies.

Consider a conservative 2 percent spent on Black businesses, as the Kellogg analysts did. Even that seemingly small amount can generate a lot of money. The Kellogg team calculated what would happen if Black households with substantial disposable income—those with a total after-tax income of $75,000, or roughly 2.65 million families—boosted their spending from 2 percent to 10 percent on Black-owned businesses. By spending just one of every ten dollars at a Black-owned business, these households would generate $14 billion in revenue.

How many Subway restaurant franchises do you think that would buy?

That's the intriguing hypothetical scenario the Kellogg team considered. They took that $14 billion, divided it by the amount it takes to open a Subway franchise—at anywhere from $81,300 to $203,000, it is one of the most economical, compared to other major restaurant chains—and found that those funds could open somewhere between 69,000 to 172,200 stores. (That lower figure is more than twice the number of existing Subways in the world.)

"Further," the report noted, "each Subway store employs 8 to 13 people. Using the model we have created, the conservative estimate of 68,965 stores can create 551,724 to 896,551 new jobs."

Half a million to nearly a million new jobs, simply by redirecting just $1 of every $10 of Black buying power in higher-income African American homes. Think about that. It's true that a fast-food restaurant job isn't exactly like being the chief financial officer of a multinational company or the superintendent of a wealthy suburban school district, but work with me here. What if a Black teenager got a job at a neighborhood Subway instead of hanging out on the corner after school? What if that teenager worked hard and became a manager and/or got tuition reimbursement to go to college and major in finance? Now multiply the possibilities by 551,724 or 896,551 or any number in between.

Imagine what could happen if all Black households, not just higher-income folks, spent 5 percent of their after-tax income on African American–owned businesses—another scenario the Kellogg team considered. The answer: $32.2 billion. That's right. Over thirty billion dollars would be thrust into the African American economy.

So do something for me right now. Pull the spare change out of your pocket or purse, or take a look at that change in the jar on your dresser. Consider what a small change in your spending habits—pun intended—could create. And then have that change be your change. Simple, right?

Chapter 6

The Turbulent Dew

CHICAGO STILL FEELS LIKE A FOREIGN PLACE TO ME. And during the months when the area is subject to wind, snow, single-digit temperatures, and gray skies, that foreign place feels like Saskatchewan. Remember, I'm from Miami, possibly the sunniest spot in the Sunshine State. In Chicago the hours of sunlight shrink so much that in December the city is nearly dark by 4 p.m. Even after fifteen years I haven't adjusted to the misery of Chicago winters, and John, the lucky guy, gets the distinct pleasure of experiencing my wretched moods from Halloween until well past Easter.

But then the weather starts to break, which means spring is on its way. John and I have our own phrase for it: The Dew. It's our capricious, catchall explanation for renewal at this time of year.

When The Dew arrives, it brings with it the anticipation of the season that liberates me, makes me feel frivolous, and reminds me of home: summer. Our private joke—and we're one of those goofy couples who have an infinite supply of them—is to attribute any unexpected pleasure to The Dew.

But this year The Dew and spring were particularly sluggish to arrive and, when they did, it was different. Something was siphoning our bliss, and its initials were EE. The momentum had stalled. Yes, we'd gotten encouragement for our efforts, but we'd also received our share of ugliness.

The most recent hit came from an unlikely source: *Ebony* magazine.

Back in July of 2008 an informal chat with reporter Adrienne Samuels was The Ebony Experiment's first official meeting, and it inspired us to move forward. Every time our confidence waned or somebody didn't call us back, we'd think, *Yeah, so and so hasn't called back, but who cares,* Ebony *is going to cover us. Once* Ebony *gives us a big splash, folks like so and so are going to be calling* us!

After our initial meeting Adrienne sent us e-mails over the next few weeks saying she wanted to do a story, had gotten approval for it, and would talk to the higher-ups about sponsorship and partnership. But by that October things started getting weird. People at *Ebony* stopped communicating, despite my entreaties. Friends with connections tried to intervene with higher-ups at the magazine, but that didn't work either.

Then, less than two months before our January launch, I realized what might be happening. Maybe it was just as Steven Rogers had warned us: Some businesses would be afraid of The Ebony Experiment. From the perspective of Adrienne, the writer, the project had obvious appeal. But the corporate honchos—those concerned about advertisers and sponsors and about being accepted into the Mainstream Media Club—might have viewed The Ebony Experiment as militant and something to be avoided at all costs. We had thought they'd embrace us because they would see how The Ebony Experiment fit neatly into *Ebony* magazine's ideals of hope and pride in Black people and its role in bringing to light the issues the rest of America would prefer not to confront.

Man, were we ever wrong. They were ignoring us, hoping we would go away.

Things deteriorated from there. On March 11, two days after the front-page *Chicago Tribune* story and the day after a live interview on MSNBC—our first major national television appearance—we were still celebrating when we got an e-mail from *Ebony*'s legal department, informing us that a lawsuit would be filed in federal court at the end of the day if we did not change the name of our project.

We'd gotten word from a very reliable source that Linda Johnson Rice, chairman of Johnson Publishing, had received calls from major advertisers asking whether the magazine was affiliated with our project. She could have said no and left it at that, or she could have said "no, but we think it's a way to open an important dialogue in the Black community," or even "no, we think it's silly, but it is newsworthy and we have a responsibility to cover it."

Instead, in what seemed like an effort to appease advertisers who may have been nervous about *Ebony*'s perceived affiliation with us, she threatened a lawsuit that could kill EE. I know advertisements pay the bills, but those ads are based on subscribers' loyalty, which stems from the relevance, reliability, and quality of content. She could have provided balanced, insightful coverage of The Ebony Experiment while still making it clear that the magazine and movement weren't affiliated. In fact, that coverage would have enhanced the integrity of the magazine and presumably drawn more readers, most of whom probably would have been interested in EE, and this could have led to more advertising interest. Seems like a pretty simple winning strategy to me. Plus, plenty of Black organizations have the word Ebony in their name and aren't plagued by infringement or affiliation concerns. Why should it be an issue for us?

At least now I knew why communications had ceased. I was a little scared but not deterred. And I was adamant: We would not back down. We started making so many calls that I'm surprised the phones didn't catch fire—to my brother, Eduardo, as well as our public relations team and lawyer friends.

Based on the information we obtained, I arranged to call Linda for what I thought would be a private conversation. Instead, she put me on speakerphone with her attorney present. I should have hung up right then. Through my tears, I made offers to place statements or disclaimers all over our website, issue a press release, and call a joint press conference.

"Please, Ms. Rice," I remember saying at one point, "if you do this, you'll shut us down."

I won't go into all of the awful things she said, but her cold tone clearly communicated that she didn't care about our project. She felt that

Ebony was her name, and she didn't want us using it. She wasn't budging, and I was done begging. That was it. We hung up.

I wanted to hold a press conference to detail what had ensued and start an e-mail campaign encouraging people to send nasty notes to the magazine and to cancel their subscriptions. But then we thought about *Ebony* and its place in our lives. It's the flagship publication of an iconic, Black-owned company that so many African Americans—including me and John—grew up with and cherished.

Although our friends agreed that we should fight, our public relations people warned us that this was a battle we could not win. They suggested we change the name, as did the attorney who had set up our foundation and registered our trademark for The Ebony Experiment.

"Why can't you guys just change the name?" she said. "What's the big deal?"

It was late on a Wednesday afternoon. John had left work early and was home with me. Eduardo and our trademark attorney were in their respective offices in Atlanta and Detroit. We'd convened an emergency conference call to plot our next move, and we didn't have much time.

I sat in a corner of the dining room blubbering. John had put the phone on speaker because I kept pacing around the floor.

"That's my fucking name!" I said. "Why did we get into this if we are not willing to fight?"

After a few seconds John came over and sat with me. He took my hands.

"Sweetie," he said, "how much worse would you feel if we lost the fight and they shut down the whole thing? Where would we be then? We have to remember why we started this journey in the first place."

I held John in my eyes a long time. Sometimes he's so clearheaded I could kick him.

"Okay, baby," I whispered. "Okay."

I'm not sure what was more painful: the dashed hope—based on the magazine's early enthusiasm—that *Ebony* would provide comprehensive, fair coverage of our project, or that EE's most ominous threat came from a Black business, one built on Black unity, culture, and pride and wholly sustained by Black consumers.

An hour before the deadline, Eduardo sent an e-mail to the legal department saying we were considering a name change and asking for more time. A few minutes later we gave birth to The Empowerment Experiment, and Eduardo sent the dreaded white-flag e-mail. The magazine gave us three months to discontinue all use of the word Ebony in our project.

I hated myself. Fortunately, we had no time to wallow in self-loathing. We had to start implementing the change. That night, we asked our web designer to rework the site. We also created a press release and prepared ourselves emotionally for the big lie. Publicly, we suggested the old name contributed to the inflammatory talk of racism that drew attention away from our true focus. Or, as I told one reporter, the new name "better articulates what's in our heart and what our endgame is."

As it turned out, the media types didn't care that much what our project was called nor did they pry too deeply into why we changed its name. The Ebony exorcism was yet one more in the series of lessons learned during the year.

Because we had to revamp the site to accommodate the name change, I also made enhancements to leverage all the traffic we were getting— several thousand hits a day, mostly because all the major press websites would include a link to our site in their coverage. The Ticker, which displayed our cumulative spending, was placed on each page of our site. I created a new page called "Our Favorite Finds," which listed about fifteen businesses and entrepreneurs we had discovered, all of which we could confidently deem EE businesses. Karriem was the poster child—or maybe poster man. Others included Jordan's Closets, a resale clothing boutique for children located in Bronzeville on the South Side; Park 52, a classy restaurant and jazz club in Hyde Park that had become our new hangout along with a WineStyles franchise, an upscale wine shop and bar in the South Loop; the African American–owned BP and Citgo gas station franchises in Rockford and Harvey—two distant towns with large

Black populations; Agriculture Crop of Style, an upscale men's clothier also located in Bronzeville; God First God Last God Always, our dollar store; Quench, our local healthy fast-food diner with seven locations throughout Black Chicago; our new wine, Heritage Link Brands, an importer of South African wines from the few Black vineyards there; Afriware, a local store that sold Africentric gifts, books, garb, and art; a Black-owned Little Gym franchise, a professionally staffed physical-education facility for kids; our dry cleaner; a movie theater; Covenant Bank; and Kimbark Liquors.

For each listing I tried to include a picture of the entrepreneur, the business logo, a personalized blurb about why I like the business or the owner, a link to their website, and basic information about the goods or services. I'd close each description with something kitschy like, "Now fill your closets with Jordan's Closets today!"

We tried to stay upbeat. Still, it had been a rough ride. We felt more than a little defeated, and it was only April. The Dew had appeared, as had a few more quality, stereotype-breaking Black-owned outlets that we depended on and were happy to support. But the disillusionment that the Linda Johnson Rice fiasco engendered stayed with me like a stain that wouldn't come out no matter how hard I scrubbed.

And then there were our children.

We were very protective of them for obvious reasons. Cara would turn four in July, and Cori was two for most of the year. Before we began our experiment we'd promised ourselves that the girls would not endure discomfort or fear. We would manage the fallout of our public pledge during business hours when, for the most part, the girls were in preschool or otherwise occupied. They were young enough that one brand of bubble bath, apple juice, or breakfast cereal was as good as another. But we knew we'd have to forgo certain family activities we'd gotten used to, like taking the girls to the Oberweis Dairy ice cream parlor in downtown Oak Park or to the River Forest Mall for pretzels, Chuck E. Cheese's and Monkey Island, all located less than four miles from us. During The Empowerment Experiment, family time meant spending a lot more hours at the park and doing arts and crafts, having a puppet show, or watching TV—which was perfectly fine with the kids—and more trips to Alan's house (John's brother), where they could play with their cousins, who were their ages. The girls had become somewhat familiar with the routes to our former recreational destinations, so we tried to avoid going down certain streets with them in the car. But when that old route was unavoidable or one of us had simply forgotten to take an alternate road, we'd endure a "Please Momma, I want pretzel, Momma."

Experiment or not, they were accustomed to me saying no to requests like that. But in the past we would follow the denial with a promise to go another time. We didn't make those promises during this year. Fortunately, their lives were still so full that they did not make much of a fuss about it. And when the four of us sat down to dinner at home, we would push the project aside and erect the Anderson Force Field that would deflect all things potentially harmful to the girls.

Our kids were one thing, but certain family outings, such as birthday parties for our daughters' cousins and friends, were a little trickier. Luckily, we had two pretty decent options for gifts. For children of our friends, who knew what we were doing, buying something from Jordan's Closets was okay. But when one of Cori's classmates had a birthday party and we didn't know her mother very well—or how she'd react if we gave her child resale clothing—we bought a wonderful children's book about Africa and the alphabet from Afriware. Another time we bought a McDonald's gift card—always a hit with the parents—for a friend of Cara's. This child's party presented another complication because it was held at Chuck E. Cheese's. This happened a couple times during the year, and we decided to roll with it—preventing Cara and Cori from attending would be cruel and pointless. It wasn't as big a deal as our friends thought. Beyond buying a gift, parents of the partygoers hardly ever had to spend money. We took the girls to Chuck E. Cheese's, and they had a ball with the ten tokens that each guest received as part of the party package. We just had to be sure the girls got the most out of each token, something John ensured by encouraging them to play the games that ran for the longest time.

John and I had to tweak our social life as well. Things we'd gotten used to—like going out for steak and cigars at Shula's, martinis at Gibson's on Rush Street, and tapas at Quattro—for the most part evaporated. But our friends wouldn't let us escape the Black bourgeoisie's life entirely. When I cohosted my close friend Colette's bachelorette party, everyone involved knew that everything—from the hotel suite and the alcohol to the hors d'oeuvres, restaurant, limo, and cake—would be made, distributed, sold, or owned by an African American, and I made sure they were. But when Colette's sister and cohost, Paulette, insisted on having the party at the W Hotel, I went, of course, and had a great time enjoying the hors d'oeuvres, cake, and limo. But I did not spend my money at the hotel, which was not Black-owned.

Our friends did make cursory attempts, out of respect for our pledge, to host events at Black-owned establishments, like Park 52 restaurant in Hyde Park and the M Lounge just south of downtown. When we had no say in how a party or outing was planned, we would still attend but not spend any money. That meant we'd go to the bar but order water, which is what happened when a close friend had his fortieth birthday party downtown at Jefferson Tap & Grill. It was awkward, but we smiled, ordered another round of "nature's champagne," and stayed true to the cause—while also avoiding a hangover. That crimp in our social life wasn't all that painful. We had two girls under the age of four, and I was traveling more often to see Mima and for the project, so it wasn't as if we were looking to go clubbing every week or even every month. We didn't have the time or the energy. Our lives were moving toward something more enduring.

The main problem at that point was clothing for our daughters. Among the businesses we had trouble finding were Black-owned shoe stores and other outlets with children's clothes. Jordan's Closets was wonderful—clean, bright, and with a wide selection—and the owners, Joslyn Slaughter and her mother, Jera, were two of the most hardworking, lovable ladies I will ever know. But the fact that I couldn't find a place that sold *new* clothes and shoes for children was aggravating. Is that really too much to ask?

Black clothing retailers of almost any kind, especially those that met our needs and tastes, were tough to find. We searched online, walked the neighborhoods, asked the Black business owners we'd met, and we still came up empty. What we did find were a few online outlets for up-and-coming designers and a couple stores on the West Side we didn't visit because they mostly carried urban gear that we did not like—bright jeans and shirts, and racy club outfits that might have appealed to us in our younger days, but not now.

We wanted a place that offered the more professional, conservative selection I would get at Ann Taylor, Macy's, Casual Corner, or from the Spiegel catalog. John's clothes came from Brooks Brothers, Jos. A. Bank, and Bachrach, and we loved shopping PaulFredrick.com for his shirts and ties. He was elated when he found Agriculture Crop of Style right next to our favorite coffee shop in Bronzeville. Their stuff was really stylish and classy, but it was too pricey for everyday items. Dwyane Wade of the Miami Heat shopped there, which gives some indication of who could afford it. I discovered Kiwi's Boutique on the West Side, but their stuff, although nice, was also a bit too hip for me.

How could it be that we were so limited, especially as Blacks have a rich history in the apparel and design industries, dating back to the 1700s in Virginia when a man named Stephen Jackson started creating hats from leather and fur? Even in the harsh climate of the Civil War and post–Civil War era, dressmaking, millinery, and tailoring were healthy businesses for Blacks. There was Eliza Ann Gardner, an abolitionist and dressmaker. African American dressmaker Elizabeth Keckley designed Mary Todd Lincoln's inaugural ball gown and supervised a staff of twenty or so young women. Ann Lowe created Jackie Bouvier's wedding gown when she married a young politician named John F. Kennedy and was also the couturier to the Astors, du Ponts, Rockefellers, Roosevelts, and Vanderbilts. Her clothing was sold in Neiman Marcus and I. Magnin. There is a long list of others: Jesse A. Terry started a shop in Alabama in the early 1960s that became Terry Manufacturing Company, grossing more than $1 million a year by selling his clothes in places like Sears and maintaining a client list that included McDonald's and the federal government. Willie Donnell Smith's famous WilliWear Limited sold $25 million a year of clothing in the 1980s. Maurice Malone's lines for men and women had sales of $8.5 million in 2000. Then there's Russell Simmons's Phat Fashions, Kimora Lee Simmons's Baby Phat Line, and Sean "Diddy" Combs's Sean John line. Sean John "Diddy" Combs, as most everyone knows, is not only an entertainment mogul but also the owner of a very hot line of predominantly men's clothing and accessories.

My guess is that Blacks don't have as many clothing stores as we need for the same reason we don't have as many grocery, electronics, furniture, or hardware stores. Perhaps we do best entering industries where the supply chain is short, where we can make the stuff ourselves and don't have to spend too much on supplies and inventories—or rely on suppliers—and we don't have to invest too much in things like real estate. That's why Blacks are more heavily into restaurants; African and African American arts and crafts, music, and books; services like home health care; barber and braid shops; and day care centers. Those are businesses we can create and maintain out of our homes.

Gary Lampley and Steven Rogers confirmed this. Lampley is the president of Black Retailer Action Group, or BRAG, a national group based in New York City that promotes African American employment in retail. He told me that having inventory and amassing the expertise that comes from years of experience are critical in the highly competitive retail industry—especially children's retail.

"There are a few children's apparel lines—Baby Phat, Sean John, Rocawear—who are doing well," he told me, although Baby Phat and Rocawear started as Black-owned and no longer are. Baby Phat was sold in 2004 to Kellwood Company; Rocawear followed in 2007, when Iconix Brand Group purchased it. They "were borne out of the hip hop music industry and [were] created after the women's and men's businesses were established," Lampley told me. "The children's clothing industry only has a few big players because that business is challenging."

He mentioned Belinda Hughes, a gifted sportswear designer who came out with the Boo-Boo Baby line of children's jackets and coats in 1987 and enjoyed media exposure in places like the *New York Times* Style section. But, Lampley said, "she, like many African American designers, has a great deal of talent but lacks access to capital."

There it was—the phrase that kept coming up in my research on the dearth of Black-owned businesses: lack of capital.

"Certain industries are just not potentially profitable anymore unless you come to the industry with a massive amount of capital," Rogers told me, "and African Americans don't have a legacy that enables us to have that massive amount of capital because the amassing of capital comes from generations."

Rogers explained that few Blacks have true "intergenerational wealth," the monster wealth that started three, four, five, or more generations ago and has been multiplying ever since; the kind of wealth that could, if the market conditions were right, start a retail chain, or buy swaths of real estate in the hottest market and develop a commercial residential complex or three.

"When you have family members who worked in America for almost 300 years for free," he said, laughing, "that's a hell of a starting point to be behind. Just imagine if my great, great, great, great grandfather had the chances that I had—if he weren't denied things because of his race— where my family could be now. My family has done well," Rogers said, "but the reality is we could be the Rockefellers. . . . The reason we're not is because my family, most African American families, didn't have the chance for that intergenerational wealth."

In fact, and maybe this comes as no shock, half of all Blacks in the United States have less than $6,200 in wealth, while the amount of wealth among Whites and Asians is eleven times higher. That means Blacks have much less money to invest in the business and less collateral to use in getting a business loan. Add lending discrimination to the mix, and it seems like an ideal setup for failure.

Speaking of business loans, research suggests discrimination in this arena is alive and well. The loan rejection rate for Blacks as well as Hispanics is abysmal compared to that of Whites. In 2002 experts from Dartmouth, Wellesley, and Williams colleges conducted a study that analyzed data from the National Surveys of Small Business Finances, finding that "[B]lack-owned firms are more than twice as likely to have a loan application rejected relative to white-owned firms." A total of 62 to nearly 66 percent of Black loans were rejected, compared to 27 to 29 percent for White-owned business loan applications. For the loans that were approved for Black-owned businesses, those firms had to pay interest rates that were 1 to 1.7 percent higher than what White-owned firms paid.

All of this—the lack of business capital and its consequences—manifested itself in our older daughter's feet, which seemed to be expanding on a daily basis.

When we made the pledge on January 1, we knew we had a three- or four-month grace period until the girls started growing out of their clothing and before they needed new clothes for spring. We knew we'd find Black-owned stores where we could purchase what they needed. In fact, the beauty of spring's late arrival was that it gave us a few more weeks to locate those outlets. But by April we still hadn't found one in the Chicago metro area or online. The Dew felt like The Downs.

Shoes were only part of the problem. Our girls' clothing shortage had become obvious, at least to me. Cara's belly started peeking out from a few of her blouses. Two or three pairs of jeans were "flood pants" that looked even worse when she put on boots. Her panties, pajamas, and socks were too tight. Her only shoes were boots, dress shoes, and corduroy or suede shoes. Now that spring was approaching, she'd need new sandals and tennis shoes.

Cori's situation was a little less worrisome. She had become accustomed to—and, bless her heart, delighted by—wearing her big sister's hand-me-downs; it meant she was becoming a big girl as well. To me it was the source of mounting anxiety.

I kept thinking how easy it would be to plop the girls into their car seats, run over to the nearest Kmart, Target, Children's Place, or JC Penney, and take care of all our shopping in one trip.

But we didn't even discuss it. We were trying to stay upbeat, aware of our commitment and proud about making it. Those mass retailers? They didn't exist. What also didn't exist was a pair of shoes for the elongating feet of our three-year-old daughter. But we were cool with that.

Until David's christening.

David is our nephew, the son of John's brother, Alan, and his wife, Pam. All the cousins were close. Cara and our niece Ashley were born two weeks apart. They were a couple of princesses who delighted in wearing all the fancy, frilly adornments they could dig up or beg us for. On the morning of her brother David's christening, Ashley for sure was going to present the full princess package in all its extravagant ornamentation. Cori and, especially, Cara had to rise to the challenge, which meant I had to rise to the challenge.

"The Dew done good," John joked when he pulled open the blinds to our bedroom the day of the christening. It was a bright May morning.

"Hi, Mommy," Cara said, wandering into our bedroom. She kissed my nose and said, "I love you."

"I love you too, sweetie." I kissed back and squeezed her. One of those magical, little mommy moments. Then it hit me. I shot up in bed, my eyes wide.

"What the hell is she going to wear?" I asked John.

He gave me a slightly perturbed look and said, "Heck . . . what the *heck* is she going to wear. We'll figure something out."

I jumped out of bed and started pacing, tugging at my hair. Cara's look went from soft and sweet to a little scared. John rolled his eyes. Sleepy Cori stumbled into the room and begged me to pick her up. Those big brown eyes melt my heart every time she looks at me the way she was looking at me that morning.

"Go to daddy, sweetie," I said, rushing past her. I hustled out of the bedroom, through the kitchen, and out the back door. The day was sunny but chilly. Cara could wear one of her winter outfits, which allowed me to finesse our EE-induced shortcomings a bit. My mood brightened. I went back into our bedroom, apologized for my craziness, and played with my babies. John made coffee.

After a few minutes I started rummaging through Cori's closet, where I kept the girls' fancier dresses, and I felt pretty satisfied with my options.

I laid out their dresses and focused on tidying up the house, cooking up a light breakfast and getting some work done on EE. The day seemed to be rolling along nicely enough. Then it came off the tracks.

Cara's shoes did not fit.

They were a pair of basic black patent-leather shoes, which comple-mented the navy blue dress with a big white bow that I helped Cara put on, along with stockings and a matching hair clip. She slipped a purse onto her shoulder and then started putting on her shoes. We discovered they were about a size and a half too small.

"C'mon, honey," I told her, trying to feign brightness. "You . . . can . . . ," I grunted as I shoved her feet in the shoes, " . . . do . . . this." With them packed inside, I sighed.

"There. See? Perfect. Okay. All set everyone?"

"No mommy," Cara said. I could see she was in pain. "They hurt."

I glanced at the clock. We were going to be late. I could envision my mother-in-law's critical expression.

"Jeeesus, Cara," I said. "Toughen up. They're a little tight. So what? You can still wear them."

"But mommy . . . " She was moving straight to whining, so I cut her off.

"You're going to wear them. Do you understand me? You are going to wear those shoes."

"Mommy . . . no . . . " She was starting to cry now.

"Please, Cara!" I shouted. Shrill Mommy, the beast, was emerging. "Just keep them on. You can take them off in the car and inside church. No one will see. Wear those shoes, girl. Do you hear me?"

John had heard enough.

"Maggie," he said, his voice a little loud—and John's voice is almost never loud. "Calm down. She's not wearing those shoes. Period. We'll have to figure out something else. Come on now. It's not the end of the world. Put some other shoes on her or let's find another dress. Let's just get this taken care of and move on."

Cara started wailing.

"No. Noooo . . . I want to wear *this* dress."

And, just like that, I was ready to bail. I thought, *I'm not prepared to en-dure this scene again and again for the next eight months. I'm not ready to force a three-year-old girl and her two-year-old sister to "toughen up." Ridiculous.*

"John," I half-whispered. "Let's cheat. We can stop at Kmart on the way and get her some shoes. Nobody has to know."

"No way."

John Anderson is many things—a detail guy; a man of composure; a deeply protective, loving father; a financial wizard entrusted with millions of dollars of people's life savings; a mentor; a weekend basketball warrior. He had thought long and hard about the commitment we'd made nearly five months earlier. I knew, in the distinct tone of that two-word response, the discussion between husband and wife was over.

I found a sundress that was too big for Cara last year but now fit perfectly. She looked adorable in it, but more like she was going to a neighbor's pizza party than a christening. I thought about her cousin Ashley, who I was certain would be wearing a long dress, accentuated by a shawl, purse, stockings, and closed-toe, shiny shoes, and Cori, who was wearing a Cara hand-me-down ensemble consisting of a white seersucker strapless dress with embroidered fuchsia-colored flowers and a white shawl, white pantyhose, and dark pink shoes. Lovely.

Cara was going to wear an informal dress with spaghetti-straps and open-toed sandals. No sweater. It was barely acceptable attire.

When my in-laws arrived at the house and saw Cara, they couldn't hide their confusion.

"Is that what she's wearing?" my mother-in-law, Debbie, said. "It's cold outside."

"Really?" I said lightly, ignoring the obvious, trying to rush us all out the door. "I thought it was warm out."

"No, no," Debbie said, and she stopped me. "It's one of those Chicago May days, you know. Looks like June. Feels like February. Let's hurry and put something else on her, okay?"

"Okay," I said, my voice flat, defeated. I took Cara into our bedroom as if I was about to change her outfit. John was there and knew what was coming.

"No," he said again. I sensed he was a little torn up inside too. "We're not going to cheat over this. She looks fine."

"John, she looks ridiculous." My voice was a mixture of pleading and anger. "You know how your family is. They're all going to be dressed up and Cara looks like she's going to Chuck E. Cheese's. Everybody in church is going to stare."

Cara was whimpering on the bed, trying to figure out which one of us was on her side so she could beat down the other with her calf eyes. We both stared at her. John waited a few moments. Then he turned to me and I could see the pain and resolve in his face.

"You really want to throw this away, Mags?" he said. "After everything we've talked about for all these years? After all the planning? After saying that folks aren't taking a stand? You're just going to toss all of it out the window over a few hours of discomfort?"

"It's not tossing it all out the window," I said. "It's just this once." But I knew as soon as I said the words that I couldn't justify cheating "just this once."

John gave me the smallest of smiles and his eyes softened. He put his hands on my shoulders. His voice was low, comforting. "We're going to do this, baby."

Look, we all know that having a little girl wear a sundress and open-toed sandals to a formal occasion isn't a scarred-for-life, "Mommy Dearest" episode. But at the time, it mattered, if for no other reason than I was the one imposing this pain on my three-year-old daughter for a reason that she couldn't understand and that plenty of rational adults thought was futile and foolish. I looked like some sort of whacked-out activist trying to make a senseless point.

Cara whimpered throughout the service. I buried my head in the Bible, dug my nails into my skin, and prayed the day would end. I kept wondering whether I had forsaken my sweet babies for a purpose to which they had no connection and from which they would never benefit.

Still, I learned something that day: My commitment to our experiment was not only as strong as the one to my family—they were one and the same. The Empowerment Experiment comes from the love I have for my girls, a love anchored in the desire to cultivate their understanding that helping others—even if it hurts sometimes—is a core value of our family.

Sure, my girls—especially Cara—would have to feel the burn before I could fully explain fire. During our Black year we all would get hurt as we grappled with the issues we had tried to evade or examine from a distance. But someday, I kept telling myself, maybe my daughters will understand that taking a stand often creates collateral damage.

Chapter 7

The Colors of Racism

SLOGGING.

That's what the middle of the year felt like, even though we were getting attention from some of the largest Black and mainstream media outlets. We appeared on CNN (twice), MSNBC, and Fox News, and we were featured in comprehensive segments for *Time* magazine and BET News. Tom Joyner and Roland Martin, the two most venerated Black media personalities, interviewed us. We'd been on the front page of the *Chicago Tribune* and received coverage in the *Los Angeles Times*. People often told us that we'd brought more media attention to the plight of Black businesses than any previous effort. Our Facebook group, "Fans of The Empowerment Experiment," earned over three thousand members between April and June—we hadn't passed the five or six hundred–membership mark in the first couple months of the group's existence. The overwhelming majority of daily e-mails I received came from supporters. We were working hard, and the results were energizing. But even with all that, there was huge anchor weighing down our high spirits.

One of our inspirations was Karriem Beyah. By this time he and his store were the spiritual and geographic center of our commitment—primarily because he was such a terrific guy and his wonderful place was on the South Side, near several other stores where we'd shop. Jordan's Closets was on 47th Street, just a mile and a half east of Farmers Best. A born "mompreneur," Joslyn and her mother, Jera, were equal partners in Jordan's Closets and Jordan's Mom's Closets, upscale resale-clothing boutiques in a still-dicey part of Bronzeville. They began planning their business in 2001 while they were working their day jobs, but they were unable to secure a bank loan—no surprise. After Joslyn's grandmother and an aunt and uncle offered financial assistance, the two women opened their first store in 2006. They named it after Joslyn's daughter, who was about five years old at the time.

"We wanted to be in a place where we could help our community," Joslyn, who was born and raised on the South Side, told me. "I didn't necessarily think I was going to get rich by running Jordan's Closets, but I wanted to give something to the community. Children around here already have a lot stacked against them."

She offered lovely, clean, low-priced clothes, but she had to educate potential customers about a resale-clothing boutique, which many people had never heard of. The community patronized the store, but the store was also burglarized three times—twice in one night—in the first couple years of its existence. Still, the business made a powerful statement: Counting Joslyn's daughter, Jordan, who helped out around the place, three generations of African American women were running a retail establishment. I wanted to support them.

As long as I was in the neighborhood, I'd drop in and visit with Milton Latrell at the swanky Agriculture Crop of Clothing. Right next door was my new favorite coffee shop, Bronzeville Coffee, which was also where I bought bagels, as I still hadn't found a Black bakery that sold them. If I had some time, I'd run four blocks east to see Nicole Jones at Sensual Steps Shoe Salon, whether or not I was in the market for shoes. She was the center of Bronzeville's small Black business community, and something interesting was always going on at her store.

Although it was five miles southeast and in an area that felt much more like the West Side, I might swing by God First God Last God Always, our household goods supplier. Like Farmers Best for groceries, it was my only option for household and personal basics. David and Michelle Powell, the quintessential mom-and-pop owners, knew their customers' names and hugged many of them—not just me—as they entered the store. Native South Siders, they were almost inconsolable over how the once-vibrant area around 71st Street had lost virtually all of its quality, locally owned businesses.

All of these entrepreneurs, my new close friends, were just two miles from Hyde Park and the University of Chicago, where only a few years earlier I'd lived for four years with John while in graduate school. I'm sure these people and places, or people and places like them, were there all the while. I never saw them back then—or even looked.

Now I was there at least once or twice a week. My trips to Farmers Best became so frequent, in fact, that Karriem set aside space in his office for me where I could conduct EE business. Stationing myself there was much less about convenience and much more about strengthening the relationship between EE and Farmers Best. We wanted everyone to meet Karriem, as he exemplified the potential of self-help economics. When the publisher of Chicago's Black Pages, the most reputable directory of local Black businesses, said he wanted to place our family on the cover of the 2010 edition and have me speak at their quarterly networking function for advertisers, I set up a meeting at the store. If the media outlets we spoke with wanted to see EE in action to help understand why we had undertaken the project, I'd tell them they needed to come to Farmers Best to meet Karriem Beyah. Nearly all of them did.

"KB" was everything we were fighting for. He sensed our respect for him very quickly, just as quickly as he perceived how serious our commitment was. He responded in kind, joining our four-member board of directors of The Empowerment Experiment Foundation, Inc. A 501(c)(3) we'd created in anticipation of funding from that group of wealthy Black corporate executives—which seems almost laughable now—the foundation was a way of assuring donors that we were going to use their contributions for research and social service–oriented projects after our yearlong experiment. We hired an attorney who specialized in establishing nonprofits, and we created the board, which consisted of John and me; a powerful attorney friend of Eduardo's; John's aunt, a highly respected public school administrator and community leader in Detroit; and now Karriem.

Sprung from a philosophical synchronicity, our relationship with Karriem was profound and deep. But at the same time, odd as it sounds, it was fraught with anxiety about our beloved Farmers Best. Odder still is that we rarely addressed it directly.

The truth was that Farmers Best was on unsteady footing from the outset and not because of anything Karriem did or failed to do. The plight of Black-owned grocery stores is similar to that of other Black-owned retailers. To top it off, the economy went into free fall about the time Farmers Best opened its doors in the summer of 2008. Not long after our very first visit to the store, we realized that we were going to have to do more to help Karriem increase traffic, and that meant devoting extra time and resources to Farmers Best.

This was a troubling prospect, mostly because financially we were floundering too. The business and marketing professionals in us were very nervous because almost none of the assistance the PBFs promised materialized. There were supporters, of course, like Cheryle Jackson of the Chicago Urban League, who had us on her TV show a couple times. Nonetheless, we felt as if almost everyone in Chicago who was supposed to shower us with love, praise, and aid was treating us like the Jehovah's Witness who rings the doorbell early on a Saturday morning.

But we had to save Karriem. So starting in April, I dove right in. Almost every day I'd ask him about his sales, what was going on with his suppliers, how much he spent on the produce run that morning. I started studying the grocery industry and became something of an informal consultant to Karriem. I begged my friends to go to his store, sending out e-blasts every week asking them to join his mailing list and trying to arrange carpools for shopping trips. The first promotional carpool e-blast said, "Did you know Chicago has a new Black-owned full-service grocery store? I'll show you AND give you a ride there!" I sent it to my EE database as well as those for a number of large Black churches, like St. Sabina, Apostolic Church of God, Salem House of Hope, and my church, Trinity United Church of Christ. My favorite e-blast was entitled "New Whole Foods Store on 47th Street. The freshest produce on the South Side!" When someone opened the e-mail, they'd find a flyer I created for Farmers Best, with pictures of all the great produce. Then right under it: "Well it's not Whole Foods, but you get the same fresh, top-quality products, and at a greater value to your wallet and your soul. Support this first-class Black business today! Click here for a ride."

We were trying so hard, fully leveraging our own networks to get more customers to give Farmers Best a chance. Nothing was working. We felt as if there was some unholy power conspiring against Karriem's enterprise and, by extension, EE. There were days when I would be the sole customer in the store.

Because Farmers Best was in a strip mall, it shared the parking lot with other stores, including a Little Caesar's pizza parlor. One afternoon in May I saw a vision in a toga-clad, sandals-wearing foam mascot: the Little Caesar's guy.

I had this "aha" moment. Farmers Best was clean, well stocked, efficient, and had competitively priced products. The reason it was struggling was simple: It lacked effective marketing. We needed to get serious about it.

Karriem fully embraced the idea and, in fact, had already planned to purchase prime-time radio spots and a full-page ad in the local Black Pages directory. I sat with him in meetings with various ad reps for the two major Black-themed—but not Black-owned—radio stations and helped decide which ads to buy. We'd advertise weekly sales and promote community events at the store with the theme "Farmers Best Springtime Series" as well as a tagline I created: "Live Your Best Life at Farmers Best." We devised promotions and gave out coupons at the store and online. I wrote the radio ads and press releases, and our PR firm sent them to media outlets. Almost every Friday and Saturday in May and June Karriem set up a tent and decorations, played music, and grilled premium meats and veggies in the parking lot.

We weren't leaving anything to chance, and Karriem was really grateful. The harder we worked, the closer our family grew to KB. He started delivering food to the house and including extra fruit and meat that was about to be tossed. We'd barbecue together. He and John would linger over drinks and cigars. Still, anxiety intruded, even in those moments away from the store when we reveled in our friendship.

"Uncle Karriem is here! Mommy, can I open the door?"

Cara peered out of the living room window and saw KB's behemoth Excursion pulling up. She was almost four years old now, and it seemed like every hour she came up with a new "big girl" responsibility she wanted to assume.

"He's early," I shouted. "I still have to tidy up downstairs. Girls, go with your dad. John, just keep him up here. Okay?"

Cara and Cori looked adorable. I'd just fixed their hair, and they were wearing pink tops and denim Capri pants—ensembles I'd purchased at Jordan's Closets.

"Yes. Cara, you can open the door," I said, "but you have to do it with a grown-up. Okay? Never alone. Now go with Daddy!"

John was looking out the window.

"Don't worry, Mag," he said. "It'll be a minute. He's on the phone in the car. You know he lives on that phone. We probably have another hour!" John broke into his impersonation of KB. Impersonations are one of John's fortes. I swear it's one of the main reasons I fell in love with him.

"*Now you make sure you get those carts out of the parking lot,*" John said in Karriem's deep, scruffy voice. "*If a cart is missing you're paying for it! And get rid of those bruised mangoes. No bruises. You hear me?*"

The girls were laughing while John paced up and down the foyer imitating KB's hulking gait and pretending to hold a phone.

Even I was laughing now, and that's exactly what John wanted. His anxious wife had been stressing about a guest's early arrival, and he had to ease that condition. He came over, hugged my waist, and whispered. "You can't blame the man for being early, right Mag? Would you want to hang around an empty grocery store in which you'd invested everything? Be nice, baby. I *know* you're going to yell at him for not calling first, but please don't. Give the po' brutha a break."

They'd made plans to watch the NBA conference finals. The game started at six, and it was 5:30. I zoomed downstairs to the TV room, still giggling and shaking my head.

When I came back up a few minutes later, four boxes of fruit, a couple cases of fruit punch, maybe ten pineapples, and three huge watermelons crowded my previously neat kitchen counter. KB was swinging Cori by her wrists, and Cara was examining the booty. John was bending over the liquor drawer, about to make drinks. I wanted them to see me with my hands on my hips, eyebrows scrunched.

"Hey, Momma!" KB said, still swinging Cori. "I brought you the Mexican mangoes you love."

"Don't give me that 'Momma' crap, KB," I said. "What's all this? Look at my kitchen. Does my house look like a Farmers Best warehouse to you?"

He smiled.

"Come here, man," I told him. He stepped toward me and I kissed him. "You crazy. You know that?"

We sliced up a couple of mangoes, put everything else away, and then sat on the deck for drinks. The basketball game was still a few minutes from tip-off. The girls were flitting around, blowing bubbles.

"So how was business today?" John asked. "Gotta be busy. Memorial Day barbecues and stuff."

I squeezed his leg under the table and didn't let Karriem answer.

"KB, did you talk to that reporter from *Time* magazine?" I asked. John kicked me back. "They going to do that follow-up story on you and the food desert stuff?"

"Oh, yeah," KB said. "I gotta call him back."

He didn't answer John's question. There was no need. We all knew that no one was coming to Farmers Best, even though we'd created radio ads, flyers, and sent out e-mails about tremendous sales on grill meats and produce, announcing free barbecue in the parking lot. It was perplexing and infuriating—but we just sipped our margaritas and ate the succulent mangoes that no one would buy.

A few days later when I was at the store, Karriem said, "Mag, I don't know what to do about this. Yvette Moyo's called like three times now, but I have never seen her in the store. Why should I call her back?"

Moyo was the founder of Real Men Cook, a national organization promoting positive Black male role models for at-risk youth. Through a series of fund-raising events, Real Men Cook raises tens of millions of dollars to provide various charities with resources for mentoring, tutoring, counseling, and scholarships. The events culminate in Father's Day picnics in twelve cities across the country, where Black men cook all day for the community. The Real Men Cook Chicago picnic is a huge affair, drawing major media attention as well as business, community, and political leaders. The mayor and governor show up every year. More county fair than picnic, the event features rides, a petting zoo, live entertainment, and several themed pavilions offering community services and sponsors' products, including those of State Farm, US Cellular, and Nielsen.

"Real Men Cook?" I said. "Calling us? This could be it! I'll see what she wants. You know Barack was a Real Man for, like, the past five years."

Yvette Moyo called Karriem because one of Real Men Cook's sponsors, Jewel, the largest grocery chain in the Chicago metropolitan area, backed out at the last minute, and she wanted Farmers Best to be the official grocery sponsor and, in effect, rescue the event.

I made the call to the organization and then Karriem received a sponsorship proposal, which included donations of cash, produce, drinks, and meats to stock several pavilions. After I negotiated to ensure his marketing benefits—a mention and the store's logo in all advertising and on their website, prime advertising real estate at the picnic, a speaking opportunity on the day of the event, and space in the health pavilion for folks to sample Farmers Best produce—Karriem agreed to be the grocery sponsor for the annual Father's Day picnic held at Kennedy-King College, located in an underserved neighborhood on Chicago's South Side.

Karriem became the hero of the day, and Yvette used every opportunity to publicly thank him for bailing her out. Karriem's Farmers Best banner was the centerpiece of the main stage. At his tent he gave out coupons and fruit cups and received much-needed exposure.

According to a jubilant Karriem, store traffic picked up over the next couple weekends. We were experiencing one of those "big possibility" moments for Karriem, and I couldn't think of a guy who deserved it more. He was the owner of a high-quality business—the only Black, full-service grocer in Illinois—a noble, courageous community leader, and role model for kids. On top of all that, the guy was working three times harder than I could have imagined. Maybe, I thought, just maybe he'd catch a break. Karriem Beyah and Farmers Best could provide the foundation on which we could build our movement.

For all the hurdles we encountered while working with Karriem, the middle of the year had its promising moments—one of the most inspiring of the whole year, in fact. That came in June, in the grandest venue I'd spoken at thus far: Friendship-West Baptist Church in Dallas. Its leader, Rev. Dr. Frederick Haynes, is another hero of mine. A frequent guest speaker at our church, Trinity United Church of Christ in Chicago, he was somewhat of an adopted, favorite son to our parish and our senior pastor, Rev. Dr. Jeremiah Wright. What so many of us loved about Dr. Haynes was that he, like Rev. Wright, is known for presenting powerful speeches that feel like riveting university lectures, which makes sense because he has a master's of divinity, a doctorate of ministry, and studied at Oxford University. He was engaging, intimidating, and committed to the life of the community. In other words, Dr. Haynes talked EE before EE existed. We were grateful when he agreed to join our roster of executive advisers, a team of high-profile academics who were known for speaking out for economic empowerment in the Black community. The executive advisers, a separate entity from the board of directors for the EE Foundation, now consisted of Steven Rogers, Dr. Michael Dyson, University of Cincinnati's Jim Clingman, and University of Texas's Dr. Juliet Walker—the latter two both acclaimed intellectuals, authors, and activists. Dr. Haynes was the first community leader to join our advisory team, but with his academic credentials, he fit right in. These advisers helped us increase the project's visibility and establish its credibility as a true academic exercise;

assist with research, data, and interviews; and make connections with other scholars and leaders aligned with EE's mission.

Friendship-West is what you'd call a megachurch. It has more than twelve thousand members and forty-five ministries, including the "adoption" of a church in Zimbabwe for which Friendship-West is building an auditorium, day care center, and school. The church also created a program to feed a minimum of 150 families in that community.

Its motto, "Equipping Changed People to Change the World," doesn't only apply to spiritual change. Located in an overwhelmingly Black and economically bleak part of town, Friendship-West has committed to being a major employer of local residents. Among other services, the church offers a business directory and career resources. It's building a co-op and community garden, and it led an effort to bring the first Black-owned grocery store to the Dallas/Fort Worth area.

As you can imagine, when Rev. Haynes invited me to speak, appear on his popular radio show, and meet with local community and business leaders, John and I were thrilled—and scared.

At any given Sunday service more than three thousand people gather in the church's cavernous auditorium. I'd never given a talk to such a large crowd. In fact, aside from presentations in business and law school, I hadn't really given a speech since high school. This had the potential to make a critical difference in the life of The Empowerment Experiment—and not just because of the size of the audience. I'd be speaking to folks—several thousand of them—ready to hear and act on what I said. And unlike the standard media interviews we'd done, I'd get to present a message of some length and depth to a captive audience.

After getting a late start writing my speech, it came quickly. Right out of college I'd been a speechwriter for the mayor of Atlanta. Later I'd done the same for McDonald's corporate executives. I flashed back to those times, which helped my confidence, and I just told myself to tell our story. I wrote about how it all started with our anniversary dinner, our feelings of doing too little, making the commitment, and preparing for the launch. I talked about the media attention and the very mixed public response. I wrote about Mima. It was redemptive, enlightening—and forty-five pages long. Over the next two sleepless nights I managed to cut it down to fifteen, but the night before I was going to speak, I got a call from Dr. Haynes's assistant while I was rehearsing in my Dallas hotel room. I had eight minutes at the most for my presentation. Eight minutes? The video I wanted to show was nine minutes. I hung up, cried, called John, and, by 3 a.m., had a ten-minute speech. I woke up at 5 a.m. to rehearse and left at 7:30 a.m. I was pleased with the speech but dead tired and angry with myself for wasting so much time.

Normally, I'm a capable driver-seat makeup artist. In fact, I've made it something of a commuter performance art. But this morning the broiling Dallas heat had transformed my hair moisturizer into warm oil. When I squeezed the container, I squirted a six-inch stream across my ivory pants. By the time I arrived at Friendship-West, I had grease slathered on my outfit. I was pissed off and slightly delirious. A beneficent church greeter directed me to the restroom, where I found an empty stall. Next thing I knew, a familiar voice called out.

"Maggie? Girl, is that you?"

It was Gisele Marcus, a friend and former Trinitarian who'd relocated to Dallas and was now a member at Friendship. She hugged me and I told her I was freaking out. Right there in the restroom, she coaxed me into prayer. Then I wiped my face and composed myself. After a few moments Gisele walked me to an office, where an associate pastor welcomed me with a hug—I must have been eminently huggable that morning— and pulled us together in another prayer circle. Before we could finish I ran to the pastor's bathroom and threw up. It was humiliating, but afterward I felt renewed.

I could hear Rev. Haynes leading the flock in singing and clapping. The place was jumping. By the time I was led to my seat in the second row, I was ready—wrapped up in the Spirit. I felt like one of those boxers in the ring moments before the bell sounds, anxious to get after it.

And get after it I did.

"Last year, my life was great," I told the audience. "Great family, career . . . healthy, financially blessed. But my blessings and my purpose were encompassed in what I had, not what I did. My life's deeds were reckless and improvised, without purpose or commitment. And then my mother was diagnosed with pancreatic cancer. She was given a month to live. All that was before The Empowerment Experiment."

Just thinking about Mima gave me the strength I needed. A couple minutes into it I was in preacher mode, bouncing around the stage, exhorting and inspiring the audience, pausing for the applause. Folks in the pews were completely engaged. The band even started chiming in at the appropriate times. I couldn't believe it was me. It was weird, it was cool— it was the speech of my life. It worked, I think, because I finally felt comfortable telling our story. As I actually said the words I'd written, it hit me that this really was a movement. Until then we kept using the word "movement," but that was more to convince ourselves.

When I finished, applause seemed to cascade upon me, and then I was mobbed. One of the first in line was a tearful woman. "You have favor," she said, meaning God's favor, and before I could get my bearings, she enveloped me in her arms and squeezed. I felt some of the air push from me. "You know that?"

"Yes," I said, inhaling, discreetly trying to pull away. "Thank you. What's your name, sister?" A high school friend, Antoine Pierre, was a member of Friendship. He started acting like a bodyguard and subtly forcing folks to form a line. He gave me the "watch her, she's crazy" look.

She told me her name and said her father was a tailor and also owned a farm equipment repair and resale business in addition to his men's clothing store.

"The White man took his tractor business away and the Black man just let the other business die so they can go to Dillard's," she said, a reference to one of the White South's retail institutions.

"I always wonder why we just don't love each other anymore," the hugger said, nodding. Maybe she wasn't so crazy after all. "I remember a day when we cared about each other and talked to each other." She paused and stared at me a moment, smiling.

"You so young, child," she said. "But if you were around back then, we'd be fighting over who got the chance to die for you."

"Oohhh, honey," I said, really touched. "That's so sweet. Please make sure you go to the website and tell your friends too. I don't need people to die for me. I just want them to help our businesses so we can have some economic power again."

That kind of thing went on for another twenty minutes. Strangers were crying and telling me stories about a failed business or humiliating treatment they received from non-Black shop owners in their neighborhood. Some asked how they could help. Some just wanted to say thanks.

During the rest of the Dallas visit I felt like I was living the EE dream. At a private breakfast with Dr. Haynes and his staff, everyone treated me like royalty. I spoke to a near-capacity crowd at the second service and hit another home run. That evening I was a guest on Dr. Haynes's radio show and then went to an event thrown in my honor at a Black-owned restaurant and jazz spot, Brooklyn Jazz. I was flattered. Dallas and Fort Worth had a few sophisticated Black-owned restaurants, but Brooklyn Jazz—a successful, elegant, Black-owned restaurant and nightclub located downtown—was a rarity.

All of the people we met were so excited that EE was coming to town solely because it represented the sentiments—love and unity—that had faded or been sold to Dillard's.

That's what our work was all about. That's why thousands in two services at Friendship-West gave standing ovations. That's why the hugger, bless her heart, wept. That's why all these strangers, from the streets to the suites, came to welcome me. I couldn't help thinking about how pointless fretting over the name of our project had been. Hell, most folks were getting it wrong anyway, but that didn't matter. Everyone understood our intention.

The Empowerment Experiment was sailing like a glorious flagship, and I was guiding it, slicing through the teal blue water. Cap'n Maggie, leader of the good ship Double-E.

While I was entertaining visions of steering our mighty cutter, the media exposure started picking up again. We were on Tom Joyner's popular radio show in June, the next month Chicago Public TV featured our story, and we spent nearly six minutes on CBS News's *Early Show*. But as with our previous media appearances, the results were mixed. We had a spike in interested visitors to our website, where they would write messages about how inspiring we were and add their names to the list of people pledging to buy Black. That, of course, juiced our engines. However, the media exposure also brought out the troglodytes from their caves, like Scott from Indiana who had this to say in an e-mail: "Ok you fuck. Buy black if that works for you. . . . This is America—one for all and all for one, but hey if you think your stupid shit is going to work. Then advertise in Nairobi because the sooner you are out of here the better our country will be. . . . Greedy Shit bags."

Richard and Mary Beth also sent an e-mail about the same time that asked a familiar question: "Why not go all the way, Andersons, and move the hell back to Africa. Take your daughters with you. This country has done everything it can in the last 50 years to give blacks the opportunity to succeed. Even at the expense of more qualified whites and other minorities. Has it worked? NO. Don't let the door hit you in your asses. Please leave."

Another sophisticate created a webpage, headlined, "The Empowerment Experiment Team NIGGERS," depicting a smiling white man urinating on my name, John's name, and the names of other supporters of The Empowerment Experiment. At the bottom was "BULLSHIT. FUCK YOU ASSHOLES!!!!" and a call to boycott the project.

That's just a smattering of what we received. Frankly, I don't know what else was written because after a while I stopped looking at the uglier sentiments. We did receive a few encouraging e-mails from Whites too, like the teacher in south central LA telling us to "keep it up," or the director of a leadership institute who said we "were so right on in many ways." I even got an offer of free help from a faith-based philanthropy and social-investing expert who called our initiative "inspiring."

But lots of otherwise sane people simply refused to set aside their anger and listen, even just for a moment. This visceral hostility became increasingly frustrating. Even we weren't naive enough to believe that White folks would "get it" from the start, and we understood that a certain percentage of folks would never get it. But I thought the kind of anger we were seeing had faded as our country's racial and ethnic mix broadened and the nation became more tolerant. I couldn't comprehend why it was okay for White-owned businesses to tailor ad campaigns to minorities while John and I were being vilified as racists for trying to raise African Americans' awareness to buy from competent, Black-owned businesses.

All of this made me think that, despite all the progress we've made toward racial tolerance in this country, maybe a lot of it is just superficial. Was that why White folks couldn't accept that Black economic empowerment was a healthy thing for everyone? And by the way, we aren't saying that *all* Blacks should spend *all* their money exclusively on Black-owned businesses. Believe me, we know it's impossible. We're simply trying to get *some* African Americans to spend *some* of their money in high-quality Black businesses. Perhaps John and I are dreamers, but we also have a pragmatic understanding of life, rooted in our marketing, business, finance, and law training. Some may even consider that pragmatism conservative, God forbid. (Note to the GOP: Make those checks payable to The Empowerment Experiment Foundation.) Either way, we viewed our project as a moderate, well-reasoned form of self-help economics, something that people across the political spectrum could support. After all, experts of every stripe agree that the problems in America's impoverished neighborhoods—Black, Hispanic, Hmong, or rural White—are fundamentally economic.

So why were we being tagged as racists?

"That's not an unreasonable response from people who are otherwise well-meaning and decent White people," said Clarence B. Jones, Scholar in Residence at the Martin Luther King Jr. Research and Education Institute at Stanford University and King's confidant and attorney. "And that's because they haven't taken the time to carefully consider the difference . . . between the general economic conditions of the White community and the Black community."

"In good faith," he added, "their judgment is clouded by an illusion . . . that there is a level playing field, that there is no significant economic disparity between the capital assets in the African American community and the capital assets in the White community."

This is a false assumption, according to Jones. The roots of that disparity date back to 1863, when four million slaves were freed—at least officially—by the Emancipation Proclamation. Two years later the "40 Acres and a Mule" order—giving freed slave families land and a barnyard animal—was established. Historians debate the scope of that specific order, but that dispute doesn't change the overall impact of slavery.

"The principal economic consequence of slavery on the African American community is the failure of them to have any generational transfer of wealth," Jones said, which reminded me of what Steven Rogers had highlighted regarding the lack of Black retailers. "Having no capital assets to transfer from generation to generation meant that you had successive generations of African Americans who were always economically disadvantaged," Jones said.

In explaining the factual and historical basis for his position, Jones pointed to President Lyndon Baines Johnson's 1965 commencement address at Howard University, "To Fulfill These Rights."

freedom is not enough. . . . You do not wipe away the scars of centuries by saying: Now you are free to go where you want, and do as you desire, and choose the leaders you please. You do not take a person who, for years, has been hobbled by chains and liberate him, bring him up to the starting line of a race and then say, "you are free to compete with all the others," and still justly believe that you have been completely fair. Thus it is not enough just to open the gates of opportunity. All our citizens must have the ability to walk through those gates. This is the next and the more profound stage of the battle for civil rights. We seek not just freedom but opportunity. We seek not just legal equity but human ability, not just equality as a right and a theory but equality as a fact and equality as a result. For the task is to give 20 million Negroes the same chance as every other American to learn and grow, to work and share in society, to develop their abilities—physical, mental and spiritual, and to pursue their individual happiness.

I think we would all agree that hasn't happened.

In search of a contemporary perspective, I sought out two people I met in the trenches: Tracye Dee, the African American owner of WineStyles in Chicago's South Loop, and Joslyn Slaughter of Jordan's Closets. I was curious about what they thought was behind the animosity toward our buying-Black effort.

Tracye told me she thought folks are fearful of a unified effort by African Americans, a group that many see—accurately—as deeply divided. "People are so afraid of something different," she said. "I think they worry that we'd take away from their patrons and their family businesses. I feel like telling them, just give it a chance. You'd find that you may even benefit from it."

Joslyn Slaughter said much the same thing. "We're not used to seeing something like this from African Americans," Joslyn said of EE. "But if we had the presence of mind . . . to bring all our talent to bear, we would be a lot further along. We're a minority, yes, but we're a big minority. We could move mountains, and I think that scares some White people."

Fear can be a powerful force. Why do you think everyone from politicians to insurance sales reps to real estate agents use it? It's effective, easy, and serves their immediate needs, but it also kills progress and opens the door to much worse. Yet the fear endures.

African Americans were brought here centuries ago as slaves, a circumstance that created an assortment of enduring emotional and psychological scars. These have been inflamed, transformed, and passed along from one generation to the next. The media basically continues the fearmongering by portraying us as dumb, loud, shiftless, predatory, and immoral, in stereotypes ranging from the obese welfare mom and the vulgar rapper to the ignorant athlete.

Fear is what prompted the "white flight," mostly in the 1960s, that occurred in the panicked home selling in Chicago and other cities. As a result, the once "good" Irish, Italian, or Jewish neighborhoods, like on Chicago's West Side, have become almost all Black and all feral.

A half century later those neighborhoods remain lost. Folks who once lived there look back with sorrow and anger at what their communities have become, and just about anybody—Black or White—who has to drive down those streets does so with the windows raised and the doors locked. Add to that the African American riots on Chicago's West Side and in many urban areas after Martin Luther King Jr.'s assassination, the Black Power movement, and the armed insurrection the Black Panthers advocated, and the fear seems justified. When some folks think about Blacks getting more powerful, they may flash on those images as well as more recent ones and think: *Those jackasses are going to be in charge? We can't let that happen. It'll be anarchy.*

There's a logical progression from fear to resentment to hate, which is, of course, much more destructive. Images of the vulgar rapper or the welfare mom quickly become what some White folks, or Asians, or Cuban Americans want—no, love—to see so they can justify and fuel the fear and anger that leads to outrage. These stereotypes become the only images those folks will let in.

The Empowerment Experiment got caught in all that quicksand. As much as John and I tried to extricate the conversation from the mud and refocus it on self-help economics and inclusion, we kept getting stuck. This emotional morass was hindering the movement we were trying to build, and it was poisoning our souls.

Chapter 8

The Trouble Is Us

AFTER THE BRIEF DAYS OF HOPE FOR FARMERS BEST, things again began looking grim, and my mood became prickly. Despite our prodding, friends were doing nothing to support Karriem's store, even though they said they would shop there. They were just telling us what we wanted to hear.

During my frequent trips to Farmers Best there were hardly any cars in the parking lot near Karriem's Ford Excursion. The entire shopping center's lot took up two blocks, and because Farmers Best was by far the largest building in the strip mall, there were about six aisles of double-sided spaces available for his customers. The other stores had no more than half that amount. Keeping my spirits up after pulling into that lot was next to impossible. I knew that empty lot meant that the inside of the store was a dead zone.

Before walking in I'd take a few minutes, clear my head, and push back the tears. Then I'd inhale and force a smile. I knew how humiliating this plight was becoming for Karriem, and I was trying not to make it worse. I'd hop out of the car, grab a shopping cart, and stroll down the empty aisles, all the while sporting a pleasant smile that bordered on the insane. And I'd buy. Then I'd buy some more. I knew my belief that buying a couple extra cans of beans or six-packs of Gatorade was going to make a difference was pathetic.

"Dang, baby," John said one afternoon when he'd come out to the garage to help me unload groceries. He was laughing. "Did KB have a sale on Gatorade?"

"Stop, John," I said. "You know exactly why I bought all that. At least I'm not wasting money. I'm only loading up on stuff that can sit for a while and that we're gonna use eventually."

"Honey, there is no more room in the garage for all this damn cereal and paper towels. You're being ridiculous."

He was right, of course.

"But John, you haven't been there in a while. You just don't know."

"I don't know?" he said. "*I* don't know. I've been there. And man, it was bad. So sad."

"So what am I gonna do? Go in there and buy some bananas and a pack of ground turkey and that's it?"

"Sweetie, you can rent a U-Haul truck and fill it up. Ain't gonna make a difference. You can't fix it because you are not the problem. The problem is not us. You gotta stop blaming yourself."

"But what about Karriem?" I said.

"Karriem's a grown man. He already appreciates us. He's facing a lot right now. But we're not his problem. The rest of them not bringing their lazy behinds into that store . . . they're his problem."

John was right—again. And I certainly wasn't fooling Karriem. We both knew that the marketing efforts, parking lot cookouts, and media photo ops weren't working.

By this time I'd gotten into somewhat of a routine. As soon as I dropped the girls at day care in the morning, the doors of The Empowerment Experiment opened. I'd check and send e-mails, tally up recent receipts, and then call KB, whether or not I was making the trek to the store. When he needed to discuss the business with someone who cared and was not too busy with a day job, he'd call. And he needed to discuss the business all the time. Having a chat at around 8:30 in the morning became standard for us.

"Maggie, you are not listening," he told me one particular morning. "It's not that I couldn't afford the meat—it's that I couldn't afford a price hike. It would've killed us."

He was talking about a wholesaler who was upset that Karriem's orders had tapered off.

"Okay, so he actually changed the price on you?" I asked. "Can he do that? We might be able to sue."

"Can he? Can he? He did. What can't he do? Those Italians own the whole strip over there. They have contracts with Certified Grocers. I'm just me. I'm no one. Just Karriem."

"But I thought they liked you. That's what you said."

"Maggie, it's not that. It's us. I need more traffic. I agreed on a price with this guy based on my ordering twice a week. I've been ordering twice a month, if that, because I don't have enough customers or money to justify those orders. So now he says he has to up my price. And I still gotta deal with these idiots at the Link office."

Link machines, the devices in stores that process the state's debit cards for customers receiving food subsidies—what used to be known as food stamps—were notorious for breaking down. Karriem's was as temperamental as the worst.

"Okay, but they're fixing that, right?" I said. "Now what about finding a new supplier? You don't have any friends from Dean's who can help?"

"Magz, let's change the subject."

I wanted to say, "*Well, what other subject is there?*" But I could tell he was frustrated. Besides, he'd already jabbed me about being an awful listener.

I knew I talked too much, but I was always trying to give him hope, a new solution he might not have considered when sometimes all he wanted was to vent. Karriem's struggles did seem to mirror our own, but at least we'd get a break every now and then—a major piece in print or TV interview, a donation to the foundation, a call from an influential business leader offering support. For some reason he was not getting any of those. I felt responsible for him barely being able to stay afloat.

As the Fourth of July approached, we were hoping for a miracle, or at least enough of a boost to keep Farmers Best open for another couple weeks. There was one reason in particular why we were optimistic: the first of the month—three days before the holiday, in this case—is one of the monthly occasions when the government refills Link accounts. The sorry fact is that those are always busy days for food stores in poor areas, which often means African American neighborhoods. Add to that the spike in grocery shopping that occurs before the Fourth, and we were fairly confident the store would be buzzing with customers. Karriem flooded the radio with commercials that week. He grilled in the parking lot again. He offered tempting sales and specials.

Then the Link machine broke—again.

When the Link machine breaks at a particular establishment, those cardholders go elsewhere. And if you're running a business teetering on the brink of insolvency, say, like a certain brave African American grocer on the South Side of Chicago, an untimely Link machine breakdown can shove you over the cliff.

On the morning of June 29, the day after my birthday, I speed-dialed Karriem's cell as I drove to the store to make sure he would be in when I got there. I had a bunch of shopping to do. The Fourth of July was around the corner, and Cara's birthday is four days after that. Then there was my best friend's bachelorette party that I was hosting later that week.

"You're coming now?" he said. He sounded exasperated, almost angry, as if I'd said something wrong. "To*day*?"

"Yep."

"I thought you'd be tired," he said. "Didn't you guys hang out late yesterday?"

"Yeah, but I'm fine. What's wrong, KB?"

He didn't answer for a few seconds. "Mag," he finally said—I could barely hear him—"please don't come to the store."

"What happened?" I said. "You get robbed?"

"No, nothing like that."

"Vandalized? Someone try to torch the place?"

"No, no, sweetie," he said. His voice sounded so defeated. "Everyone's okay. I just don't have everything. I couldn't make my orders and I told everyone to stay home. I don't want you to see the store like this." He explained that he did not have the funds to pay for his meat and frozen food orders. His suppliers would not let him pay on credit, so they would not deliver, and Karriem could not replenish his stock.

I hung up. Saying it was too painful for him, but I knew what had happened: He'd closed. It was over. How in the hell could we have let that happen? I pulled over. It was too much. I shut my eyes and shook my head. Then I pressed down on the accelerator and headed for the store. I had to see what was going on.

As I drove those fourteen miles through some of the most desirable and most forlorn neighborhoods in America, I kept replaying the events of the past few weeks. The brisk traffic at the store that we'd worked so hard to create had dissolved. Many folks who came for the promotions would buy only the items advertised or just redeem the $5-off coupons. Some showed up for the barbecues but never stepped foot inside the store. Or they came once and never returned.

When I arrived the parking lot was empty. I found Karriem sitting in his Excursion and I hopped in.

"Mag, I can't keep throwing money into a black hole," he said. He looked drained, resigned. "I have to close down. I'm ordering some of those 'Going Out Of Business Sale' signs, and I hope they'll clean me out. At least I won't have to throw away my inventory."

I didn't know what to say. I looked at him and just started weeping. Karriem hugged me. After a few moments I calmed down.

"Where are you going to shop now?" he asked. "I can't believe I did this to you."

I turned to him, wiped the tears away with the back of my hand. I was amazed at what I was hearing.

"*You?* Did something to *me?* KB, you are the project. I'm the failure, not you. Remember all that crap I told you about all those folks I'm going to bring in here? That you weren't going to be able to handle all the customers? Remember all that? Dammit, Karriem! Don't you see that we failed you and not the other way around?"

"Yeah, I remember," he said, laughing ruefully. "You said we were going to have a ribbon-cutting ceremony for my second location as the EE Victory Party. That there was gonna be a flood. Black customers from

Oak Park, Bolingbrook, South Shore, Harvey flooding into the store. Big flood! Yeah, I remember."

He laughed louder, holding his stomach. He wasn't being mean or insensitive. This was his way of maintaining sanity.

"And I believed it too. I was all in that Kool-Aid!"

I looked at that beautiful, empty store and was disgusted with myself. Then I started blubbering, and this time, a full-fledged weeping-Maggie avalanche erupted. John and I told Karriem we would change the world—one entrepreneur, one business, and one community at a time—starting with him, his store, and this community. The premise was simple and straightforward: Black entrepreneurs hire Black people and the dismal Black unemployment rate starts to drop. The neighborhood improves. People see what's happening in that store and other establishments take root and grow. Momentum builds from the sidewalk up. That was EE's promise—our promise to Karriem. I made him believe everything we'd told him. I poisoned him, his store, and his dream with our hopes and naiveté. I misled and let down this honorable man.

I ended up shopping that day anyway in a nearly dark store. I felt like I was grocery shopping after a nuclear apocalypse, as if I was rummaging through the lone food store on earth.

Karriem did order the signs, and he let everyone go except two employees he needed to help break down shelves, coolers, and other equipment to liquidate assets as part of the bankruptcy. In those few weeks after he closed I stocked up on whatever I could store in my house and whatever I could give to John's brother and sister-in-law. Karriem would bring cartons of dry goods like chips, pasta, condiments, peanut butter, soda, and beans. It got to the point where he was stopping by almost every day on the way to his home, just to bring over some of the inventory he could not liquidate.

And the produce! We gave away cases of mangoes, oranges, and pineapples to family and friends. We spent an entire weekend peeling, cutting, bagging, freezing, and juicing. We had fruit smoothies for weeks. We tried to make the most of a depressing situation.

What was most agonizing about Karriem's closing was the realization that no one but Black folks was to blame—Not *'da man*, not *'da gub-*

ment. Us—the customer base that should have flocked to his place was apathetic, cynical, and otherwise missing in action. How much effort we as a people invest in denying the possibility of a successful Black-owned grocer was amazing.

My encounter with a lady in the store's parking lot was typical. One summer afternoon prior to the store's closing a pretty woman wearing a sundress and floppy hat approached me. She was holding a bag from the dollar store next to Farmers Best.

"Do you shop here a lot?" she asked. I was ready to give her the whole Farmers Best–EE story. I was already digging for my card.

"Yes! And I love it . . . "

"You know that place ain't Black-owned," she said. "No way is that big store Black. I ain't stupid. Did you hear that on the radio? That it's Black?"

I couldn't believe it. Although I wanted to scream at her, I took a breath and launched into the details about Farmers Best and EE—our pledge, the businesses, Northwestern's study. She listened to all of it and then, in a staggering display of ignorance, said, "I'm not giving them crackuhs a dime of my money."

It was maddening.

"Alright," I said, feeling exasperated. "I don't want to argue with you about this. I'll pray for ya."

Sometimes I wonder whether something in our DNA prevents us from working together, whether the cultural liabilities we've experienced and, yes, cultivated over the decades have become the essence of who we are.

One of my favorite examples is the bullshit hoax of glorifying the ghetto. We love to do that—to boast about "keeping it real." It makes me roll my eyes and want to stick a finger down my throat. The truth—and we all know it—is that ignorant perspectives like the hollow "keeping it real" refrain guarantee that our neighborhoods will stay chaotic, impoverished, dilapidated, violent, and hopeless. But those neighborhoods are ours, baby. They're all ours, glory hallelujah, and as long they're ours, we've got something. *Da hood is ugly, broke down, and scary, but it's all mine!* Now isn't that something to crow about? If it weren't so painful and embarrassing, it'd be funny. Well, here's something else to consider: We never talk about *why* it's ours. Pretty simple, really: The ghetto is ours because no one else wants it. Who would?

Then there's the ridiculous line of thought used to justify our complacency—a forced, slightly twisted logic that links our inertia with our spirituality. You know the phrases: "Blessed be the meek" and "The more we suffer here, the greater our reward in heaven."

In her book *Talking Dollars and Making Sense: A Wealth Building Guide for African-Americans,* Wall Street veteran Brooke Stephens comments, "From the days of slavery, African-Americans have bought into this bizarre fallacy that there was something noble about poverty and suffering, and that the only comfort we should expect will be in an afterlife." In other words, be proud to be poor. We are not supposed to prosper: Our honor is in our exploitation and suffering.

Really? So why didn't Rosa just stay in the back of the bus and suffer proudly? Why didn't our mothers and fathers in Selma quit at the Edmund Pettus Bridge? You know why? Because they understood that the time to act had come. They knew they had been denied basic human rights for too long and that the only course to take was to dig in their heels and say, *Enough. No more will we take this humiliation and denial. We must stand—whether it's claiming a place on the bus or marching to guarantee safe entry into the voting booth—and seize our God-given rights.*

Since then things have gotten a little complicated. We've allowed ourselves to compromise. We've been seduced—maybe sedated is a better word—and we've lost focus. The humiliation endures, but it's more nuanced, more insidious, and the big difference is we've perpetrated it. We've betrayed ourselves and then directed our bitterness at everyone else. Time to take ownership, folks. Time to take action—again.

I also hear this crap about "them"—White America—stepping on us because they want to be us. We get all righteous about how they exploit us and condemn us but never will be able to be us. *Let them have all the prosperity and power,* this ludicrous riff goes. *They can't take our soul. We've got our soul power!* Translation: You're lazy and don't care anymore. You don't believe we can make things better, and you've found a way to contort that into some kind of warped pride—the triumph of failure. How whacked out is that?

"To go on blaming society, the white man, recent immigrants, Congress, the 'establishment' for one's lack of prosperity is good for venting one's frustration," Stephens writes, "but what are you going to do about the situation once you get past the talking stage?" This line of thought is just "another category of Black paranoia and a set of excuses not to make any effort to change and stop being a willing victim," she continues. "Our ancestors bought and paid for our success—it is time to claim it as being long past due."

Fear—not all that different from the fear in the White community and fear among Prominent Black Folks—is a powerful, hope-killing force in the African American psyche. "The bottom line is that most Black folks are scared to talk about money," Stephens notes. "Scared to admit they've made dumb choices with it. Scared to take risks as entrepreneurs. Scared to trust and respect each other as professionals in business deals. . . . Scared to challenge outdated beliefs about prosperity and economic well-being. Scared to stop blaming racism for all the financial problems that exist in the Black community."

Amen, sister.

Stephens' words made me think about all the Prominent Black Folks who took a pass on supporting EE. Were they afraid of taking a bold step that somehow might offend Whites? Were they cynics who believed that most Blacks were incapable of running successful businesses? Regardless, their sense that their position is precarious seems to motivate their behavior. Dr. Walker told me, "I have found that the most wealthy and most prominent blacks achieved their wealth and power by placing themselves in the mainstream of American life and, for the most part will stay away from anything that can be considered racially divisive." They flourish as long as they succeed in treading lightly—acknowledging they're Black but not so Black that they jeopardize business relationships with well-heeled Whites.

By way of example, Walker pointed to the rushed firing in 2010 of US Department of Agriculture employee Shirley Sherrod, an African

American woman whose out-of-context remarks at a speech twenty years ago depicted her as unfairly dealing with a White farmer. The Obama administration couldn't get rid of her fast enough, but then they were embarrassed when the media revealed that, in fact, Sherrod had treated the man with dignity, had actually helped save the man's farm, and had become friends with him.

According to Clarence Jones, no empirical data exist to show that the Black power-elite is lagging in its support of impoverished Blacks, but he thought that this lack of support might exist, and it might be generational.

"My gut feeling, strangely enough," he said, "is that . . . except for Bill Cosby and Oprah—I don't think [it is] on [the older Black elite's] radar. I really think that the predominant mindset is that 'I did it so anybody can do it.' And . . . there may be a sense of not wanting to put what they have at risk."

However, according to Jones, the new generation of African American sports personalities "really have a sense that, 'I want to give something back.' They feel much more of a connection and they're more proud from whence they came. In many ways, they're much more secure in what they've acquired than some of the older ones."

With all due respect to Clarence Jones, given our experience I believe that part of the reason Black people can never earn their rightful place in society is because we do not support each other. This failure does not have to do with our history in this country, racism, or discrimination. This failure is about whom we have chosen to be.

I had a strong sense about all this before embarking on The Empowerment Experiment, but I refused to acknowledge it. Once we got rolling I wanted to believe that the desire to empower ourselves was latent but strong in all of us. If we just had a spark to ignite it, we could overcome our ingrained, destructive history. Maybe our belief was a survival tactic. Or chalk it up to our guilelessness. Or maybe I just didn't think that the defeatism would be so intractable that it could kill Karriem's store.

What made it worse, if that's possible, was reflecting on all the empty promises people—Prominent Black Folks and not so prominent—made to us regarding their support of Farmers Best. I call it the "art of civilized hypocrisy." Basically, folks were lying to our faces, especially people in Bronzeville and Hyde Park, vibrant neighborhoods with substantial Black populations near Karriem's store. People there had no excuse to bypass the place except for the obvious reason: racism among our own people, against our own people.

Then, once the stored was closed, folks would respond in shocked disbelief and ask why it had closed.

"What?" I remember one guy telling me. "No way. It's gone? I didn't even get a chance to go. Damn. That's rough."

"Wow! He should've been a little more patient," somebody else said. "I was going to come and bring some folks with me. He gave up that quick?"

That question would really light my fuse.

"Not enough support," I'd say, trying to stop the burning between my ears. After a while I stopped being polite and let them have it, which is what happened with a congregant of Trinity United Church of Christ who made the mistake of asking me about the project after she recognized me from the CBS *Early Show* interview. When she suggested that I ask Pastor Moss to include Farmers Best coupons in the church bulletin, I told her it was too late: The store was closed. She reacted the way everyone else did—with surprise.

"It's your fault," I told her, "and everybody else in this church's fault who didn't have the simple decency to empower one of our own brothers by doing nothing more than shopping at his beautiful store once in a while."

Poor woman never knew what hit her. But I had all these other thoughts—questions, really—about what went wrong for Farmers Best. Why would folks like this seemingly well-intentioned woman never, ever wake up on a Sunday morning and drive a few blocks to Farmers Best but instead drive eight miles to the closest Whole Foods or Target Greatland? Why do we spend our hard-earned money in those disgusting neighborhood minimarts, owned by people who live in prosperous suburbs with high-performing schools and who treat us, their customers, with contempt while offering overpriced, inferior goods? Why are we so willing to help send their kids to college instead of supporting someone like Karriem, a caring, committed, hardworking role model who provides a wonderful store employing and mentoring at-risk Black youth?

Are we that ignorant? Are we that comfortable with our misery? Do we really hate ourselves that much?

After our Black year ended, the *Chicago Tribune* ran a second article reflecting on what had transpired, including the closing of Farmers Best. Karriem publicly pointed to the rough economy, deep-pocketed and not always upright competitors, and the unavailability of capital—there it is again—as the culprits. His love for us and his appreciation for our efforts on his behalf were strong, which was noble of him. However, his feelings for The Empowerment Experiment and the notion of Blacks supporting Black-owned businesses were ambivalent. Grudgingly, he acknowledged that the lack of community support was a factor in shutting him down.

He said, "The Empowerment Experiment . . . made people aware of the lack of support for Black-owned businesses and aware that there was a Black-owned fresh market. What people chose to do with that remains to be seen."

Then Karriem said something that encapsulated his—and our—experience. He suggested that being highlighted as a Black-owned business might have hurt Farmers Best.

"If you're under the radar," he said, "then maybe you won't get that belief from customers that the other guy's ice is colder than yours."

What happened to Karriem still keeps me up at night. The whole episode highlights one of the most enduring problems of this odyssey: I was enraged at the people I wanted to empower. I hated the people I wanted to help the most. That love-hate dynamic made me want to slap or spit on somebody, to burn something to the ground—and this lasted a long, long time. When it finally started to dissipate, it morphed into cynicism, which is debilitating when you're trying to sustain a movement and instill hope.

I almost felt as if Karriem's closing, the PBFs' rejection, and the overall Black divisiveness were signs from God that we were not meant to win this fight. I came to this bizarre conclusion that we Blacks suffer from a paralyzing psychosis brought on by a cancer, and that cancer is not the leakage, nor is the racism or the exploitation at the hands of other ethnic groups who had raided our neighborhoods and industries. We were the cancer. We were sick, poisoned, dying, and choosing to ignore the symptoms.

I learned that it was going to take a lot more than a fantastic store and a dynamic entrepreneur to shake my peoples' paralysis, to cure the cancer. And I couldn't stop myself from coming to another conclusion: Farmers Best was everything EE could be and everything we in the Black community would never be.

<hr>

Although the Farmer's Best closing knocked us on our rear ends, we were getting signals that we had at least piqued people's interest. The e-mails, T-shirt orders, and registrations kept coming—between the website and the Facebook group, about eight thousand official EE members by August—and so did speaking requests. We received awards from or invitations to partner with several key organizations—from the United American Progress Association, a grassroots organization based on Chicago's South Side, to the NAACP, National Urban League, and National Black Chamber of Commerce.

Throughout this time we were reevaluating our media strategy, which had been focused on getting as much national, mainstream media exposure as possible, sometimes at the expense of neglecting smaller Black outlets. Our PR firm had to focus on paying clients, and it was not doing much in terms of promoting our story. So other media's coverage triggered most of the media we got, and that made us think we may have been spending too much time explaining and defending instead of sharing and inspiring. Educating outsiders who wanted to understand the issues was important, but we wanted to spark real change, and nothing was going to change unless Black people were inspired to act. The result was that we altered our media strategy: We would focus our efforts on predominantly Black outlets.

Which was why meeting Doug Banks, one of the most popular Black radio hosts on the air, was so invigorating.

We crossed paths a few weeks after my June speech at Friendship-West Church, when I attended the National Urban League Conference in Chicago. Apart from being a radio giant, Banks is an author and public speaker, though he is definitely not your typical talking head. He presents a full-bodied, nuanced portrayal of the issues and believes in intelligent conversation—as much as can be achieved on a radio call-in show, anyway. In other words, he's smart, articulate, and takes seriously his role as cohost of the nationally syndicated radio show, *The Ride with Doug and Dede*. Because of all that, people view him as a leader in our community.

When I told him about The Empowerment Experiment, I could almost see the wheels clicking. That happened with lots of people. And, like lots of people, he said he supported the project 100 percent. What made Doug different was that he immediately took action, inviting us to be on the show, which airs in the all-important 2–6 p.m. weekday time slot. We set it up for August 18, a Tuesday. John and I were ecstatic. Every day on the show Doug submits a topic for discussion on "The Adult Conversation," and folks call in. We thought Doug and Dede would interview us for the standard few minutes, which is what happened with most of our other media appearances. Instead, they called us at home and kept us on the show for an unprecedented three hours. The topic was "Should Black People Do More to Support Black Businesses?"

We got our answer in a hurry: no bleeping way.

While John and I passed a phone back and forth between us (there was better reception if we didn't use separate receivers), we were subjected to an audio lashing. Only one caller supported self-help economics and pledged to do more to spend his money at local, Black businesses. The rest tore apart the ideals behind our mission, usually by recounting a story about a disappointing experience at a Black business and then swearing off ever patronizing one again.

"Yeah, every time I go to my Black Popeye's, they don't have chicken," the typical caller would say, "or I have to wait ten minutes for my food."

Someone said they were cheated at a Black-owned business; another claimed the customers at the establishment scared her; a third said the owners did. A caller complained that the Black-owned stores didn't look like Wal-Mart. "Bottom line," another critic pronounced, "is that Black businesses are always dirty, and the prices are too high. Black people are just greedy."

And then there was my all-time favorite: The Black folks who want credit for trying to buy Black once, ten years ago, and having an unsatisfactory experience, which leads them to dismiss the entire race as being incompetent business people. This old saw invariably triggers one of my loud, crazy-lady laughs.

We'd gotten some of these reactions before, of course, so we were prepared with data about leakage, stories about encounters with high-quality, Black-owned businesses, and our suggestion to support only reputable Black businesses as a way to lower unemployment, strengthen the tax base, improve schools, and provide good role models. We told the one-time buy-Black shoppers to keep trying, that even Sam Walton started as a small-time retailer who needed customers from the community.

I remember asking the Popeye's caller whether he knew if the place was really Black-owned. "I bet you it's not," I said. "Have you ever considered who the owner is and what kind of service and quality he'd deliver to a Popeye's in one of those nicer neighborhoods on the North Side?"

To another skeptic I said, "But doesn't it bother you that all your hard-earned money is sending everyone else's kids to college, and our kids are the least educated and most likely to go to jail?"

Doug and Dede kept up the same approach, trying to steer the conversation back to the bigger issues, but the critical calls kept flowing. We were back in the quicksand and sinking fast.

"Guys," an exasperated Dede said at one point, "why are y'all spending so much time talking about why we can't do this instead of why we should?"

The very next caller ranted about how Black people have no respect for each other like we used to and that's why our businesses fail.

"Welcome to my life," I told Doug during a break.

"Mrs. Anderson," he said, "I really did not think it would be this way. I'm so sorry."

We finished "The Adult Conversation" feeling like we'd been shoved onto the sidewalk after being roughed up in an alley for three hours. That beating reinforced another lesson: the myth that "The Black Community" is a monolithic, unified culture moving to the same beat, almost like a single-minded church parish. The cult of Black—we all still vote Democratic, right? But what surprised me was just how divisive we could be. Has it gotten this bad? Do Black folks hate each other that much? Are we that narrow-minded and ignorant?

Maybe The Empowerment Experiment was doomed to fail. On the one hand, we had angry Whites calling us racist, and on the other, we had Blacks tearing into us for a number of reasons, saying we were ignorant for believing that Black-owned businesses were competitive with White-owned ones—or could ever be. It was our own Perfect Storm.

In my despair I reached out to Dr. Juliet Walker, who, as the only female member of our Executive Advisory Team, had become a mother figure to me. She said Black divisiveness must be viewed in the context of what is known as "crabs in the bucket" or "crabs in a barrel." The story is that Booker T. Washington formally coined the phrase and used it in one of his lectures to point out how Blacks were holding each other back. Picture a bucket of crabs. None of the crustaceans will allow the others to climb out. Any time a single crab attempts to get out, the rest pull the lone crab back down. This was one of the theories we were trying to examine in The Empowerment Experiment.

Booker T. may have coined it, but the phrase, used most often to describe the plight of our businesses, has been around for about as long as Africans have been Americans. Lately, Black folks have used it—mistakenly, I believe—in reference to commentators and intellectuals, like Tavis Smiley and Cornel West, who publicly criticize President Obama. It's not that Smiley and West expect to be president, the misguided thinking goes; instead, it's that President Obama was making it out of the bucket, so they will attack the president, pulling him back in because he is Black and successful and that bothers them, and doing so benefits them personally in the form of more listeners, viewers, and readers.

You see it in other cultures too: Hawaiians call it Alamihi Crab Syndrome, the Swedes and Scandinavians know it as Jante's law, and in Australia and New Zealand it goes by Tall Poppy Syndrome. I even found a reference to it in a 2006 International Monetary Fund essay on why poor countries stay that way: "Citizens, fearing that the advantage gained by one group may come at the expense . . . of the other, become like crabs in a bucket, preventing each other from getting out," writes Raghuram Rajan, director of the IMF's Research Department. "Uncertainty about who will get the benefits of reforms can further compound resistance."

I call it the "Advancement is betrayal" perspective. It is about as defeatist an outlook as you could conjure.

Others have remarked on the by-products of this syndrome. In *Talking Dollars and Making Sense*, Stephens writes, "African-Americans have such a strong historical identity with poverty that we seem to define ourselves by what we don't have rather than what we do have. . . . If and when a brother or sister finds a way to create a profitable life, that person is immediately looked upon with suspicion and condemned as having 'sold out.'"

That identity with poverty leads to laziness and, in Stephens's view, "is a self-fulfilling prophecy." People think, "The few dollars I make don't mean anything, and I'll never have anything, so why try?"

Complicating matters is the fact that White efforts to derail Black economic empowerment have existed for about as long as "crabs in a barrel." Laws to discourage Black entrepreneurship were established "almost as soon as the first settlers came to America," according to Jessie Carney Smith, editor of the *Encyclopedia of African American Business*. "From the end of the Civil War to the modern civil rights era, whites drove blacks out of their trades."

So Blacks found other ways to survive, most notably the aforementioned fraternal societies that became banking and insurance companies as well as businesses like shoemakers, draymen, and liverymen that Whites were reluctant to enter.

But the Black community remained fragmented. Some of this divisiveness, Dr. Walker told me, is borne of hopelessness, which was a product of all that formal opposition and something else: the horrifying widespread practice of lynching.

"It should be mentioned," she pointed out, "that during the age of massive lynching of Blacks—according to the findings of Ida B. Wells— the largest number of Black men lynched were those businesspeople who competed with Whites"—not those facing the already highly suspicious charges of raping White women.

That wasn't only Ida B. Wells's conclusion. In a landmark 1931 report, two prominent sociologists—one White, one Black—studied thousands of lynchings in the South and refuted the impression that these horrific crimes were meant as punishment for those dubious allegations of rape. In fact, fewer than 20 percent of all lynchings stemmed from rape or similar charges; many were attempts by largely rural, poor Whites to fend off what they saw as economic and political competition from their poorer Black neighbors. In my research I found repeated references to an estimated two or three lynchings each week in the late nineteenth and early twentieth centuries in the South, and every reference listed economic competition from Blacks as a leading reason for the crime. Lynching was economic terrorism.

White violence against Black economic empowerment didn't end with lynchings. Look through enough African American history and you can find all sorts of violence perpetrated against successful Black businesses. In 1859 Black furniture maker Henry Boyd, considered the most successful African American manufacturer before the Civil War, closed his Cincinnati plant after it had been burned three times. In 1860 arsonists destroyed the elegant Sea Girt Hotel in Newport, Rhode Island, owned by African American hotelier and civic leader George Thomas Downing. The 1906 race riot in Atlanta, in which at least twenty-five Blacks were killed, and the 1919 race riots in Chicago, where twenty-three Blacks were killed, were directly traced to White tension over economic competition from Blacks.

I've never been one of those people who blame everything on slavery and the especially harsh realities for Blacks through the late-nineteenth century; I do believe, especially now, that hundreds of years of slavery, slaughter, open and covert hostility, and various forms of exploitation have plenty to do with it. In any case, the result is that Blacks now have very few businesses, and most of them are concentrated in a few markets and industries—like hair braiding—and in a few locales—in poorer, predominantly Black neighborhoods. This would not be so catastrophic if those businesses were successful, expanding, employing more than one or two people, and dominating lucrative industries. You know where that's happening? Among Koreans, who have taken over the Black hair and beauty supply industry, which generates over $9 billion a year.

To make matters worse, only a small percentage of the Black-owned businesses that do exist are high quality and competitive. That condition perpetuates a debilitating cycle, Dr. Walker notes. Most Black businesses don't survive, and those that do survive can't generate enough money to expand, which often leads to their eventual demise. That environment plays into the cynicism, suspicion, and divisiveness among our own people.

Clarence Jones, the scholar in residence at Stanford's Martin Luther King Jr. Institute, told me that African American disagreement over buying Black is a result of the struggle for civil rights, a desire "to be considered and treated as part of the mainstream. . . . They don't want to be reminded of the economic disparities. They mistakenly don't see Black empowerment as a positive step. They see that as somehow a denigration and denial of their status as 'equal' in this society and they, too, are living an illusion."

As Jones pointed out, slavery exacted an incalculable psychological toll on Blacks, and segregation "scarred our psyche." The overall consequence—apart from the lack of intergenerational wealth—was a lasting sense of lower social status.

"They should see [buying Black] as an act of pride," Jones said, "as a validation of their self-worth, but some of them don't see it that way." And so they resist. "That resistance must be challenged . . . in a sympathetic way," he cautioned, "because you are dealing with a Black people who are inflicted with their own sense of inferiority."

Chapter 9

In the Groove

THIS IS THE PART OF THE STORY WHERE OUR MARRIAGE falls apart; where the strains of driving thirty-six miles for paper towels, the realization that despite our best efforts we couldn't keep Karriem's business afloat, and the stress of forcing two little girls into an arrangement they couldn't possibly comprehend all combine to ruin a family.

Except they didn't. Thank God, exactly the opposite occurred.

While the jalopy that was The Empowerment Experiment was sputtering along, the four Andersons took hold of one another and drew closer. Maybe this was due to a feeling that we were alone in this, and despite the disillusion, we still believed in the experiment. Maybe it was anger with the rest of the world or a shared sense of heartbreak and loss. I'm not really sure. But I like to think it stemmed from the love John and I have for each other and that our values are so closely aligned. Although we might not have begun with the best-laid plans and things weren't working out the way we had hoped, that didn't change our belief that we needed to do something and that *this* was the something we both felt was right.

I know it's a cliché, but the hardship made me appreciate John's character even more. Those traits that drew me to him—his dependability, intelligence, trustworthiness, calm demeanor, and devotion to the girls, the community, and me—shone through during these trying months. He told me that he grew to appreciate even more my prowess as a writer, my feistiness, smarts, and ability to work a room.

As for the girls, Cara and Cori were still young enough that they viewed EE as an adventure, for the most part, and this was helped by my ability to, uh, market the project to them. Plus, they had made some new friends and were treated like princesses in just about all the stores we frequented.

"Do it like Zinga, Mommy!" Cori said one Saturday in July while I worked on her hair. This hot summer day was going to be full of fun, food, and frolicking—EE style—for the four of us. "Zinga" was Nzingha Nommo, owner of Afriware Books, one of the few EE stores we'd found in Oak Park. Cori absolutely loved Nzingha's Afro, which was easily seven inches in radius. And both girls adored Nzingha, who always showered them with kisses. The cute bubble blowers we bought whenever we visited the store gave our daughters hours of joy.

I had promised the girls that we'd finally visit their new buddy Jori, and her mom, Ms. Faye, my tech-support person and the owner of a Quiznos franchise. Ms. Faye, Jori, the Quiznos store, and their backyard pool were all in Calumet City, a predominantly Black suburb far southeast of Chicago—almost in Indiana. Because the route from our place to theirs cut through much of the South Side, we were going to get the most from that hour-long trek by stopping at a few of our favorite businesses, starting with Afriware Books.

"Cori," I told her. "Mommy really wants to braid your hair today, sweetie pie. We're going in the pool and I don't want your hair to get in your eyes."

"Mommy, but can I wear it loose? To show Zinga?"

"Okay, baby," I said. "Okay." A mom has to pick her battles. "You can wear it like Zinga."

We met Nzingha during those first research-driven weeks in January. When I used Google to look for "Black businesses" and "Oak Park," up popped a link to Afriware's website. Under the store's Helpful Links tab was a list of other local Black-owned businesses. We thought we struck gold. The majority of them were restaurants and some professional services we didn't need—an accountant and a lawyer, for example. But the bakery, dry cleaner, two shoe stores, coffee shop, convenience store, and ice cream parlor definitely piqued our interest—until we started calling and found that all but one of the numbers had been disconnected. I called Afriware Books and left one of my trademark long-winded messages outlining our project.

That evening John was checking the messages as I was getting dinner together.

"Dang, John, you still on the phone?" I called from the kitchen.

"It's the lady from that bookstore," he said. Then he listened for another full eight minutes.

"Yup," John said to me, one ear to the phone. "You guys are gonna get along just fine." He laughed. I knew exactly what he meant. Nzingha possesses a similar propensity for leaving long messages.

A couple days later our family was standing in Afriware's doorway. Greeting us was a statuesque goddess sporting a large Afro, shell necklace, kente-cloth wrap skirt and a tight T-shirt with the red, black, and green map of Africa. This was the image I had in my head when I first heard her smooth late night–radio DJ voice on my voicemail. She was so striking that I felt a little outdone in my Oak Park mom getup of baggy jeans, worn-out sweatshirt, and my hair balled up in a bun.

"Greetings, sister and brother," she said, a warm smile spreading across her face. "What a beautiful family! I am so honored to have you in my store."

The place housed Black classics—from *Roots* to *The Color Purple*—and all the hot reads from the Black intelligentsia, including Cornel West, Tavis Smiley, our pal Dr. Michael Eric Dyson, and Dr. Na'im Akbar, the prominent scholar and psychologist. The celebrity stuff was there too, including LeBron James's book and Steve Harvey's self-help digest for Black women. And, of course, there were T-shirts, dolls, figurines, books, and posters depicting our new president. The room was clean and bright, just like the surrounding area. Afriware was in a prime spot—across the street from the high school and just a couple blocks from downtown Oak Park. The store became our go-to place for children's books, birthday presents, and the like.

That Saturday in July, Cori's hair was a hit, and Nzingha was flattered. We bought a special-edition Michael Jackson T-shirt for my mother, who is a huge MJ fan, and picked up more bubble blowers for the girls. We told the girls it was time to wave bye to Nzingha, and they were about to protest until John told them we were going for ice cream and to see Ms. Tracye.

Tracye Dee, another vivacious beauty, owned the WineStyles franchise in the South Loop, a very hot, upscale neighborhood a few blocks south of downtown Chicago. In the last few years stylish new condos, eclectic restaurants, bars, and boutiques had transformed what had been a somewhat seedy, largely overlooked section of town. Now the area was teeming with young, cultured professionals. What John and I found so exciting was that Tracye's place was in the center of a cluster of Black-owned businesses. What the girls found exciting was that Tracye also had a gigantic Afro, she smothered them with love, and her store was right across the street from a Black-owned Cold Stone Creamery. While John and the girls headed for treats, I crossed the street and went into Tracye's fine establishment. I loved shopping there, and the timing was ideal. We were planning a wine-tasting fund-raiser to be held here in a few weeks.

Tracye came into our lives in May at a party and awards ceremony that Nicole Jones, owner of Sensual Steps Shoe Salon in Bronzeville, had set up to celebrate the four-year anniversary of her business and to single out a few noteworthy African American businesspeople. She'd asked me to present awards, one of which went to Tracye for community stewardship.

As the owner of WineStyles, Tracye loved interacting with her customers.

"They are always surprised," she told me, "when I say, 'Hi, my name's Tracye, and if you need anything, let me know.' I hand them my business card and they say, 'Oh, you're the owner?' and then the questions start. That is really fun."

She was also able to keep her sense of humor during insulting encounters, like the times Tracye would be working with her manager, who was White, and a vendor would direct his sales pitch to him. "My manager would point to me and say, 'She's the owner,'" Tracye recalled with a chuckle. "Needless to say, they didn't get a sale." She sighed and smiled. "People need to break out of these boxes."

The interior of WineStyles looked just like all the fancy shops on Oak Park Avenue and in downtown Chicago. Hundreds of wine bottles in wood and marble-trimmed cases lined the walls, complimenting the oak barrels that doubled as bar stools. Leather couches and high tables were placed throughout. That day an older Black couple sat in one of the couches, with two bottles of wine on the coffee table in front of them. But most of the customers were White. The bar was full of White patrons, who seemed like they were all together for a tasting. They laughed as Tracye charmed them. I picked up two bottles of wine from Black-owned Heritage Link Brands—the Mhudi and Bukettraube—and came over to the bar to say hello.

"Hey, girl," I said to Tracye. "You do your thang. I see you're hosting a tasting right now. I'm gonna leave you exact change, okay? Just mail me a receipt."

She poured them all another round, excused herself, and then stepped around the bar.

"Child, please," Tracye said. "Give me a hug, honey." She moved gracefully and seemed so happy. I wished all my EE entrepreneurs looked that way.

"I heard Cara's party was awesome," Tracye said, a reference to Cara's fourth birthday party, held a week earlier at a Black-owned Reggio's Pizza parlor about a mile and a half from WineStyles.

"Honey, if you get me started on that party," I said, "I'll keep you here all day. Go back to your customers. You got me forever, girl. I want you to get *new* business."

I pulled out my credit card to buy the wines.

"We're definitely going to feature the Bukettraube at the EE fundraiser next month, right?" I said. "I just love this stuff. You know what? Just charge me for three and I'm gonna' grab another one on my way out. Thanks!"

We kissed each other's cheeks. John and the girls were standing outside with shakes. Tracye waved at them.

"Alright guys," I said. "I got the wine for Faye. Did you find some cupcakes for Jori?"

"Mommy!" Cara said. "Remember I told you how Jori kept eating all the Oreo cookies off my birthday cake?"

"Yes, baby."

"So Daddy found an Oreo cupcake, and we found strawberry for Cori too!"

"And I got the perfect present for Auntie Faye," I said, holding a bottle over my shoulder. "Yay!"

John was cracking up.

"You got her the Mhudi?" he asked. I nodded. "She's going to love you."

"Okay, girls, let's go to Jori's!"

Faye, a tech professional and freelance programmer—and Karriem's younger sister—crossed our path in April right after we had to revamp the website. I had been complaining to him about how difficult updating the website was and how I wanted a more functional database for our new registrants, and he referred me to her. After a few e-mail exchanges, Faye and I met at Bronzeville Coffee. She was a much prettier version of Karriem, but in every other way they were exactly the same. Smart, driven, and a die-hard, loyal South Sider, she told me what growing up there was like. Neighborhood kids worked in the grocery stores, ice cream parlors, diners, drugstores, and clothing stores—all Black-owned. But, as she said, "When the businesses died, the community died. The riots and all that stuff just put the nail in the coffin. We were already lost."

We moved on to other topics, scrolled through the website, and discussed what she could do for us. Then I asked how her business was going.

"Oh, this is okay," Faye said, "but the sandwich shop pays the bills."

"You have a sandwich shop? Like a café or a deli?"

"It's a Quiznos," she said, and sipped her tea.

"You're kidding me, right? Why didn't KB tell me?" I was pretty aggravated. Here we were looking to support Black businesses and Karriem didn't think to tell me his own sister had a sandwich shop. What was wrong with that man?

"I would have been supporting you all this time," I said, my voice gaining volume. I stood up and started pacing. "We love Quiznos and haven't had any since the experiment. What is with your brother?"

My demonstrative demeanor took Faye aback, and she seemed a little embarrassed.

"I guess he thought it was too far," she said. "The store is past my house in Calumet."

I decided to sit.

"Doesn't matter, shuga. Do you sell gift cards?" She nodded. "Well, I'll just buy gift cards from you and buy the food over by my house."

From that point forward we would buy two $25 gift cards from Faye every month and use them at the Quiznos near our house and in Oak Brook, where John worked. Because she and I lived so far apart, I didn't get to see Faye very often, but we talked a lot on the phone and became friends, even meeting a couple times with our daughters to shop at Jordan's Closets. Jori was a year and a half older than Cara, and they had the same long, curly hair. What Cara loved the most about Jori, though, was that her bedroom was the size of our living room and that she had her own pool and swing set.

We approached Faye's corner lot, and the girls started squealing about what they were going to do once we arrived. Faye and her husband, Gerald, greeted us warmly, and we went inside. While the moms got the girls into their suits, John and Gerald were in the kitchen making drinks and heating up some frozen Reggio's Pizza. As the girls splashed around in the water, Faye and I relaxed on lounge chairs, drinking Tracye's wine from Heritage Link Brands.

"This is nice, isn't it?" Faye said, enjoying the breeze, the wine, and the company.

"Yeah, it really is." We let the sounds of the shrieking girls pass.

"By the way," I said, "did you find a sitter so both of you can come to the wine tasting at Tracye's? And you can't let me forget to pay you for that database program you built. I didn't get to test it but—"

"Mag, slow down," Faye said, chuckling. "Can we just sit here and chill out? Everything doesn't have to be about work. Damn girl, relax."

I smiled. "Never."

She reached out for my hand, and I took it, squeezed, closed my eyes, and wondered whether I had gotten back to the caterer for the wine tasting. Then I made a mental note to call the photographer from *Black Enterprise* magazine to schedule a photo shoot.

The other thing I should have been thinking about was grocery shopping. After Karriem closed his store in July, the arrangement we had to buy food from him became increasingly awkward. For weeks we were living on whatever food was still fresh, using up as much of his inventory as we could. The rest we stored in our freezer and four coolers we borrowed from friends.

After Karriem had to shut off the power and clear out his place, he bought food from his wholesale suppliers and sold it to us—simple enough, except for the delivery part.

We originally chose to do the first drop at one of our favorite spots, C'est Si Bon!, a gourmet caterer and restaurant in Hyde Park. Over the past couple years Renee—the owner, my friend, and a true-blue EE believer—had essentially closed the restaurant and focused on the more lucrative catering operation. But I had been eating there since 1999, when I was a grad student at University of Chicago, and had hosted John's twenty-ninth birthday party and our engagement party there. So Renee, the sweetie, would direct her chef to whip up my favorite—fried chicken and waffles with extra honey butter—whenever I asked.

While I was enjoying my meal with Karriem, the staff was preparing for a big wedding and the place was bustling. Renee came by to apologize for the noise and offer her condolences to Karriem. "Oh, Karriem," she said. "We tried, baby."

Renee definitely was one of those who had. She purchased her produce from Farmers Best and had complimented Karriem on how punctual and professional his guys had been.

"I know, Renee," Karriem said. "It wasn't your fault. I feel bad I can't hook you up anymore. Where you gonna find your sweet potatoes for that cheesecake?" C'est Si Bon! was famous for its sweet potato cheesecake.

"Oh yeah," I said. "Renee, do you have any extra? And some collard green rolls I can take home to John and the girls?"

Renee said she'd have to check.

"Between you and KB giving me stuff," I mock-complained, "I'm not gonna have any room in the truck."

Karriem shot up straight in his chair. "Shit, Mag," he said. "Your stuff is in the other truck. Paola needed it today to pick up her family from the airport." Paola, Karriem's wife, was pregnant, and the baby shower was that weekend. "I forgot to take your stuff out."

He was silent for a second and then asked if I could come to his house, which I couldn't. I had interviews set with the *Charlotte Post* and on a radio show, after which I'd have to rush to pick up the girls from day care.

So we came up with Plan B, which really was Plan I-294/I-88, the spot where those two interstates cross. It's reasonably close to my house and a relatively easy drive for Karriem. He left C'est Si Bon! right away and headed for home, where he'd grab the boxes and drive to the appointed spot. I was going to meet him, but getting there took me a little longer than I'd expected. The result was that I arrived late. I felt awful. Karriem was doing us this huge favor while he was dealing with professional devastation and a baby about to be born. And it was raining. We stood there on the shoulder of the highway, cars and trucks roaring by us, as I kept apologizing and trying to explain.

"Mag, all that's fine," Karriem said. He was shouting in part to be heard over the rain and traffic and in part because he was a little pissed—and had every right to be, which made me feel worse. "But I do have stuff to do. I'm late for a meeting now."

"Karriem," I shouted back. I was waving my hands. "We'll get it later. We can get it Sunday at the baby shower. Go to your meeting."

"No!" he said. "Now. Get back in your car. I'll do it."

I did what he said, feeling lousy while this generous, hardworking man loaded boxes of cereal, beans, and rice into the back of my truck in the rain. I couldn't help feeling like this was some sort of illegal, clandestine operation, as if we were food smugglers.

After that we clearly had to come up with a Plan B for Plan I-294/I-88. This ratcheted up the pressure—at the precise time we were getting into the groove of the movement. I have to admit: I liked the feeling. EE wasn't necessarily where I wanted it to be, but it was moving forward.

People were responding and that was at least something. Entrepreneurs and directory publishers were making business propositions. They wanted to partner with The Empowerment Experiment to help their business grow or direct more traffic to their directory. Some of our favorite business owners, including Selena Cuffe, of Heritage Link Brands, and Tracye at WineStyles, were planning that fund-raiser for our foundation. I had set up a visit to Mima in Atlanta and had agreed to give a big speech while there. We had several other major interviews lined up too, as well as requests for me to appear on a panel or give a lecture. Now I was CEO of The Empowerment Experiment, not just this suburban homemaker with an idea.

Meanwhile, movement or not, we still needed food. So I cobbled together a supply system that involved shopping at dumps like J's Fresh Meats and using our gift cards from Black-owned gas stations to shop at other stations' minimarts. Our original intention had been to use the gas cards to buy gas, but as our food options dwindled, we started depending on the gas cards to buy food as well. Some of the minimarts were clean and well stocked. Some were nightmarish. And because we needed the cards for both gas and food, we started buying $300 and $400 worth of plastic at a time. A family friend who owned a Citgo station far from our home first suggested the idea; we sent her a check and she would place that value on a card from her station, thereby receiving our support. Then she mailed the card to us.

This strategy became a lifesaver as the year progressed, and we branched out to use it at fast-food restaurants and the like. Of course, the approach only worked with Black-owned franchises of companies that sold gift cards. Sometimes we'd find a franchised company that sold gift cards, but we couldn't find a Black franchisee, which was the case with Pizza Hut. Other times we'd find a company with a Black franchisee, but the organization didn't offer gift cards, which was the case with Popeye's Chicken and Biscuits.

We also found another place to shop—a cramped, disappointing joint called Woods Grocery, on the South Side, just a few blocks north of Farmers Best but in another retail hemisphere, the one in hell. It was J's Fresh Meats with a couple more refrigerators, a slightly improved grocery selection, and much higher prices. I'd drive about fourteen miles one way to Woods because it had some cold cuts, cheese slices, a large selection of sugary cereals and sodas, and a wide array of frozen TV dinners, the new staples of the Anderson household diet. Driving to Woods, I took the same route I used to get to Farmers Best, longing for Karriem's store every minute of the journey. Thinking about spending $40 at Woods on what typically would cost roughly $15 elsewhere made me angry. This was insane: two boxes of cereal at $6 each; pancake mix for $3.69 when, prior to our experiment, I had never paid more than $2 a box; a pack of bologna for $3.99. We don't even eat bologna; we eat turkey. Bologna, in my mind, is a distant, suspicious cousin to meat, but under the desperate circumstances of The Empowerment Experiment in the third quarter of the year, it qualified.

In retrospect it sounds exactly like what it was: ridiculous. But when I was driving all those miles and paying all that money for primarily substandard food, I mostly thought about the people who live around Woods and had to shop there. It was pretty much their only option in what otherwise appeared to be a food desert. But I didn't feel burdened, nor—and this sort of shocked me—did I feel like giving up. If anything, I felt like it was my duty to keep shopping this way. If a point was going to be made, maybe it was good that I didn't have a wonderful option like Karriem's store because most Black Americans don't.

One thing about an adventure like this, if ever there was an adventure like this, is that you make discoveries about the world and about yourself. Some are dreadful; others are awesome. And some are just curious. As our bologna saga illustrated, finding meat was particularly challenging. Once in a while we'd find something in the small refrigerated section at Woods—cold cuts, bacon, a cylinder of ground beef. On a good day we'd find a bag of frozen chicken wings. But usually the case was picked clean. We might as well have become vegetarians, except we couldn't find vegetables either. Is there something like Bar-b-cue-nacho-chip-arian? Frozen-burrito-arian? Those might have been closer to our status.

On one of my increasingly rare online searches, I stumbled across a meat distributor that looked promising, Israel's Clean Meat House, which, near as I could tell, was also a church, or maybe a Bible study group, on the far South Side. You don't get that very often—butcher and Bible. But the word "clean" appealed to me, and it looked legit. I was a little surprised that I hadn't come across this outfit in my previous searches, but I'd never looked specifically for meat packers or meat distribution companies. Israel's had only recently begun selling directly to the public, I learned, to help bolster lagging sales. When I called to check it out and explained our project, the person on the other end of the phone knew of us.

"So that's you?" he said, his voice probing. "Is that really you? And your husband? I saw y'all on TV, but I'm one of those folks who's less likely to believe something just 'cuz I saw it on TV? You know what I mean?"

"Yes, sir, I do," I said. "Everything feels like a show now."

"But you. Y'all for real," he said. "God Bless it! This is real. And I'm talking to you."

"Yes, sir. And I called you because I want to support you. It's for real."

"Well, that's good. He may not come when you want Him to . . ."

"But He's always right on time," I said, finishing the popular Christian axiom. "Speaking of being on time, this talk is really on time. You know that our grocery store closed down? I need food. And I need it from a quality Black business. Now, is that you? Was He on time?" I said, chuckling.

"Yes. He is an on-time God." I think he'd had enough of the unnecessary religious banter. "You said you went to our website, right?"

Then he explained how retail worked with Israel's Clean Meat House. It was an education in resourceful, if somewhat elemental, African American food procurement.

First, you call or fax in your order from a fairly wide selection of cuts—turkey, lamb, and beef products—including burgers, hot links, Italian sausage, bacon, breakfast sausage links, and patties. On Israel's Meat Market Day, the second Sunday of each month, you could pick up your order at their main location, which was an annexed part of a church on the South Side. Or if you ordered enough, the drivers would meet you at one of a number of different locations. The church was about twenty miles away from us. So I drove to the parking lot of a Black-owned bank, which was only a few miles closer on the South Side but a little more conveniently located right off the expressway. Locals could walk up and purchase products on the spot on Market Day, but only those who ordered and paid in advance were entitled to the big discounts. The first hour was reserved for those customers; Israel's handled walk-up customers in hours two and three.

I was hoping to see a huge crowd, something akin to the famous scene from the African American classic *New Jack City*, when neighborhood drug kingpin Nino Brown, portrayed by Wesley Snipes, sets up in an abandoned lot and passes out turkeys and boom-box radios to the adoring residents and throws money to the kids.

Fortunately, the people of Israel's Meat were not wealthy drug dealers, giving out turkeys in exchange for pumping drugs and crime into the neighborhood. They were the exact opposite, really, but seeing a similarly appreciative crowd would have been nice. I noticed one man, dressed in a short-sleeved white shirt with a bright purple tie, leaning on an old Ford Taurus with a large cooler at his feet. He was fifty maybe, clean-shaven, with shockingly bright eyes. The day was hot, and he was sweating and looked uncomfortable—until I got out of the car. He smiled a Jimmy Carter smile and started walking over, arms outstretched. I returned his hug, pointed at the cooler, and said, "That for me?"

"Yes, Ma'am. And we threw in a little extra so you can sample the beef products. You okay with beef?

"Yes, and thank you so much." I hugged him again. He took the bags out of the cooler and loaded them into my backseat. He was closing my door and about to turn away. "Sweetie," I said, "I need a receipt. You know we're saving the receipts for the study."

"Yeah, yeah. Man that's great," he said. "We all need to save our receipts." He shook his head, went to his car and returned with a receipt. "Here you go. Take care nah."

I felt a moment of sadness, overwhelmed by the knowledge that he would never grow his company into something like Johnsonville Sausage or Hillshire Farm. Then I looked at the backseat and saw all of those boxes of turkey burger patties, hot links, and Italian sausage, and I felt overjoyed. "Thank you, Jesus!"

For my next Israel's order, I did venture to the church after stopping at God First God Last, which was only a few blocks away. I wanted to see whether more folks would show up at the church office. Much to my satisfaction, they did. It was not like the crowd who came out for Nino Brown, but there were about fifteen customers standing in line when I arrived. Just like me, they were picking up food they had already ordered. The parking lot took up the corner of Kingston Avenue and 75th Street, a busy thoroughfare of the South Side. It was one of those streets camera crews filmed when they wanted to show a gritty Black neighborhood. But this working-class area lacked the suffocating depression of Madison Street on the West Side. People here were shaking hands and waving at each other, working, or walking with their kids and coworkers. Every store on the block was open. The owners weren't Black, for sure, unlike every person you could see, but at least the stretch wasn't full of abandoned storefronts.

The back door to Israel's refrigerated eighteen-wheeler was open, and I saw my friend from the bank parking lot there behind a small desk placed next to the truck. The operation seemed very organized. Customers provided their name, and the nice fellows from Israel's, all wearing white, short-sleeved shirts and bright purple ties, handed them the meat from the back of the truck. Everyone in line engaged in small talk while waiting. As each customer reached the desk, I could see that patrons and employees knew each other. *Yes! Repeat customers*, I thought. I was happy to support an honest businessman, although buying meat from a truck instead of at a major retailer did feel a little pathetic. But then I thought, *maybe this is how Johnsonville started decades ago. We just have some catching up to do.*

We availed ourselves of Israel's finest for a while, but the process was so cumbersome and, in truth, I wasn't that crazy about the taste of the meat, except for the turkey Italian sausage. In September we stopped buying there.

———

While we were foraging for food and building the movement, Mima's health was in rapid decline. Most days she'd make it out of her bedroom to the living room, but she would just lay on the couch all day watching TV. These were sad and desperate times, when she was lucid enough to talk about the fact that she wasn't going to be with us for much longer and to wonder about what came next.

In August the Black Business Network, an online community of nearly thirty thousand Black supporters of African American businesses, asked me to deliver a keynote address during the conference celebrating its official launch in Atlanta. Though BBN's organizers had been operating for a couple of years as TagTeam Marketing, a resource for Black entrepreneurs to grow and showcase their businesses, this event would celebrate the official launch of TagTeam's new offspring, the Black Business Network. BBN's focus was to facilitate buying Black, and its launch coincided with my scheduled trip to visit my parents.

BBN, like most Afrocentric community-based activist organizations we encountered, was a robust supporter of The Empowerment Experiment. Although the group couldn't offer funding or the connections we needed, their faith in our movement was unmatched. John referred to them and other Black economic power groups as "the base," "doers," and "the soldiers." I called them the "wall peeps" after one supporter told me during a BBN event: "Mrs. Anderson, I'd go through a wall for you!"

What BBN lacked in corporate sponsors, university affiliations, and media recognition, they made up for in passion, hope, and a willingness to do what needed to be done. Headquartered in an impressive facility in Atlanta, BBN had its own store, classrooms in which to teach successful business practices and train sales reps, and a state-of-the-art auditorium where businesspeople could make their pitches and others, like me, could speak. Those sales/motivational sessions could get pretty emotional, with lots of hugging and clapping.

My plan was to spend the weekend with my parents and then give my speech on Sunday afternoon. But Mima wasn't doing well. On Saturday she was having trouble keeping food down, and we were getting conflicting instructions from the on-call nurses. That night, when Mima finally fell asleep, I resumed working on my speech. When she awoke in pain about four hours later, I gave her meds and we talked about my plans to write this book. She said I should dedicate it to Cara and Cori and made me promise to include lots of pictures in it.

"Some people don't understand your writing," she added. "Make it so everyone understands."

Mima, I thought. *Even now, she's offering blunt, constructive criticism like only she can.*

The morphine tabs kicked in as we cuddled, and I told her repeatedly that I loved her as she drifted off. The next day, when I was getting ready to go to the meeting, it was clear that the intense pain had resumed. Unfortunately, we could do nothing about it because it wasn't time yet for the next dose of medication. I didn't want to leave, but Mima and Papa insisted. They were scared, but they were also adamant that I was going to give that speech.

I cried when I left them, cried during the drive to BBN headquarters, and kept at it as I walked toward the building. I was trying to prepare myself for the energetic reception I knew awaited me. I tried to take deep breaths, but the heave-filled sobs overwhelmed them. Just as I placed my hand on the door, I heard my name.

"Are you ready for Maggie Anderson?" an amplified voice said. "Are you *ready*?" I heard shouts and clapping. "Y'all ain't ready," the man's voice said. "This queen is coming all the way from Chicago to be with us and that's all you got?"

Standing in the doorway, I should have smiled, but I couldn't. My mind was locked on Mima.

My host had been doing a good job of pumping up the crowd. Music was blasting, and the DJ was mixing in excerpts from Dr. King's last speech, the one in which he asked the people of Memphis to take their money out of downtown banks and put them in Black-owned banks like he had done. Did these folks at BBN believe I was part of all that? It was overwhelming.

A homeopathic doctor I'd met before happened to be one of the first people I saw when I entered the building. She pulled me aside and directed me to a corner of the lobby.

"How's your mom?" she asked. "Is it your mom? I remember she had pancreatic cancer because my aunt has it too."

I hugged her tight and just wept.

"C'mon, sister," she said. "Let's get you outta here."

She took me in a bathroom, and we sat on a couch in the lounge area while she consoled me. She told me the presentations were running behind so I had time to regain my composure. We talked about her aunt and my mother, the hospitals and treatments. Then she gave me some space.

I just sat there sobbing. In a way I didn't want to calm down. I was overflowing with sorrow. And I was angry at everything—at the disease and at myself, angry with The Empowerment Experiment and at having to give another damn speech. After a few minutes—I don't know how long, really—the doctor came back to check on me. She sat down and took my hand.

"I know you're in pain," she told me softly, "but that pain is nothing like what your Mima is enduring right now and what she has already suffered. You need to change your focus, away from your pain and worries, and think about her and what would comfort her. You think running back home now and crying at her bedside would make her and your dad proud? Or would she be happy if you got up there, made a great speech, then rushed home to tell them all about it? I don't really have to tell you the answer to that, now do I?"

That's exactly what I needed to hear. She stood up, rubbed my back, and told me to push on, that it would be fine. After a few moments I stepped into the auditorium, finding a seat toward the back. Several people recognized me and gave me hugs. When I was called to the podium, I went right into my speech, knowing I was among friends. I was in the zone, or whatever you want to call it. When I said that I was beginning to understand the power of God because he saved my mother from death three times, everybody leapt to their feet, cheering. Again, it was overwhelming.

And then, for an instant, time stood still.

I thought about how none of these people knew a thing about my mother, aside from her illness, and I wanted them to know more about her. But everyone kept clapping and I started weeping, and the more I'd tear up, the louder they cheered. I flipped over my papers, placed my hands on them and waited. Then, I spoke from my heart.

I told them about my mother, how she taught me to fight for what I believe in. I wanted them to know that without the little woman who peeled shrimp and cleaned fish for a living, The Empowerment Experiment wouldn't exist. I could see that some members of the audience were crying. Evidently I wasn't the only one with a passionate, strong mother. I wasn't the only one who was sick of the economic neglect, exploitation, and insult that manifest themselves in so much human destruction. A bond was forming among all of us in that room. I felt like Mima was there too, and that, finally, everybody in the room understood what she was about. I stopped crying, flipped the pages back over, and continued my speech.

When it was over, the audience erupted in a standing ovation. I was so proud to be Luisa Maria Palacio Waite's daughter.

By the time I got home Mima was feeling better. The pain had subsided and she was asleep. I knew she'd want to hear the full story, so I kissed her forehead and woke her up. She opened her eyes and smiled.

"Ay, m'hija, como te fui?" (Oh, child, how did it go?) she whispered. "Lo hiciste? Lo hiciste bien? Y los gentes? Lo senti?" (You did it? You did it well? And the people? Did they feel it?)

"Si, Mima. Todo fui bien. Como siempre," (Yes, Mommy. Everything was great. Like always.) I said. "Tu sabes cómo lo hago! Les pedí que grabarla, paras usted." (You know how I do it! And I made them tape it, for you guys.)

The tape was the most important part. Along with game shows, re-runs of *Good Times* and *The Fresh Prince of Bel Air*, and *Caso Cerrado*, a Spanish-language court show, my parents would watch videos of their little revolutionary explaining EE on the news and in other venues. Over and over again. Every day.

Mima smiled, squeezed my hand, pulled me close, and kissed me on the cheek.

"I'm proud of you, m'hija," she said. "So proud." She said that in En-glish, except that it sounded like, "I so prow de ju."

And then she drifted off to sleep.

A few minutes later, after packing, I walked out of the stillness of my parents' house, got into Eduardo's car, and felt restored by Mima's strength and courage. I boarded the plane and relaxed. Some semblance of peace with this overwhelming effort was sweeping over me. With her words echoing in my mind while the plane cut through the darkness to-ward Chicago, I was ready to continue our mission.

"Lucha, m'hija."

Around this time I received an e-mail about a Black grocery store, Graf-fiti and Grub, which was opening at 59th Street and Wells, on the bor-der of the Englewood and Washington Park neighborhoods on the South Side. The owner was promoting Graffiti and Grub as a store em-phasizing hip-hop and a healthy lifestyle while trying to increase aware-ness about the area being a food desert. On its website the pictures of a prelaunch community event showed lots of people and produce. The store would be small, only open a couple days a week, and would feature produce and cooked food from Illinois Black farmers. How cool was that? I e-mailed them information about EE and received a call within minutes from the owner's assistant. The owner, LaDonna Redmond, president and CEO of the Institute for Community Resource Development and a self-proclaimed "food justice" activist, was out of town, but her assistant said LaDonna was excited about EE. We set up an appointment to meet.

At this point, however, I was more interested in seeing the store than meeting the owner. So I checked the site for the store hours and called KB, who agreed to visit it with me. We met for lunch at Third World Café, a Black-owned place in Hyde Park about two miles east of Graffiti and Grub. I hadn't seen him in a few weeks, and it was good to catch up. We talked about the new baby. He sounded a little more upbeat, telling me he'd survive financially and would continue pursuing his dream of owning a successful grocery store in the community. He shared plans about being a minority partner in the reopening of a huge grocery store in Hyde Park, and that he was working out deals with creditors. We were skeptical about Graffiti and Grub, only because Black entrepreneurs had not had a great track record with opening grocery stores, and we tried to set our expectations accordingly.

"Maggie, be ready, okay?" KB said. "It might not be much better than those bodegas you found on the West Side. I don't care what the website says. It's just too hard to get in the supply chain as a newcomer and get good quality stuff."

"But their hook is that they get direct from the farmers," I said. Nothing could top Farmers Best, but I was desperate. I just wanted to be able to find decent food for my family and never have to go to a wretched minimart again.

We jumped in KB's truck and headed for 59th and Wells, but we had trouble finding the store. The address was adjacent to the expressway, literally on the service road, in an uninviting industrial stretch of real estate comprised of a few abandoned lots and warehouses. We kept calling Graffiti and Grub but got no answer, and finally we spotted a steel door with a number that corresponded to the address.

"You stay in the car," Karriem said. "I don't like how this looks. Let me check it out."

He left the Excursion running and banged on the door. Nothing. He walked around the back of the building and yelled, "Is anybody here?" Again, nothing. He headed for the truck and shrugged.

"I don't know what to say, sweetie," he told me when he stepped inside. "Could they have closed before they opened?"

He wasn't joking. I called the assistant's cell phone and complained that I made this twenty-mile trip specifically to support this store, and it was closed during its advertised hours of operation.

"Oh," she said, "I guess he had to make a run. I'm sorry. Someone should be there any minute. Please don't give up on us, Mrs. Anderson."

"Baby, I have no choice," I said. "I depend on you. But y'all sure don't make it easy."

"Can you just wait a little bit?"

"For what? This is not how you run a business." I was getting a little steamed—and for good reason. This is the kind of operation that instills a spark of enthusiasm and then, when it can't deliver, so much cynicism in Black folks.

"Where is the sign?" I asked. "Is there any food in there? I mean, how do you expect anybody to . . . "

Karriem yanked the phone out of my hand.

"Hi, this is Karriem Beyah," he said in a calm but firm voice. "I'm a Black grocer too. There is no excuse for this. Please let your boss know that we will not be back until she gets her act together. Have a good day."

I took a deep breath, closed my eyes, and leaned back.

"Thanks, sweetie," I said. "I just can't take it anymore."

"But you can't yell at that lady," he said. "*You* took this on. *Your* pledge is not *her* problem."

"What are you talking about?" Our brother-sister squabbling had become a normal part of our relationship. "Hell yeah, she is the problem. Look at us, KB. We're sitting on the side of the expressway, in a dangerous neighborhood, banging on doors, and waiting on folks so we can support them. Are you kidding me? That's the problem."

He laughed. "No, Maggie," he said. "Your problem—*and* my problem—is that we thought this would be easy. We thought that things should work out because they make sense. All that win-win bullshit. That's *our* problem. And that's why we're sitting in this fucking truck."

We sat in silence. Then KB said, "Let's go see my guy, the farmer who gets to sell his stuff by Walgreens. We'll get you some produce. Don't worry about it."

Our visit to the farm stand was much more successful than our previous stop. I bought bags of grapes, bananas, potatoes, and apples. When I got home—in a much better mood now—I Googled "Black farmers markets" and "Black farm stands" and made the happy discovery that several outdoor produce markets operated in the city, mostly on the South Side, usually set up after a church service.

We found another one in Austin, at Madison and Central, about four miles from our house. That corner had a small outdoor play area, although it looked like someone had started building a park and then quit. Still, I thought taking the girls with me and giving my husband a little "John Time" would be great. He'd earned it.

We arrived at around noon on that Saturday in mid-September. The weather was somewhat brisk, so the girls were wearing sweatshirts and jeans—perfect play gear. They started cheering as soon as I pulled into the lot next to the jungle gym.

But Cori and Cara were still too young to play on these recreational structures alone, and I was nervous about the asphalt base. The setup seemed dangerous.

"Mommy, mommy," Cori said as I pulled her from the car seat, "I wan do slide!"

I thought, *How can they have a slide leading onto rough asphalt?* I added this to my mental list of "What Happens on the West Side Doesn't Happen in Oak Park."

Cara tapped my arm. "Me too," she chimed in.

"Sweetie pie, I don't know. There's no grass around here. If you fall, you are gonna hurt yourself."

That was not the answer she was hoping for. Cori started crying.

"Okay, okay, hush child," I said. "But Mommy has to stay close."

I surveyed the layout. The farm stand was too far away for me to shop and monitor them playing at the same time. Fortunately, the lot was pretty clean, and no one was just hanging around.

"So that means you are going to have to come with Mommy to get the fruits and vegetables first, then we can play a little bit. How's that, angel?"

After a few more minutes of whining, I knew I had to become Enforcer Mommy.

"We end this discussion right now," I told them. "I said you are going with me. That's it."

When we arrived at the farm stand—three six-foot-long tables loaded with about fifteen different crates of produce—five or six elderly customers milled about. Barrels of apples and strawberries had been placed next to the stand.

A plump teenager with large, warm eyes, who I later discovered was the niece of the older gentleman running the stand, smiled at us.

"Welcome to our urban farm," she said. "Please look around and tell me what you like."

She was tending to an adorable older couple who were dressed alike in jeans and sweatshirts from a family reunion. The woman was huge and huggable, like the mother from the movie *Soul Food*. Her mate was tall, thin, and very handsome in a Billy Dee Williams kind of way, and he had his arm around her shoulder. I was staring at them, thinking about John. I noticed her glasses were broken and his shoes were worn. Then I scanned the lot and realized my car was the only one in it, aside from a big truck that was parked next to the stand, which obviously belonged to the farm family. *Did they all walk here?* I thought. *I hope these people live close.*

"And look at what I have for you," I heard someone say.

The elderly farmer had stepped from behind the stand to greet us. He had two baby pumpkins in his hands for Cara and Cori.

"It's Black Santa Claus!" Cori exclaimed. She had softened up, but Cara was still in a funk. The old man, with his white beard and short Afro, bright red overalls, black lace-up boots, and long-sleeved white shirt, did look like the Black Santa Claus from a poster at their day care center.

I laughed and apologized.

"She knows better," I said. "Is this your stand?"

"Yes, ma'am," he said proudly, and then he noticed Cara's sad face. "What's wrong little cutie? You don't like pumpkins?"

"Oh, they're upset because I wouldn't let them play over there," I said. "It's too far for me to watch them. So I told them we gotta get the produce first. She'll be alright."

I hugged Cara. She took the pumpkin and smiled.

"Keisha, I need ya', honey," he called. The niece came close. "You take the babies to the park over there. Make sure you watch 'em now."

She stood in front of the girls and stuck her hands out. Cara and Cori gave me the "Is this okay?" look, and I nodded. Keisha put the pumpkins in her pockets, took the girls' hands, and they pulled her toward the playground. We all laughed.

I shopped and got to know the old farmer. He told me he lived near Kankakee, about sixty miles south of Chicago. Jeremiah Wright, our pastor at Trinity United Church of Christ, had spoken about the plight of these farmers, who had been working that area since the late 1800s, and how they were losing their land to consolidation by big, White-owned farms and the growth of Hispanic farms. In 1920 there were 820 Black farms in the state; now there were fewer than 50. Our church raised money for the Black farmers, signed petitions, and hosted their stand after services.

I told him all this, and he thanked me for our efforts.

"It's because we don't have reliable customers looking for us and helping us build a brand," he said. "The other groups got contracts with big grocery chains. Why they gon' do business with us, except as a token display of charity from time to time, when they can go to the White farmers they like and the Hispanic farmers?"

He went on as I held his hand and nodded.

"We need more Black business in the food industry. We can't keep fighting for White folks' scraps. Some of us can't survive on that. And then, they just don't want to do business with us. But Trinity and other churches are really helping us out."

We had not been to Trinity in a long while. We loved it, but it was far from where we lived. Once the babies came, getting there every Sunday became difficult. We kept saying we were going to start going back now that the girls were older, but we cherished our Sundays at home, especially during the time crunch that was The Empowerment Experiment's inaugural year. Still, I was proud to be able to tell this noble man that we were Trinitarians and that we created EE.

He was really excited, which got me pumped again. "Y'all have done so much to let people know that Black farmers is about to be extinct," he said. "It's so tough on us now. It was tough before, but at least there was enough of us that we could stand up for each other. Now we just trying to hang on. These weekend markets really help. And what you doing is really going to help us believe in the grocery stores again."

I kept turning around to check on the girls, who were just fine, laughing and playing. No other customers had approached, and he offered to help carry my bags to the car.

It was a bright, enriching EE day, and so was every other weekly Saturday visit there. That farm stand became our produce lifesaver, offering a great selection—beautiful squash, apples, bananas, strawberries, grapefruit, and fresh greens—at really low prices. Apart from that, it was fun. On any given visit the farmers would toss us a couple extra apples and joke around with the girls. But when November arrived the farmers told us they were moving on for the season. This set up an anxious final few weeks for EE.

Chapter 10

Our Problems, Your Solutions

BY EARLY FALL WE'D FINALLY BEEN ABLE TO TRANSFER some of our investment and retirement savings to a Black-owned financial firm, Ariel Investments LLC, where owner John Rogers Jr. is chairman, CEO, and chief investment officer. We encountered so many restrictions on accessing and moving these funds that making the switch took until October.

At the same time, generating ongoing attention for our cause was proving to be a challenge, at least with the mainstream media. We had received an enormous amount of press, but it did not lead to the groundswell of support or the corporate sponsorship we'd hoped for. Eleven months into the project the media inquiries were fading, in part because we'd decided to focus on the Black community via speaking engagements and events. Between running The Empowerment Experiment on a daily basis, managing our appearances and speeches, and trying to deal with our growing anxiety over Mima's condition, we were on overload.

Plus, as the harvest season ended, the farmers' markets disappeared, which meant once more we were having trouble finding decent, nutritious food at Black-owned stores. Facing our own version of a food desert, we resigned ourselves to completing this journey right where we'd started: J's Fresh Meats. It was dreadful, yes, but it was relatively close and we basically had no other choice.

One morning I hopped in the truck and headed for the West Side. About a half block away from the store I slowed down, scanning ahead for a parking place as close to the door as possible. The sidewalk and curb were clear. There were no unsavory characters or cars—just space. I pulled up right in front and then I saw why. J's was closed, and not just for the day.

I jabbed the button for the hazard lights and peered inside the store. No lights. No people. Nothing on the shelves but a few six-packs of what could have been applesauce, fruit cocktail, or pudding. Whatever they were, they were probably expired long before J's did. The dust-caked ATM looked right at home. I didn't see a "Closed" or "For Rent" sign. Why would I? No one cared that J's was gone, and no one was rushing to rent the space. Just to be sure, I called J's phone number and was greeted by the all-too-familiar EE refrain: "The number you have reached . . . " Another one of Austin's sorry, Black-owned grocery stores was gone.

Of course, I thought. *It's just so fitting that this place closed.* This is what our businesses had come to—a dilapidated, poorly run convenience mart that, inevitably, was doomed along with the battered, forgotten neighborhood around it. That deserted, forsaken store said it all.

And it's part of an ongoing trend. According to a 2007 article published in the *Journal of Labor Economics,* the probability of a Black-owned business closing is nearly 30 percent, compared to less than 23 percent for White-owned businesses. In addition, average sales for Black-owned businesses are often only 25 percent of the average sales for White-owned businesses.

Here are a few other unsettling findings reported in that article:

—Only 13.9 percent of Black-owned firms had annual profits of $10,000 or more, compared to 30.4 percent for White-owned firms.

—Nearly 40 percent of all Black-owned firms operated in the red.

—White-owned firms hired nearly three times as many employees as Black-owned firms, and median sales for Black firms were one-half that of White firms.

The reasons for that dismal scenario, according to Robert Fairlie and Alicia Robb, authors of the study, are the lower education rates among African Americans compared to Whites, the scarcity of resources—meaning money—in Black homes, and the much lower rate, compared to Whites, of Black business owners who had worked for a family member's business before starting their own.

The authors also cite US Census Bureau figures from 2005 showing a household net worth gap. According to these data "the median level of net worth for black households is $6,166 as compared to $67,000 for white households." As staggering as it may sound, more recent figures indicate the gap is widening. In 2009 median net worth for Black households was $2,200. For White households, that figure was nearly $98,000.

These statistics bring to mind another fraction: our status as three-fifths of a man during and right after the era of slavery. Almost 150 years later our wealth remains ridiculously low compared to our former owners. We were worth more as slaves.

Figures like these not only demonstrate why we can't start businesses, but they also show why we so badly need our businesses to succeed: so that we can economically empower the community with better jobs and higher salaries.

But research highlights the sorry conditions for Black start-ups. Consider that the survival rate for non-minority-owned businesses was nearly 73 percent from 1997 to 2001, compared to 61 percent for Black-owned companies. Business expansion rates for Black-owned businesses during that period also were disheartening. About 26 percent of Black-owned businesses expanded from 1997 to 2001, the lowest expansion rate of all ethnic groups. The highest was Hispanic, at 34 percent, followed by 32 percent of Asian- and Pacific-Island-owned businesses and 27.4 percent of non-minority-owned businesses. Key factors for Black-owned businesses continue to be less access to capital and less management and technical training.

Further, Black-owned firms trail well behind White-owned firms in that important category of start-up capital. In general, businesses perceived as having a greater potential to succeed can generate more of those essential funds. According to the article in the *Journal of Labor Economics,* just "8.1 percent of Black-owned businesses required at least $25,000 in start-up capital as compared to 15.7 percent of white-owned businesses." Don't let the word "required" throw you; the salient fact is that far fewer Black-owned start-ups were viewed as potentially successful compared to their White-owned counterparts and thus fewer Black entrepreneurs received crucial start-up capital, even though they still needed it. These differences, Fairlie and Robb write, "explain a substantial portion of the black-white gaps" in the success and failure of small business ventures. "Clearly lower levels of start-up capital among black-owned firms are associated with less successful businesses."

Experts note the absence of role models within Black families and posit that the lack of family business experience may contribute substantially to the sorry number of Black-owned businesses. Research shows that 12.6 percent of Black business owners had worked for a family member's business, whereas the rate for White business owners was 23.3 percent. Experts call this "restricting [the black business owners'] acquisition of general and specific business human capital." In other words, as Black people living on the West Sides or South Sides of America can tell you, we view each other as workers, not owners. Only Whites, Asians, Indians, or those from the Middle East are perceived as business owners capable of powering a family enterprise. It's so damn discouraging.

When I speak around the country, I don't need to cite these statistics or detail what the experts have discovered because people in the Black community witness these phenomena every day. There is nothing revelatory about the fact that most young Black kids do not have family members or neighbors in business—aside from the in-home day care proprietor, barber shop, or braid salon owner.

I'm grateful that some government, philanthropic, and academic institutions have explored the reasons behind Black business failure and have responded with lending assistance and training programs. But we need to pay more attention to the cyclical, interrelated, and interdependent nature of the problems the Black community faces. Difficulty obtaining capital, lacking family business experience, and lower educational attainment aren't only causes; they are also *effects* of centuries of racism, exploitation, and sabotage.

That's one dark place we hoped EE would illuminate. Sure, we want more consumer support of Black businesses, but we also want to spark real conversation about the reasons behind the reasons, and we want to do something concrete about those core issues, not tinker at the periphery.

Not that any of this information would save J's Fresh Meats, obviously, but it did suggest that the place was probably doomed from the start. What the data did not explain was why Farmers Best suffered the same fate. If anyone could defy the statistics, it would be Karriem. For a while after his store closed, I thought that Black business owners had no way to succeed unless they were rap stars, super athletes, corporate sensations, one of their offspring, or just plain lucky. John saw things differently. He felt that KB was proof-positive of our original point—that many quality businesses exist and are critical to rescuing our community, but they are dying solely due to a lack of support.

Either way, I still needed groceries.

In my files I found a default grocer of sorts, Community Mart, another Black-owned store a little over a mile from J's Fresh Meats. Our friend Terry Dean, a reporter from the *Austin Weekly* who wrote about EE early in the year, had been sending us articles about local Black businesses. One of those featured the headline, "Corner Store Teaches Youth about Business: Minister Operates Grocery with a Sense of Mission." That was Community Mart. From the picture in the article I could tell the store was pretty small. In fact, it was really nothing more than a convenience store like J's, which meant that it, too, probably resembled something out of a postapocalyptic minimart.

Community Mart was in Austin, the same distressed neighborhood as J's, but the church next door, New Philadelphia Christian Ministries, owned it, and they also operated a soup kitchen and homeless shelter. To the hardworking people of the West Side, New Philadelphia's pastor, Bobby Butts, was a true hero. He took in drug addicts, at-risk youth, and felons, and he helped them change their lives for the better. I really wanted to believe in the place and would have spent more time at Community Mart just to support Pastor Butts. But too many raggedy, unsteady-looking men always hung around the store and the area in general. John was so concerned that he wanted to inspect it before I went there by myself. After stopping at Community Mart on his way to an appointment downtown and checking out the men hanging around the store, John declared it a danger zone.

"Baby, if they were sitting on a bench reading a paper, or even waiting on a hot and a cot, that might be different," he said. "But man oh man, when I got out of the car, they were sizing *me* up."

I went anyway because I had no choice. One afternoon in the late fall I drove there to buy a few basics, but the milk cooler was empty. The cashier, a hulking teenager, said the delivery guy had missed last week's drop but was supposed to come today, except that he hadn't. We got to talking—him, mostly—and the kid told me about his life. He had been an abused foster child turned gangster until the pastor gave him a second chance. The story wasn't the only thing that stole my heart; he was so anxious to tell me about it. So when he said the milkman would probably be there in the next few hours and that I should drop by later that afternoon, I gave him my cell phone number and asked him to call me either way. Then I reached in my purse for a credit card to buy the couple of things in my basket.

"Cash or Link," the cashier mumbled. "Cash or Link."

I sighed and reached into my wallet for a few dollars.

About four hours later I drove back to Community Mart. At this time of year it gets dark pretty early, and I questioned my decision to go trekking back as the sun set just for a jug of milk. I knew John wouldn't be happy about it either. But I wanted to support an honorable venture and a fragile kid, and we needed milk.

I walked in and found no milk. My shoulders slumped. I sighed as I stared at that refrigerator case and thought about Pastor Butts, the church, the men outside, Karriem, John, the girls, and driving home without milk, past all those clean, well-stocked stores. I cursed under my breath. I was about to walk over to the cashier to scold him for not call-ing me, but he was a long-winded kid and I just didn't have the energy for an extended encounter. I was done.

Then I remembered I had a Citgo gift card with some money left on it and that there was a Citgo station with a small convenience store a couple blocks away. I drove over there.

By this time it was dark, casting a fairly frightening aura over the place. I could taste the gas fumes. Like so many of these stations, unset-tling characters were drifting in and out of the store and through the half-lit parking lot. The second I stepped from the car, some shabby, eld-erly guy hobbled over and started hassling me. He was shorter than me, missing teeth, and had an extreme, almost exaggerated limp. I could de-tect a fairly strong odor of what I thought was vomit. I felt sorry for him, thinking maybe he was a lost vet. But at that point, even if he was one of the Tuskegee Airmen, I didn't want to talk to him. I just wasn't in the mood. *Please, oh Lord,* I thought, *please don't let him bother me.*

"Fittee fuh twunee," he sputtered. "Fittee fuh twunee."

I looked at him like he was speaking Mandarin. For a few seconds I couldn't figure out what the hell he was saying. Then it dawned on me.

Fifty for twenty. Fifty for twenty.

More victim than predator, the poor hustler was selling food stamps—$50 worth of food stamps for $20 cash—so he could buy liquor, which you cannot do with food stamps.

Dudes like him—and women too—roam the parking lots of retail food establishments in devastated urban landscapes across America. They find someone who looks like he or she doesn't rely on food stamps and then they make that someone a profitable proposition. Lots of people take up the offer, which only expedites the drunk/junkie/thief's down-ward spiral and helps entrench neighborhood rot. It makes me crazy.

I just stared at him. And then I let loose. That he was old, tiny, and harmless must have had something to do with my sudden burst of courage, that and the fact that I was beyond pissed.

"Do you think I'm going to give you *my* money so that you can go out and get drunk?" I yelled. "How stupid do I look?"

I pointed at the food stamps in his hands. "Why don't you quit hassling people and use those things for what you're supposed to use them for? Just for tonight, for a change," I said. "Get yourself some food and take a break from the drinking. Just for one night. Okay, sir? Make an effort. Just this once."

He didn't say anything, just looked at me with yellow, bloodshot eyes, and I knew he was gone, lost a long time ago, and I felt bad. But the ire wouldn't pass.

"Unbelievable." I just about spit the words at him. "Get out of my way."

I stomped past him and headed for the lights of the store. Feeling the anger begin to dissipate, I started babbling to myself about the miserable history and the dreadful current conditions that put this guy in this predicament: the racism, the poverty, the lack of jobs, the hopelessness. And I started to feel ashamed of myself for yelling at him.

Inside, the mart was filthy, impersonal, like some store you'd see in a war zone, which I guess wasn't all that far from the truth. The cashier was walled off by what looked to be six-inch-thick bulletproof glass. He spoke to customers through a speaker linked to a mike on his side of the barrier. The only thing close to actual contact could occur through a slot at the bottom of the glass where money exchanged hands.

I sighed, shook my head again, and went looking for milk and any other reasonably edible food. I did locate milk and Pop-Tarts and knew the girls would be excited about the real cheese I found. Near the line at the cashier, some large, menacing guy was speaking in a loud, deliberate tone, talking smack about "the A-rabs." Of course, the cashier, who was probably the owner or a relative, looked Middle Eastern.

"I don't want to be givin' my money to these people," Angry Brutha said. It was obvious why he was upset. Like a lot of Black folks in these areas, he was disgusted with how his neighborhood looked and how everyone in it was poor and suffering. Seeing these thriving business owners making money from him and his community, coupled with the certainty that they did not employ locals, live, or otherwise reinvest here, fueled an ugly anger. "For all I know, they're turnin' right around and givin' it to Osama. Shit."

As I stood in line and tried to tune out his tirade, all I could think was, *What are you doing to change that, asshole?* Angry Brutha was still going on about "motherfuckin' terrorists" when I reached the front of the line. I used my gas card, and the cashier slipped me some plastic bags through the slot at the bottom of the glass.

Angry Brutha abruptly stopped his rant and came over. He started helping me bag my groceries. I just looked at him and thought, *So much is wrong here.* His small gesture of kindness, helpful as it was, seemed to serve as more evidence of my growing belief that the situation is intractable. Here is this angry, hate-filled man who has stopped to help me. Despite his animosity, he clearly has a basic desire to lend a hand. I'm sure he has a sense of community spirit too, somewhere deep within him, and yet he is so frustrated. He's expending so much energy on the bitterness that he is incapable of focusing on the bigger issues.

Or maybe he isn't. Maybe he understands but he's overwhelmed. As much as his behavior infuriated me, I got it. In fact, he and I might not be all that different after all.

I trudged back to my car, dropped the groceries in the backseat, and drove home, all the while thinking that what we're doing isn't going to make a difference. The Community Mart will probably be closed in a month, and why am I helping that place, anyway? I don't want it to grow. The lost brothers and sisters who wander in and out of that place, other shops like it, and the miserable Citgo will always be there. Everything is so messed up and has been for so long. Once home, I walked in the door and collapsed in John's arms, sobbing.

———◇———

That time of year, maybe more than at any other point in our odyssey, was full of contradictions. One moment I'd be foraging for food in a frozen, gray urban landscape. The next moment I'd be attending or planning an event at a swanky establishment. Our latest was another wine tasting and fund-raiser, envisioned as an EE victory party, to be held in December in Bronzeville, the South Side neighborhood known in the early twentieth century as the Black Metropolis. The neighborhood became a haven for thousands of African Americans fleeing the hostilities of the South. Over the decades it developed into a vibrant community, home to some of the most famous African Americans, including Joe Louis, Richard Wright, Gwendolyn Brooks, Ida B. Wells, and Andrew "Rube" Foster, founder of the Negro National Baseball League. At that time, apart from those folks, Bronzeville supported several Black newspapers, 731 businesses—including several Black banks and seven insurance companies—106 lawyers, 192 churches, and one of the top Black hospitals in the country. By 1929 Bronzeville Blacks had accumulated real estate holdings totaling $100 million.

After World War II, however, Bronzeville started slipping, in part because of less restrictive housing elsewhere in the Chicago area, and the community became one of those rough, somewhat deserted sections of town. Things started picking up again in the mid-1990s, when folks began to appreciate its undervalued real estate, battered but beautiful houses, and its proximity to downtown, McCormick Place, the University of Chicago, US Cellular Field, and the beaches along Lake Michigan. That residents had easy access to a pair of major expressways didn't hurt either. All of that blended together to make Bronzeville a textbook example of gentrification, one of the thornier issues for Black America.

In Chicago much of the gentrification of the 1990s first occurred in neighborhoods like Bronzeville, places close to the Loop that were low-income and predominantly Black. That revitalization sparked a huge jump in home prices. According to Derek S. Hyra, an associate professor at Virginia Tech University who studies gentrification in Chicago, "Between 1990 and 2000, real estate prices in Douglas and Grand Boulevard, the two contiguous districts that make up Bronzeville, rose 67 and 192 percent, respectively."

The population of Bronzeville, while still 92 percent Black, has become increasingly White. In 1990 census figures showed that a total of 2.5 percent of the community's population of 66,549 was White; by 2000, when Bronzeville's population actually shrank to 54,476, the White population grew to 4 percent. Some research suggests the White population is now closer to 6.6 percent.

Though we're all for diversity, the mix doesn't necessarily mean that Whites are being inclusive and welcoming Blacks to their neighborhoods. Rather, what seems to be happening is that Whites are coming to an all-Black neighborhood on its way "up" because of the amenities it offers.

The problem, according to Professor Hyra, is that "we typically see whites moving in and taking over all the public spaces and putting [in] their own cultural values, and making the community their own, as opposed to integrating the values of individuals who have lived in these communities." Professor Hyra and other experts have noted that retail growth in urban areas is occurring where the White population is rising. The research says that those merchants are following the money. I say that they are following White money.

And it's not only middle- and upper-class Whites who are elbowing out lower-income Blacks; it's also middle- and upper-class Blacks too. In fact, researchers suggest that middle-class Blacks are playing a larger role than Whites in driving out lower-income Blacks from once-impoverished neighborhoods like Bronzeville. Members of the Black middle class have had their options limited due to discrimination from banks and realtors, what scholar Sheryll Cashin calls "integration exhaustion." As a consequence, those Blacks are moving to poorer, predominantly African American neighborhoods and exerting their influence.

When wealthier newcomers push for economic growth so that property values will rise and more upscale businesses and restaurants will be lured to the area, it's often done with complete disregard for the original residents. Large financial institutions, government agencies, and land developers also influence the changes that occur in a neighborhood. According to Professor Hyra, "it is undisputable that the black middle class and their preferences for 'community improvement' are associated with rising property values and the displacement of the poor."

The efforts to drive out poor Blacks along with the threats they supposedly represent to property values are becoming less and less covert. Hyra affirms that upwardly mobile Blacks cooperate with various entities in gentrifying neighborhoods to exclude the most impoverished Blacks, so that those who have enjoyed "individual success and achievement" have pushed the neediest to other high-poverty neighborhoods.

The situation obviously generates a fair amount of hostility between longtime residents and the recently arrived middle-class Blacks and Black professionals, but some neighborhoods are working to minimize the tensions. In Bronzeville, for example, several African American community groups started collaborating in 1990 with the city government and private entities to encourage economic development while retaining longtime residents. Together they devised a plan, "Restoring Bronzeville," which emphasized "historic preservation and racial heritage tourism." The tours of "historic Bronzeville" featured signs and monuments paying tribute to local entertainment, business, and political heroes as well as pointed out sites of civil rights and music history interest. The plan also called for mixed-income housing and pushed for owner-occupied units.

Longtime residents and recent transplants liked the idea of economic development because they agreed that Bronzeville was dying economically and had been for some time. Instead, their goal was to attract members of the Black middle class, which is why their campaign emphasized, in part, racial heritage tourism.

The logic, as I see it, was to honor Bronzeville and to restore some cultural identity, which would prevent outsiders from taking over and converting the neighborhood into just another pretentious, overpriced, pseudosuburban enclave. The strategy did foster a sense of ownership in Bronzeville that only the people who were from there could feel, while indicating to the gentrifiers that the pride of Bronzeville was not for sale.

To ease low-income residents' concern of being displaced just when the neighborhood was becoming a safe, desirable place to live, supporters of that middle-class influx promoted the belief that middle-class folks needed to embrace "group advancement" as part of their civic responsibility—a version of the "rising tide lifts all boats" aphorism.

According to Michelle Boyd, an associate professor of African American studies and political science at University of Illinois–Chicago, there is an assumption "that whatever class differences do exist among blacks are easily overshadowed by similarities. Blacks were united by the common threat of whites. . . . [But] the problem lies in how reference to these commonalities can be used to sidestep the issue of competing interests" between middle-class and low-income Blacks. Poor families in Bronzeville and other low-income neighborhoods want affordable housing, jobs that pay a living wage, and child care that suits their schedules in those jobs. Owners of higher-priced housing "want to increase the price of housing as well as the quality and cost of neighborhood goods and services," Boyd notes.

The two often conflict. Guess who loses?

"One reason poorer residents do not present sustained opposition," Boyd writes, "is that they are filtered out of the community development process." Not only were their needs less likely to be discussed, but they experienced a great deal of friction with more affluent residents during the planning process. This "homogenizing" is a classic political technique used not only with gentrification but also in any process in which lower-class Black buy-in is needed to achieve the goals of others, including middle- and upper-class Blacks. Politicians, both Black and White, use it to get votes. Likewise, gentrifiers, both Black and White, use it—the "we're all in this together" line or the "we are doing this to create jobs and improve schools" cant—to get approval for the profit-driven upheaval in their neighborhoods.

The Black middle-class alliances with outsiders complicate the dynamics of gentrification. Often White-owned development firms, financial institutions, and political power brokers convert middle-class Blacks into what sociologist Mary Pattillo calls "brokers." Perhaps a better term would be sellouts. They bridge the gap between powerful Whites and neighborhoods looking to catch a break.

As Pattillo explains, "disputes between black residents with professional jobs and those with no jobs, between black families who have been in the neighborhood for generations and those who moved in last year, and between blacks who don fraternity colors and those who sport gang colors, are simultaneously debates over what it means to be black."

This is exactly what is so disturbing about gentrification: its tendency to divide Blacks along economic lines. Wealthier Blacks need to be concerned about the displacement and exploitation issues that affect poor Black people in neighborhoods with rising property values. It is our duty as members of the Talented Tenth. Our ascendance was supposed to facilitate new systems and ideas, like gentrification, that would lead to our collective advancement. Instead of ensuring a higher quality of life for all of us, those developments created an environment that breeds the perpetual Black ghetto.

See what I mean about how complicated this can get? You have these honorable folks like Joslyn Slaughter of Jordan's Closets and Tracye Dee of WineStyles scratching out an existence as they present wonderful role models and clearly help their neighborhoods. Yet conditions being what they are, the people most in need seem to have been abandoned.

These two women had slightly different experiences with gentrification. By the time Tracye had moved to the South Loop, it had already been gentrified, and she was grateful, as a businesswoman, for the neighborhood's new cachet that, in her opinion, helped with community building. Joslyn, however, had located her boutique on the outskirts of Bronzeville because that was pretty much all she could afford. She witnessed former residents of the 'burbs rehabbing and inhabiting the buildings.

"They would go to work and go home and that was pretty much it," she recalled. "They still didn't feel safe shopping in the neighborhood. Their disposable income was not being spent here." Part of the reason, Joslyn said, was that higher-end stores in Bronzeville were somewhat scarce.

Then the recession hit, and rehabbing slowed before stopping altogether. Now, in Bronzeville at least, gentrification is mostly theoretical.

"I had mixed emotions [about gentrification]," Joslyn said. "Bronzeville had been a beautiful area and . . . I'd love to see it return to that," but she worried about a nicer neighborhood forcing out residents who'd lived there for decades. Still, she thought gentrification would improve the area.

"Things need to change and evolve," Joslyn said. "As African Americans, we need to learn that we deserve to live in a different environment."

And then there is my buddy, Mell Monroe, who has lived in Bronzeville since 2002. With nearly three decades of corporate, entrepreneurial, and community-organizing experience, Mell moved to Chicago in 1992 and then to the South Loop. In 2002, nudged by his wife, Angela, they moved to a historic, seven-thousand-square-foot, red-brick Romanesque Queen Anne in Bronzeville. He fell in love with the history, beautiful homes, and prime location of the neighborhood. Mell founded and became president of the Bronzeville Area Residents and Commerce Council and created the Annual Historic Bronzeville Bike Tour. In 2006 he ran for city council. We met him in the middle of 2009, when he'd heard about us and asked, through a mutual friend, if we would have brunch at his home, which he was converting to a B & B. We enthusiastically accepted. He liked what we were preaching and, a few months later, agreed to host the December wine tasting at his elegantly restored home.

The buzz happening in Bronzeville excited Mell—and us too. It was hard not to be excited. He also bristles at the word gentrification, but for slightly different reasons than we do.

"I don't know how to respond to that word when I hear it," he told me. "It actually puts middle-income people on the defensive. I think a better way to put it," he said, "is that middle-income people want neighbors to behave in a manner that doesn't interfere with the public or social order, just like in any neighborhood. We would like to have nice amenities like everybody else."

Low-income residents concerned about middle- and upper-income folks' supposed plans to push out the less fortunate should stop worrying, Mell said. In Bronzeville the objective—as in virtually every neighborhood that may be experiencing the G-word—is safe, clean streets with decent services and businesses that provide jobs. Forget about all the class warfare, he said. If everyone pulls together to tout Bronzeville's rich history, location, and housing stock—and everybody behaves—everybody wins.

Here's the real rub for us: By patronizing businesses in Bronzeville and the South Loop, we were part of the problem.

Yes, those businesses needed our support and we loved them. The more their businesses grew, the greater the chance that other Black businesses could find success too, and probably, the more the neighborhood would improve, which would create the wonderful ripple effect John and I like to talk about.

But like I've said, we were hoping The Empowerment Experiment would reach those most in need of help. Supporting Black-owned businesses in gentrifying places like Hyde Park and Bronzeville funnels dollars to those businesses that, in effect, would expedite the displacement of the most vulnerable folks. By no means were the African American entrepreneurs of the South Side's Bronzeville any less or more courageous and committed to the community than those on the West Side's Austin, Lawndale, or Garfield Park, and neither one was more deserving of our support than the other. But for every leg up the owners in gentrifying areas received, in effect, the West Side lost something. Blacks from the South Side and West Side have a long-standing disregard for one another that boils down to class distinction. But both were once at least united in the struggle—win or lose. Gentrification was eroding that, and fast.

I wanted to shop on the West Side but just couldn't. At the moment our objective to reach brothers and sisters who most needed a hand was looking increasingly improbable, which brings me back to a variation of the question I posed earlier: Where does gentrification leave places like the West Side? Who is going to rescue the children there?

Gentrification is not designed to preserve a neighborhood's racial and socioeconomic demographics, which is why I'm highly suspicious of it. Virtually everything I've read indicates that it works to drive out the economically distressed, not empower them, so that they won't impede the economic development that'll elevate property values. It's a calculated, even heartless scheme. At worst, it is a modernized form of racist economic exploitation.

I can no more be a proponent of gentrification than I can be for giving tax cuts to the richest 1 percent as a way to build small businesses, infuse more money into the economy, and counter unemployment. Gentrification resembles the false promise of trickle-down economics: It just doesn't work. The wealthy folks, politicians, and groups that back these tax cuts are adamant, as if our very liberty and democracy were at stake. But when it comes to the trickling part, folks seem to just sort of wait and hope, and the trickle turns out to be more like a single drop. I'm all for waiting and hoping as long as we eventually ride the river of prosperity.

One of my biggest fears is that in promoting gentrification as a means to rescue underserved Black areas, its shortcomings would become acceptable. We'd expend all this energy and celebrate the benefits of the "urban pioneers"—the arrival of locally owned businesses, stable home ownership, a general cleaning up of the neighborhoods—but somehow ignore the needs of the residents who were there to begin with. That's unacceptable in my book.

I don't want to minimize the impact gentrification can have on the residents of these areas, but I can't get on board because it does not respect the people living there nor does it acknowledge the potential of these communities. These locales aren't being valued for what they are but only as a "blank canvas" on which the developers, businesses, and corporations can build.

However, if gentrification can be used to *improve* the welfare of those who would be displaced, then I think it can help achieve glorious things. If more Black people—young professionals, grad students, and even older, middle-class Blacks—take charge of the gentrification process with that overall goal in mind, this would fit The Empowerment Experiment's ideals and the essence of Du Bois's Talented Tenth doctrine. This is possible, but it will take a lot of sophisticated thinking, hard work, and, maybe most difficult of all, trust. If gentrification can't accomplish economic development in distressed areas via empowering "indigenous" residents and businesses—especially the least powerful—then it contradicts what we stand for.

In thinking through these issues I've found it useful to keep in mind the words of Sudhir Alladi Venkatesh, a professor of sociology and

African American studies at Columbia University. In a 2007 piece for the *Boston Globe,* he wrote, "What is the responsible position of the black middle class? . . . The question goes back at least to the 1890s, when W. E. B. Du Bois wrote his seminal study of urban development, 'The Philadelphia Negro.' Du Bois wrote that the indigenous and more cosmopolitan Black middle class will forever oppose the newly arriving Southern migrant, unless the two recognize their conflicts only serve to strengthen the whites in power."

Chapter 11

A Rewired Family

ALMOST EXACTLY 177 YEARS AFTER MARIA STEWART GAVE her landmark but largely forgotten speech in Boston, I stood, possibly just as pissed off, in front of 350 members of Northwestern University's Kellogg School of Management Black Alumni Club, of which John is an active member. As guest speaker at a November evening reception thrown in our honor and dubbed "An Evening with the Andersons," I was trying to convey all the frustration and fatigue we'd experienced during the past months so the audience could understand my pain and anger. In a sense, that indignation, mostly due to Karriem's store closing and the herculean task of simply trying to find food, was pushing us toward the finish line.

The Empowerment Experiment had gained a certain amount of clout—or maybe it was notoriety—mainly on the Black speakers' circuit. In mid-September I was the opening speaker at the Illinois Black Chamber of Commerce Annual Conference in Chicago. A week later I was in Washington, DC, addressing the Congressional Black Caucus Annual Conference, where, predictably, I got a "you go, girl" and little else from Illinois US senator Roland Burris.

A couple of weeks after that I lectured at Georgia State University. It was my first speech to a crowd that was mostly White, and I was a little nervous about how I'd be received, but it went well. In fact, a faculty member said that the "students have been fundamentally transformed by their brief exposure to her project. She definitely made an impact."

A few days later the United American Progress Association honored John and I with their Man and Woman of the Year award at their annual awards banquet, which turned out to be even more uplifting than it sounds, mostly because of one brief comment from a ninety-two-year-old man, Dr. Webb Evans, UAPA founder, who had marched with Rev. King. During my acceptance speech to five hundred community activists, I saw him weeping. Later he uttered the one sentence that seemed to make all the hassle, heartache, and anger of the year dissolve: "Maggie," Dr. Evans said, "you are his [King's] dream come true."

November was bananas. I was giving speeches every week. Jim Clingman, who was featured in the March *Chicago Tribune* article about us, arranged my first visit to Ohio. I spoke at the University of Cincinnati, hosted by its chapter of the Kappa Alpha Psi fraternity, and to the Cincinnati/Greater Kentucky African American Chamber of Commerce.

Then came the Kellogg event, followed by my speech at the University of Chicago's African American MBA Association's annual conference. Close to Thanksgiving, I gave a big speech in Beaumont, Texas, at the annual "We Are One Power" Conference, presented by one of the most successful Black businesses in America, Compro Tax, our version of H & R Block. Two weeks after that we helped coordinate the Philadelphia Chapter of the National Alliance of Market Developers' annual three-day buy-Black holiday shopping event, where I was the keynote speaker. Norm Bond, one of our advisers, was the NAMD national president.

In mid-December I was on two of the most famous Black radio shows, *The Steve Harvey Morning Show* and *The Eagle with Joe Madison*, talking about buying Black for the holiday season, and we did the wine-tasting event at Mell Monroe's in Bronzeville. We stuffed hundreds of Chicago's Black business elite into his elegant home and the tent outside. Guests made reservations to stay at Mell's new B & B, Welcome Inn Manor, when it opened in February, and they bought Selena Cuffe's Heritage Link Brands wines. It was all very energizing.

At all these events I gave some variation of my basic speech, in which I discussed how this experiment had transformed a sweet soccer mom into a somewhat bitter warrior on a rampage. Sure, I wanted to inspire people to give back, but I also wanted folks to know that they were the problem. I told them that our generation had gotten lazy, accepting as status quo an unacceptable situation. How can we can have a Black man in the White House, but I can't shop at a full-service Black-owned grocery store? After exhorting the audience to take action, I concluded my talk with the following words: "Just care about justice. Just yearn to be part of something. Just know and believe we have all the talent, smarts, and resources we need to put our community back on track and pass on a greater story and legacy to future generations. Just realize that our kids won't do better unless they actually see better."

As I spoke I sometimes felt as if I was conjuring the ghosts of African American economic empowerment, from Maria Stewart and Marcus Garvey to Rosa Parks and Dr. King. I guess the ghosts were working their magic during my talks—especially at the end of the year—because I'd receive thunderous applause and move folks to tears. Then came the standing ovations, after which I'd be mobbed and would receive two or three more invitations to speak.

Back on the ground, in the real world, we were running low on produce. Like I said, by this time the Black farmers markets were gone. Our only option for buying produce in the entire Chicago region was Woods Grocery, on the near South Side close to Bronzeville, in a basket near a washing machine. That's right, a washing machine. Sometimes that basket had apples, bananas, or oranges in it, and sometimes it didn't.

We were stuck. We really didn't know what to do.

That's how, one freezing, late November morning, I found myself in the parking lot of Fair Share Super Market, a Hispanic-owned grocery store a few blocks from our house. We could have gone to a Jewel, the popular Chicago-area chain, I guess, or anywhere else with produce. But Fair Share was smaller, more of a fresh mart than a full-fledged grocery store. We were restricting ourselves to buying non-Black only for what we absolutely couldn't find—produce—and Fair Share was the closest thing to a farm stand in our area.

How insane is it that we couldn't find a Black-owned store in all of Chicagoland with a consistent supply of fruits and vegetables? In some ways I still can't believe it. I felt terrible about shopping at a non-Black-owned store like Fair Share, but we just couldn't go the final weeks without produce, especially with young kids. Dressing my daughters in weird, ill-fitting outfits was one thing; risking their health was altogether different.

John helped me through it. He said this was no different from paying the ComEd utility bill or buying a ticket on American Airlines. We had no choice.

"You know, Mag," he told me one night while I was agitating about what to do, "this is not just about taking a stand. You've got to get away from that mind-set. This is an exercise too, an experiment, like we've been saying all along."

The project, he reminded me, was supposed to bring forth greater understanding. That's why we were keeping notes on the experiences, whatever they might be.

"If we can't find produce in the Black community, we can't find it," John said. "So we'll document it. It doesn't mean you have to go without everything. This is also about a study and our study revealed this: After exhausting all of our options for produce, we had to buy it at mainstream stores. It's that simple."

He brushed his palms together. Then he looked at me hard and held my shoulders.

"Look at me," he said. "Maggie, it doesn't mean you're a sellout, okay? It doesn't mean you're a hypocrite. We've been at this for eleven months. That hardly suggests you're weak. It means we can't get produce from Black-owned stores in Chicago. That's a very important piece of data, but that's all it is."

Lord, I'm glad I married that man.

Still, sitting in the car in that parking lot was tough—after everything we'd done to stay true to this cause, to live our commitment. What propelled me out of the seat was the vision of coming home empty-handed. I knew that John and the girls were waiting for some fresh fruits and vegetables. I'd promised them, and I couldn't bear the disappointment—even anger—that I'd face.

When I stepped into the store, it was like walking into a fruit and vegetable Mecca, a Broadway musical of earthly delights. Aisles and aisles—or was it miles and miles?—of fresh, colorful, bountiful lettuce; green, red, orange, and yellow peppers; onions, carrots, tomatoes, asparagus, strawberries, plumbs, mangoes, oranges, apples, bananas. I felt overwhelmed.

Of course I went crazy. I Probably spent $80 to $100 on produce. The experience was intoxicating. And when I got home, the girls were jumping up and down at the sight of plums and oranges and mangoes and all that good stuff. That response helped a lot. I was hero-mom. For once in a long time I didn't have to deny my family something. It felt wonderful. But for the rest of the year, whenever we went to a mainstream grocery store, we never—ever—bought anything other than produce, much as the girls wanted Goldfish crackers or Oreos, and John would have loved a piece of salmon.

Fair Share was a tough place to be in other ways, apart from feeling a little sting of betrayal and the temptation to buy whole-grain cereal or chicken breasts. The place made me angry. That feeling had nothing to do with the fact that it was Mexican-owned—and everything to do with it.

Statistics show that although Hispanics fare only slightly better than Blacks in terms of social and economic progress, they still possess enough resourcefulness to open many grocery stores. Hard numbers are tough to find, but Fyple, an online business directory of more than one million companies, lists 309 "Mexican Grocery Stores" in the United States, six of which are in Chicago. In Colorado, one of several states experiencing dynamic Hispanic business growth, eleven large, Hispanic-themed grocery stores opened between 2003 and 2010. Dozens more are open for business in the southwestern United States and other areas of the country with large numbers of Hispanics. Maybe not all those are Hispanic-owned, but I'd wager that the vast majority are.

Though the main clientele at Fair Share was Hispanic, people of all colors shopped there. Every employee was Hispanic, and the store boasted a wide array of Hispanic-themed products from Hispanic producers and distributors, stuff you wouldn't find in a White-owned mart. With all those Hispanic customers, Fair Share was able to give valuable shelf space to products that wouldn't be given that amount of space in a mainstream store. That shelf space strengthened those Hispanic businesses so they could hire more Hispanics and expand their reach—a beautiful example of self-help economics. Every time I went in, the place was buzzing. Seeing this was inspirational and joyous, yet it filled me with sadness—and envy.

I kept asking myself, *Why can't we have something like this—a nice Black-owned grocery store right here in Oak Park?* Given what I've learned about the relative success of other ethnic groups in this country, the family who owned Fair Share likely only arrived in this country a few years earlier and, with the help of a relative or friend, started their business. African Americans have been here four hundred years, and we still don't have anything like this to show for it. These immigrants, not so different from my parents, seem able to set up shop soon after they land here and become successful. We can't even make it work much longer than a year, as in Karriem's case.

Fair Share is just a grocery store. But in the context of The Empowerment Experiment, it is a tangible representation of everything we're fighting for and of our failures as a people. In twenty-first-century America, don't you think the Black community should also have at least a few successful grocery stores?

About the same time as our Black-supplied produce was running out, Mima's pain and nausea increased dramatically and her weight dropped quickly. After many inconclusive tests, doctors finally determined that the cancer was back and had spread throughout her body, so much so that in bone scans it was impossible to distinguish cancer cells from healthy ones. This time, doctors told us, she had weeks, maybe a couple of months, to live. One thing was sure: She was still fighting.

On our Facebook page I dedicated my Christmas message to her. I wrote about how we almost lost Mima last Thanksgiving but that she was not giving up. If she could wage her fight, we—all of us who wanted to help lift up our community—could use her example as inspiration.

While doing your holiday shopping on Black Friday, I urged our readers, just buy one item on your Christmas list from a Black-owned business. Don't run to the mall like everyone else. I even gave tips on how to do something for the community—like buying books from Black-owned bookstores written by Black authors; gift certificates for Black-owned restaurants, beauty salons, and spas; gift cards from Black-owned franchises like McDonald's or Burger King—and I also listed a bunch of websites with decent Black-owned business directories. A lot of this information can be found in the appendix of this book.

I received dozens of notes from supporters who said how touched they were and that they did support Black businesses on Black Friday. This was one of my favorites:

Nov. 26

God Bless You Maggie! I thank him for keeping Mima alive as a testimony of his faithfulness. God will never put on us more than we can bare [sic]. He knew how much strength you draw from Mima. I promise to buy black this season and going forward as a lifestyle! God Bless you! Thank you for your passion.

Your Sister in Christ:)

LaTissha Kandrell Moore

Amid all the hectic flutter of EE, we had to start making our own Christmas plans. My holiday shopping normally starts in the second week of December, and most of it occurs online. I can't stand the malls, and going on those adventures with the girls is so difficult. This Christmas was completely different. We were so worried about Mima, first and foremost, that the holiday spirit was in short supply at our house. Plus, I was still touring, making speeches, appearing on radio shows, and participating in various community events. It was more than a full-time job.

And I still had to be a dutiful daughter, spouse, and mom. That left me with almost no time to shop, but I had to, and not just because that's how the holiday is celebrated. We wanted to prove that it could be done the EE way, that we could have a wonderful family holiday while supporting our community.

As we considered the people on our list, deciding what to buy for the men was easy: Sean John. We could have held a Sean John fashion show with what we bought that year, and finding it was relatively easy because a store in a mall near us had a wide selection of his apparel. For teenage girls on our list, we sought out clothes from Kimora Lee Simmons, the model and TV star who also had a chic clothing line, Baby Phat. For other kids in our extended family we gave gift certificates purchased at a Black-owned McDonald's.

For Cara and Cori, shopping was a little tricky. We could find no Black-owned toy manufacturers, and our only African American–owned retailer, God First God Last God Always, had a selection limited to stocking stuffers like water guns and packs of cards. I did find Black dolls, but I was hoping for something like a Black Barbie knockoff. These plastic ladies looked like streetwalkers. We found a Black Monopoly game, but the girls were too young for that. So no toys. We bought books at Afriware, where we also found cool ethnic jewelry made for little girls. We loaded up on clothes at Jordan's Closets because, as a resale boutique, the prices were unbelievably low. We didn't put any restrictions on what other people could buy for our kids.

Even with its limitations, Christmas shopping the EE way was manageable. Mima's downward spiral, of course, was much more challenging.

We opened presents on Christmas Eve and a few more on Christmas morning at home to give the girls some semblance of a normal holiday. Later on Christmas day we hopped a flight to Atlanta and I moved into my parents' house, where my mom was on hospice. My dad, my brother Eduardo, and I took care of Mima around the clock. We changed her tubes, fed her, gave her medicine, and cleaned her. John and the girls were staying at Uncle Eduardo and Auntie Deidrea's house, so the kids could have a less fraught experience, go to the park, and play with their cousins. But I wanted the girls to spend time with Mima while they still could.

It was really hard. Cori and Cara saw their once-vivacious grandmother edging closer to death, and it scared them. All of the sadness and confusion swirling around Mima ruined the holiday for them. I don't think they even thought about the kinds of gifts they did or didn't receive. If they remember anything from that point in their young lives, it will be that their mother was so sad and their grandmother was extremely sick.

As hard as being in Atlanta was, leaving Mima on New Year's Eve, knowing that this time she was not going to spring back, was wrenching. We'd run out of miracles. Now all we could do was wait. I remember arriving home exhausted, the four of us just relieved to collapse in our house.

As 2009 became 2010, John and I spent some time reflecting on what The Empowerment Experiment had been like for us. We seemed to have made an impact or, at the least, planted a seed in peoples' minds. Millions had been exposed to our message through the media, our speeches, or the conferences we attended. In twelve short months we built an influential network of supporters who believed we were going to last. Although those connections might be hard to quantify, the possibilities are infinite.

But we also recognized how naive we'd been when beginning our odyssey, which may have been a helpful thing. Had we known what we were getting into and how hard it would be, well . . . perhaps that's better left alone. Let's just say we'd have done a few things differently.

On New Year's Eve we were not contemplating all the things we could get in a few hours now that our year of buying Black was over. We were too busy. Our attention was focused on Mima and the practicalities of getting the girls ready for their return to preschool. Besides, we were different people now. This wasn't like some diet where I'd lost twenty pounds and was planning to gorge myself on a banana split and chili cheese dogs to celebrate. This was a paradigm shift, as they like to say in the business world. Our hardwiring had been reengineered. We couldn't go out on January 1 and do something ludicrous like drop $300 at Wal-Mart; doing that would make us feel sick. And for this we were glad: Heightened awareness and the wisdom of experience are healthy things.

We felt liberated too, but perhaps not in the way folks would think. Knowing we could buy Black without the scrutiny and pressure was a relief. We were so knowledgeable now; we could do it with a laserlike focus. And we could enjoy it. Buying Black would be fun and fulfilling— not so much an obligation. That was what we were looking forward to.

Groceries, however, were a different story.

We did not feel guilty; in fact, we were ecstatic about buying what we needed at the nearest grocery store. As a mom, I was thrilled to be able finally to get my girls the food I wanted for them, to spoil them a little for enduring their parents' zealous mission. I did feel a pang for all those moms who don't have that luxury. But to be honest, the joy and anticipation washed that sentiment right out of me. We talked about what a fresh piece of salmon would taste like as well as spinach, feta cheese, whole-grain bagels and cereal, olive oil, and skim milk. It made me grateful for those things, which was an unexpected benefit of EE.

So I went back to my neighborhood Jewel, a mere six or seven blocks from our house. Before The Empowerment Experiment, I'd be there two or three times a week. Those shelves were almost as familiar to me as my own pantry. I had figured out which cashiers were friendly and which weren't, which were fast and which dawdled. I even knew when produce arrived and when the deli was least crowded. I was so psyched about going that I caught myself humming.

This was not where I figured I'd be in early January 2010. I was meant to be shopping at Karriem's store—or maybe at a second store of his— or at another bustling Black-owned grocery store I'd discovered the next town over from us. A strange mix of emotions—sorrow, failure, and remorse—rose in me when I walked in the store.

And then something clicked in my head: my EE training. I started hunting for the products that were Black-made. I remembered that Real Men Cook, the charitable organization that hosted the annual picnic Karriem had sponsored, published a cookbook of "Real Men's" recipes, which mentioned a couple of their products. I took a few extra minutes to locate the Real Men Cook sweet-potato pound cake mix and dropped it in my cart. I knew where to find the Heritage Link Brands they stocked. The owner, Selena Cuffe, had sent me a note telling me I could find it in my local Jewel. She even told me what aisle and shelf. I seized a couple bottles of the Seven Sisters Bukettraube. Then I looked in the freezer case and found Reggio's Pizza, owned by local entrepreneur, activist, and former US Department of Commerce Minority Business Owner of the Year John M. Clark Jr. In another freezer case I found Baldwin's Ice Cream, owned by Eric Johnson, a fellow University of Chicago Booth Graduate School of Business alum. I tried to find ComfortCake, whose founder and CEO, Amy Hilliard, is a Harvard Business School graduate and entrepreneur extraordinaire. *Maybe*, I thought, *I'll ask the manager to stock it.*

I bought a lot—and I mean a lot—of food, about $220 worth. Doing the best I could to support Black food producers made me feel a little better. Until I pulled up at home, got out of the car, and, holding a few of those grocery bags, saw John coming out to help me. Something in his expression had the whole year in it—all the hard work, the disappointment, the stress, the nasty e-mails, the encouragement, the survival, and the heart. I fell into his arms, weeping.

"I know, baby, I know," he whispered over my whimpering, his big hands rubbing my back. "Let's just get this stuff in the house."

It seems so foolish now, to be crying over a mundane event like a trip to the grocery store—unless you poured your heart into something the way we did and understood how powerful a simple run to the grocery store could be. Then it makes complete sense.

Just like when I came home from my first trip to Fair Share, when we walked in the door with the bags from Jewel, the girls went nuts. They tore through the paper, squealing when they got to the Starburst and Pop-Tarts and juice boxes and brand-name chips they love. My little babies were cheering for applesauce, jumping up and down for yogurt. If you were a fly on the wall, you would have seen John shaking his head, the girls squealing every time they pulled another item out of the bags, and me blubbering. It was one authentic, uniquely rich, Anderson-family EE moment, and it is forever stored in my memory.

Over the next few days John and I examined our spreadsheets—we'd logged everything over the course of the year—did some number crunching, and found our unofficial tally: We'd spent about 70 percent of our after-tax income, or about $70,000, with Black-owned businesses. Then we took a look at how our spending had trended pre- and post-EE. In general, we spent less in nearly every category except gas, which isn't surprising considering all the driving we did.

About three-quarters of that percentage was spent on child care, automotive needs, restaurants, and food. Fortunately, we had started with our child-care provider a year before the experiment. We chose it, from about four local centers, because it was a quality institution, we liked the teachers, and it had a high proportion of Black children. We had no idea who the actual owner was. When we checked, for purposes of the experiment, we were happy to learn that it was a Black woman from the Austin neighborhood.

As for the rest of our spending, here are some of the highlights:

Groceries. Overall, they accounted for 5 percent of our spending in 2009; a year earlier it was 10 percent. When Farmers Best was open, though, we spent as much on groceries as we had the year before. After it closed and we struggled to find decent, Black-owned food stores, our spending dropped significantly. And the kind of food available changed too. We couldn't buy ground turkey, frozen bagels, fish, whole-grain bread, yogurt, fresh deli meats, bleu cheese, healthy snacks, or olive oil. But we could find cereal, pizza, beans, soda, sugar, chips, Chef Boyardee canned pasta, condiments, and lots of junk. Recall the research linking food deserts and poor health, mentioned in chapter 1? Imagine how much health care costs would drop if a few quality, Black-owned grocery stores could establish themselves in predominantly Black neighborhoods.

Fast food. In 2008 we might have let the girls eat a fast-food dinner twice a month. In 2009 they ate fast food three times a week. We found a bunch of Black-owned McDonald's and Burger Kings, a few Popeye's chicken restaurants and Subways, and, of course, Quiznos sandwich places. The fast-food binge began after Farmers Best closed and we were pressed to find anything decent to eat. For John, who works in a virtually all-White suburb, no Black-owned restaurants existed. He used gift cards from Black-owned fast-food restaurants to purchase his fast-food meals at franchises near his office, a big change from the year before, when he'd rarely eat a fast-food lunch. It was pretty much the same for me. A year earlier, while working for the business strategy consulting firm, I'd come to the downtown office for weekly meetings and then I'd stop at a Panera Bread, Chipotle, or Cosi's, or maybe the Bennigan's or Friday's on the concourse level of the office building. In 2009, when I was working on EE from home, I would usually eat lunch there or grab a fast-food meal on the go. Overall, casual and fine dining dropped to 7.5 percent of our spending in 2009, compared to 20 percent a year earlier.

Clothing. In 2008 I bought our clothes at the mall or online. In 2009 we did not find a Black-owned clothing outlet until late spring. We had Sean John and Agriculture Crop of Style, but the prices were much higher there than what we normally spent. I bought very little clothing for myself that year. Spending on clothing for the girls went up after I found Jordan's Closets, but it was my only choice and required a long drive to get there. In 2009 our outlay for adult clothing accounted for 7.5 percent of our overall expenditures, down from 10 percent the previous year. We spent more on children's clothing—20 percent in 2009—compared to 10 percent in 2008, but I think that was because John and I spent so much less on ourselves.

Toiletries. We found no Black-owned drugstores and no Black-owned drug or personal hygiene company, like Dove, Suave, or Oil of Olay. We were able to find some no-name brands at our dollar store, God First God Last God Always, but those products were lower quality than what I normally buy. We did find small containers of brand-name, over-the-counter drugs at gas stations. Later in the year we found a couple of

Black-owned "bath and body" companies—Soul Purpose and Carol's Daughter—but their products cost much more than what I would typically pay. Again, we spent less overall. Toiletries, cosmetics, and over-the-counter drugs totaled 2 percent of our spending that year, down from 5 percent in 2008.

Here's the rest of our spending comparisons:

In 2009 gas totaled 25 percent of our spending; 2008: 10 percent
In 2009 housewares were 2 percent; 2008: 10 percent
In 2009 toys, books, children's gear totaled 2 percent; 2008: 5 percent
In 2009 entertainment/nightlife totaled 5 percent; 2008: 10 percent
In 2009 children's entertainment totaled 2 percent; 2008: 5 percent

Crunching the numbers and seeing how the experiment influenced our spending habits was illuminating, to say the least.

Today, our new consciousness about buying Black extends to other areas of our lives. When we need work done on the car, instead of dropping it off at the local Firestone shop, which is owned by a skilled, conscientious White man, we drive the forty-five minutes to Advantage Chevrolet because the proprietor, Desmond Roberts, is a strong African American role model and supporter of worthy causes in the Black community—and equally skilled and conscientious. Yes, it's a nuisance to travel that far for an oil change, but it's become second nature to us now. Some people might protest that we are taking business away from a local establishment, but the need is great, our purpose is worthy, and our consciences are clear. Besides, what do you think most Hispanics, Polish-, or Asian-Americans would do?

We buy John's clothes from Sean John, and he recently purchased a suit from Steve Harvey's new clothing line, the Steve Harvey Collection. We have a friend who is an independent reseller of J. Hilburn custom shirts, and she stops by John's home office. He doesn't even have to leave the house. We found a Black-owned shoe store with a selection for the whole family in Hyde Park, right down the street from Kimbark Liquors, which we still frequent when we need to restock our liquor cabinet.

Afriware Books moved to a less expensive location, but Nzingha is still around, and so is her Afro. This has been another benefit of The Empowerment Experiment: When we shop at Afriware, my daughters get to see another positive Black role model. That's no small thing.

Our home security company remains Black-owned Foscett's Communication and Alarm Co. of Chicago, and we still use Covenant Bank, an African American–owned institution a mere five miles away on the West Side. Twice a week we drive five miles in the opposite direction to Black-owned Evans Cleaners in Maywood. We still buy the gas cards and the McDonald's, Burger King, and Quiznos cards from Black-owned franchisees. For the rare times we go out for a nice romantic dinner, we stick to Park 52 and Market, both Black-owned. But a couple other options have turned up, including Fleming's in downtown Chicago and the five-star C-House, owned by Ethiopian celebrity chef Marcus Samuelsson, known for his philanthropic work and social justice activism in his homeland and for funding food justice and mentoring programs for urban youth in America.

And we keep our eyes open for other opportunities to do what Maria Stewart, Booker T. Washington, those resourceful heroes from the Black Wall Streets, and so many others before us have done. We're carrying on as best we can.

Couldn't do it any other way even if we wanted to. We're walking up this path now, forever.

Epilogue

MIMA DIED AT HOME ON FEBRUARY 13, 2010, AT 2:46 p.m., while I begged her to live. She'd started a steep descent in mid-December, and by January I felt as if I was spending all my time on the phone, yelling at somebody—the doctors, the nurses, the hospice coordinator. It was my way of protecting Mima, and I was going to do so even if it killed me or anyone who crossed me.

E-mails, phone calls, messages, and invitations for The Empowerment Experiment were piling up since we completed our historic year. I ignored all of them during Mima's final weeks while I focused on managing her illness and shuttled between Chicago and Atlanta. My life and my family's life felt very frayed.

At this point the disease so ravaged Mima and she was so heavily sedated that I don't know what registered for her. But of this much I am sure: She hung in there until we had completed the year of EE. Although I did everything I could to help her, the overall lackluster outcome of our Black year made me wonder whether my time would have been better spent just being with her. It still weighs on me. The only consolation I have is that Mima survived with pancreatic cancer for nearly two years, a miraculous length of time.

In the first few months after her passing I kept thinking about the authenticity of her life, something I'd grown to appreciate after The

Empowerment Experiment ran its course. During that year I could have filled a house with all the pretension, deceit, and artificiality I encountered. The thought of her living with such purpose and unwavering love yields profound admiration in me. It always will.

Impervious to heartache, time passes. We buried Mima on February 17. The next day John and I returned home to the girls, to the harshest month of Chicago weather, and to whatever was next in the life of The Empowerment Experiment.

What followed—after making and fielding phone calls about Mima, responding to the condolences, and excavating the mountain of e-mails, phone messages, and other business for EE—was the report from the Kellogg School of Management at Northwestern University, twenty-nine pages that analyzed our adventure and offered a broader perspective. An uplifting compilation for the most part, it made us feel that we'd contributed by providing data for some academic gravitas that was, at the same time, anchored in the real world. The complete report can be found in the appendix, but here are a few of the highlights.

"Over the course of 2009," the report states, "the Andersons made 513 purchases and spent approximately $48,943." That total actually represented what you might consider spending money. If you include our mutual fund investments and other money we transferred to Black fund managers and financial institutions and deposits, we ended up "spending" about $94,000 that year in African American businesses that we otherwise wouldn't have.

It was especially interesting to see the pie chart (see appendix 2) indicating how we spent our money day to day at Black-owned businesses or elsewhere when we could not find a Black option. Our biggest expense, 37 percent, was child care. Automotive came in next at 18 percent, followed by restaurants at 11 percent. Almost as telling was the list of products and services that Black-owned businesses didn't offer—things like car seats, appliances, lawn treatment services, basketball shoes, cell phone service, utilities, bed sheets, hair clippers, a treadmill, and vitamins. Seeing this in black and white made it all the more clear how barren the landscape is of African American businesses.

Calling business awareness "a significant hurdle," the researchers encourage Black-owned businesses to "leverage on-line Black business search engines and ensure that their business websites clearly highlight Black ownership," something with which Karriem might take issue. Word-of-mouth referrals are also important. In addition, the report urges Black-owned businesses to "maintain high levels of quality and service in order to capture and maintain" consumer awareness, determine service and product needs in predominantly African American communities, and establish neighborhood businesses to fill those needs. Black businesses should target "industries where there is severe Black owner underrepresentation," which would offer entrepreneurs a unique advantage and a potentially lucrative opportunity, especially where their diversity can be seen as valuable and appealing.

That was pretty logical stuff, but my favorite part of the study is a little blue-shaded box buried in the back of the report (see appendix 2) where the researchers calculated the impact of all fifteen million Black households in the United States spending 2, 5, 10, and up to 68 percent of their after-tax income on Black-owned businesses. As discussed in chapter 5, a few pennies here and there can create tens, maybe hundreds of billions of dollars in economic empowerment for folks who could use it in productive ways.

"The Empowerment Experiment has laid the foundation for leveraging the economic power of the Black American consumer," the report notes. "Although the breadth and depth of the experiment were limited, it reinforces key issues and opportunities within this large consumer base that have direct implications for the growth of Black entrepreneurs and ultimately for 'self-help' economics."

"Ultimately," the report concludes, "successful execution of The Empowerment Experiment on a larger scale, consistently, throughout the nation will create generations of financial stability and wealth in the Black population that have yet to be achieved."

The report brings up a key factor in empowering Black businesses: the importance of capital. Our friend Steven Rogers and others are aware of this problem and discuss it in public forums. According to Rogers, few people know of the successful fund management companies dedicated to providing money to minority entrepreneurs and that those companies are profitable, safe places to put money to work. There is even a consortium of the most credible of these funds and equity investors, the National Association of Investment Companies, which includes Yucaipa Johnson, owned by business magnates Magic Johnson and Ron Burkle; John Rogers's Ariel Investments; and Goldman Sachs's Urban Investment Group Companies. For Black entrepreneurs and emergent businesses it is a network (and gold mine) of funding sources and venture capital firms specifically focused on creating and growing Black businesses. NAIC has successfully invested funds in *Essence* magazine, Black Entertainment Television, and TV and Radio One.

As proof of the consortium's performance, consider the 2003 report by the Ewing Marion Kauffman Foundation, which analyzed funds operated by NAIC and found that "investments in minority business enterprises resulted in healthy returns equal to, if not slightly higher than, traditional investments by mainstream venture capitalists."

"We have to educate the White community," Rogers told me, "the ones who are the holders of capital, that this is good business. . . . Look at investing in minority-owned businesses as a competitive advantage. Do it with the expectations of market rate returns, and one of the benefits will be social benefits. Don't do it from a philanthropic kind of mindset. Every argument has to be an economic argument that says this is good for business."

I couldn't agree more. It's supporting the Farmers Bests of the world versus the J's Fresh Meats. We want to support only those businesses that make the grade, which brings up another important point: training. As Rogers and other experts note, research shows that a lack of training— sometimes more often than a lack of capital—is a critical factor in why entrepreneurs fail. Entrepreneurial training for Black businesspeople can be achieved through partnerships, not charitable handouts. These partnerships—with universities or other institutions—can teach small businesses and entrepreneurs how to grow.

Based on what we've learned through The Empowerment Experiment, the best way to get started is by creating more Black-owned franchises of major consumer brands, including food and clothing stores, hotels, and household and professional services. We need to offer consumers convenient ways to make the small changes in their lives that result in economic empowerment for underserved neighborhoods. Sure, we want to establish Black-owned grocery stores, hotels, retailers, banks, and law and accounting firms, but let's begin with what already exists. Consider McDonald's, KFC, Foot Locker, and Jiffy Lube. The franchise model enables Black entrepreneurs to enter a market with a known commodity, consumer demand, and quality products.

Unfortunately, at the moment too few Black-owned franchises exist. The biggest hurdle is the initial investment required to acquire the franchise. But franchisors can help with that. At McDonald's, the most successful franchise in the world, I worked on this very issue, researching and presenting a report to senior management on the importance of franchisee diversity. That report offered strategies on recruiting, retaining, and establishing parity between the Black consumer base and the restaurant owners.

In fact, programs like this exist now and they work, but not enough companies have them, not enough money is being invested in them, and not enough attention is being paid to them. One fantastic example is Marriott's Franchise Diversity Initiative, in which the chain partners with the National Association of Black Hotel Owners, Operators and Developers (NABHOOD). Through it, in July 2011 Marriott had 586 women- and minority-owned hotels nationwide, including 126 owned by African Americans. That number surpassed the goal of the program, set in 2005, to have 500 women- and minority-owned hotels by 2010. The objective was part of a larger diversity agenda that included a pledge to spend $1 billion with minority suppliers, a goal Marriott has surpassed by $1.3 billion.

Another worthy program is New York Life's $50 billion Empowerment Plan that seeks to persuade two hundred thousand African American families to purchase at least $250,000 of life insurance. Yes, it's a savvy sales strategy, but that doesn't detract from its broader value. The idea, as New York Life states, is to show African Americans "how other cultures use life insurance to protect income and to build multigenerational wealth." The company wants to challenge Blacks "to be wealth creators, instead of wealth spenders." However, the wealth creators are not just the consumers who are able to create and transfer wealth with life insurance and annuities; the $50 billion Empowerment Plan also calls for targeting Black entrepreneurs as agents and brokers: "New York Life's 900+ African American agents have pledged to help empower the communities they serve." Eugene Mitchell, SVP of the African American Market Unit, describes these reps as "quasi business owners," something akin to being a New York Life franchisee. In effect, the Black entrepreneurs, their families, and their neighborhoods reap the same benefits that occur when major franchisers recruit, train, and support Black franchisees. As an advocate for African American economic empowerment, I like that concept—a lot.

If other corporations, like Pepsico's KFC and Pizza Hut, Procter & Gamble, Toyota, Home Depot, Kmart, and The Athlete's Foot, were to allocate one-tenth of the money they spend on advertising to Black consumers on advertising to Black entrepreneurs, they would attract some of the most talented, driven, and hardworking franchisees, suppliers, and vendors on the planet. The money they would invest in training the new franchisees—which is what the companies would invest in any potential franchisee—along with offering financing, extended repayment periods, and that critical help with start-up costs—would get the attention of Black consumers, who would support those stores in big numbers. The same would happen if these firms were to put more money into finding Black suppliers and vendors or enabling quality Black companies that may not be big enough to serve as subcontractors or suppliers to their partners or their own suppliers. Progressive organizations engage in Tier 2 supplier diversity by requiring that their main suppliers meet certain levels of spending with minority suppliers.

I don't think you need an MBA to understand that those companies that market their franchisee support with a little savvy would earn extremely robust returns. So many of these companies already have commercials showing Black managers and employees in their stores, and they show off their high-ranking Black officers in *Black Enterprise* and *Ebony* magazines.

Imagine what an impact they could make by showing off their Black *owners.* Consider the example of stores Magic Johnson owns. I'm pretty sure Starbucks never considered pushing its overpriced coffee in the Black community, and Black people always had to go to the suburbs or downtown to enjoy T.G.I. Fridays. Then Magic Johnson opened Starbucks and Friday's outlets in underserved Black areas, and they are some of the most successful stores in their corporations. That's because Black consumers love to say, "I'm going to Magic's Starbucks" or "I'm going to the Magic Johnson Friday's." Lots of Black folks patronize those businesses, even when they cannot find a Magic Johnson–owned outlet, because they know those companies have made an investment in the Black community. It's called customer loyalty, and it is invaluable. Starbucks is a great example. The coffee company started a partnership with Magic's Johnson Development Corp. (JDC) in 1998 and has opened more than one hundred of what Starbucks calls "Urban Coffee Opportunities" locations in underserved neighborhoods from Los Angeles, San Francisco, and Seattle to Denver, Chicago, Detroit, Atlanta, Washington, DC, and New York City. Those stores have helped jump-start economic development and strengthened the sense of community in neighborhood after neighborhood.

What else did we learn in our yearlong odyssey? Despite some of the ugly stuff we encountered, we learned that we had lots of supporters, the great majority of whom are Black, which I guess should come as no surprise.

Between April and December I spoke at six conferences, five universities, three churches, and was honored on six different occasions. We also organized six of our own events, like the wine-tasting fund-raiser at Tracye Dee's WineStyles and the holiday celebration at Mell Monroe's Welcome Inn Manor. That's twenty-six speaking engagements, not to mention dozens of media interviews that gave us broad exposure and got people thinking about the issues, even if a fair number of folks got angry. Because of how we positioned our experiment, because of the viral nature of our interviews and stories, because the centerpiece of our movement was the website, and because most of EE's exposure came from mainstream media coverage, our supporters were people who spend a lot of time online, watch the major news networks, or read the papers and who were accustomed to social networking. There are about fourteen thousand now between the Facebook fans and the more than eight thousand folks registered on our website, and at least half are business owners and professionals. Our Facebook group is larger than that of the National Urban League and the Rainbow PUSH Coalition, two established organizations with millions in their coffers, chapters all over the world, and dozens of major corporate sponsorships and celebrity endorsements. I think that's an indication of how serious people were about our effort.

Thanks to The Empowerment Experiment, our network has multiplied, and we've connected with many visionaries, activists, and business and community leaders. Between April and August of 2010 I spoke at twenty events, including giving keynote addresses at events hosted by a couple of prominent business groups—the FraserNet PowerNetworking Conference in Atlanta and the National Alliance of Market Developers annual conference in Baltimore. As for 2011, I racked up more than eighteen speaking engagements in the first seven months, including major addresses at the National Urban League's national conference, the National Association of Black Accountants' national conference and expo, FraserNet again, and the US Black Chamber's annual conference. I'd have hit a few more, but I had this little story to write, and I promised to avoid being away from the family every week. I still find time to visit my father twice a month in Atlanta.

In addition to the speeches I've been serving on panels and speaking for the community as an expert on economics, entrepreneurship, and business. In the summer of 2011 I represented EE at the inaugural White House Briefing to Community Leaders, where the president—my old law school prof—offered his support to community activists like me. Michael Blake, the director of the White House Office of Public Engagement and President Obama's liaison to the African American community and minority business, invited me. Donald Cravins, the chief of staff and chief counsel for the Senate Committee on Small Business and Entrepreneurship, has asked me to testify to the Senate on behalf of Black businesses and economically distressed Black neighborhoods that need more local businesses investing in the community. In addition, the chief diversity officer at Office Max asked me to deliver a keynote address to their minority suppliers and the company's senior management during a swanky all-day event the company put on specifically to recruit high-quality minority prospects and create a forum to enhance the value of the supplier diversity program. They could have asked a celebrity to do it, but they asked me, and it was the first event of its kind. I shared our journey and delivered a business case for supplier diversity that explained how substantive supplier diversity can increase sales. I received a standing ovation after closing my speech with these words, "Do Good. Make Good. Make Good Money." Office Max received letters from Hispanic, Asian, and White women business owners praising the company for partnering with The Empowerment Experiment and supporting EE's vision of conscious consumerism. Kraft's Supplier Diversity Lead was there. She has decided to have a similar event for their suppliers, and guess who will be delivering a speech urging Kraft's executives to invest their marketing dollars in supplier diversity? That's right.

That investing simply isn't happening fast enough, as the plight of so many Black-owned businesses we came to know painfully demonstrated. My favorite wine store, WineStyles South Loop, run by my dear girlfriend Tracye Dee, closed in August 2010. She just didn't have the liquidity to keep the store afloat. Jordan's Closets couldn't make it either. The same month Tracye closed, Joslyn and Jera converted to an online-only operation. Then, in the spring of 2011, they closed altogether. When she explained, "We just weren't getting the business we needed," I felt my heart drop into my stomach.

The same fate struck two of my other favorite Bronzeville establishments: Sensual Steps Shoe Salon, which had survived five years under my beloved Nicole Jones, and Bronzeville Coffee Shop. David and Michelle Powell at God First God Last—God bless 'em—keep plugging away. But the last time I drove by what was Farmers Best, it was a barred-up, hollow shell. I had to turn my head.

There have been uplifting moments too, often in the form of individuals touched by the hope that The Empowerment Experiment can spark. Corey Tabor heard me speak in February 2011 at the University of Texas at Austin. Tabor, an African American preacher at a multicultural parish and a car sales rep—I love that combination—grew up in Abilene, Texas, in a mixed-race environment. Not until he attended the University of Texas at Austin did he start investigating more deeply his African American heritage. He ended up establishing a ministry for Black students at UT. He told me he'd always wanted to commit to buying Black, and he did patronize the one Black-owned business that all Black men commonly patronize: the barbershop. Doing much more seemed overwhelming and pointless to him.

But something about seeing the stand our family took gave him pause.

"The first thing that caught my attention was how one family could make that big of a difference," Tabor said. "It was one decision made by two people that began this movement, and I think we often forget that movements start with individuals who are not comfortable with the status quo."

Two days after hearing my talk Tabor lined up quotes from a Black-owned insurance agency and a Black-owned lawn-care provider. He checked to see whether a Black physician had room for an additional patient and contacted a Black accountant. Corey Tabor is one man making a difference in large part because he believes he can, and so often, that belief is just about all it takes.

I'm also inspired when I help White folks understand that this idea of ours is not racist but rather something that adds to the universal good. For example, when I gave that speech in Austin, almost everyone in the audience of about 250 people was White. Like the talk at Georgia State and another one at Belmont University in Nashville, looking over that audience in Austin was a little unsettling at first. But it went well. Afterward, a couple of White students told me they'd originally come with the intention of publicly declaring that I was a militant Black racist. Instead, they listened to my talk and apologized. Then they asked where they could find businesses to support. I nearly cried.

A similar scenario occurred when I was invited to speak to the faculty members of the Chicago chapter of Network for Teaching Entrepreneurship (NFTE) during their annual retreat held at Northwestern University. A mostly White organization, NFTE is a popular, well-funded, and corporately sponsored global initiative that concentrates on teaching minority youth entrepreneurship in high school and helping them create their own profitable businesses before they turn twenty-one. After the lecture to approximately fifty teachers, the great majority of them White, I received a standing ovation. The president asked me to stay involved with the group and serve as a judge for their business plan competition.

Beyond individual transformations, larger efforts to foster buying Black are cropping up. One of the most exciting is a program sponsored by the Houston Citizens Chamber of Commerce, the second-oldest Black chamber of commerce in the United States—with ties to Booker T. Washington's National Negro Business League—and the National Black MBA Association's Houston chapter. Called the Economic Empowerment Initiative, it's like EE on steroids. One hundred members of the Houston chapter of the National Black MBA Association are looking to buy Black and track the experience, and the program is spearheaded by Eric Lyons, president and CEO of the Chamber of Commerce. He told me he was inspired when he saw John and me on CBS's *Early Show* in July 2009.

Another example is our partnership with the nonprofit Powered by Action, founded by Andre Hughes, global managing director of Accenture and Cisco Business Group. PBA's mission is to mobilize people, companies, and institutions to transform distressed communities around the world into self-sustaining entities. Although new, PBA is already operating in a remote village in Ghana, where the organization is employing local residents to build a school as the first step in overhauling that community, as well as in the troubled Chicago suburbs of Ford Heights and Chicago Heights, where PBA is helping with an incentive-based student-performance plan.

We are working to integrate EE's mission to help people find and support quality Black-owned businesses into PBA's creation of self-sustaining communities. We could do that by designating a struggling neighborhood, like Austin on the West Side, as a PBA target community and including self-help economics as a component of the blueprint for making it self-sustaining.

Beyond all that, EE has fans in the pop-culture world, including singer and music producer Kandi Burruss and singer Tionne "T-Boz" Watkins, who have hosted EE events and made public statements of support. We are discussing corporate sponsorship of an EE National Tour with General Motors, Walgreens, OfficeMax, Kraft, Pitney Bowes, American Airlines, Bank of America, Delta, Dell, Exelon, and UPS. The plan would involve barnstorming in ten or so markets with high concentrations of African Americans and feature upscale events at Black-owned venues where we would use Black vendors, products, and professionals. Those companies would promote their supplier diversity initiatives, and our entrepreneurs could get some face time with major corporate prospects. These companies sponsor events like this all the time in order to market to Black consumers. By working with us, they'd get the chance to promote and facilitate their supplier, franchisee, dealer, and vendor diversity.

We did one such event, supported by General Motors Southeast, in August 2010 in Atlanta, where we featured local Black GM dealers, an upscale woman's boutique, and a cognac company. The hosts were *Rolling Out* magazine, a top-quality, national weekly found in twenty markets across the country, and the Atlanta Metropolitan Black Chamber of Commerce. *Rolling Out* has since become the official media partner of the EE National Tour, promoting and covering all my speaking engagements, showcasing EE entrepreneurs in the magazine and on its very popular website, and helping organize events. Owned by Munson Steed, a community and business leader, friend, and EE entrepreneur, *Rolling Out* is located in and employs from the Black community. The magazine and its parent company, Steed Media, fund entrepreneurship and educational programs that help the African Americans they serve and represent in their media.

So in some ways prospects look encouraging. I'm constantly turning down invitations, trying to limit them to twice a month. Next year, if we get some help tending to Cara and Cori, I might be speaking to groups once a week.

Despite all this I can still get trapped in gloomy places. I sometimes wonder whether our very public pledge and all that came with it has done nothing more than drive a wedge between different groups of Blacks and separate us even more from the rest of America. I worry that EE should have been a little smarter and more sophisticated but wasn't because of something we did or didn't do, that these small but encouraging endeavors and partnerships will wither. That's a very discouraging little space to occupy.

Although some might disagree, we did not want EE to reinforce the problems that set Blacks apart in the first place. We weren't out to stir up that kind of trouble. But I know we've done a little of that. Having Whites *and* Blacks hammer us for being racist is confounding. As soon as we prove we're not militant, we then have to begin demonstrating we're not sellouts. It's a corrosive, no-win predicament.

So, yes, EE is about race, but not racial divisions. Labeling The Empowerment Experiment a racist endeavor is an easy way to shift the focus away from honest discourse. It hardens people's souls and preserves the ugly status quo in which Black businesses, neighborhoods, dreams, and children die. I'd go so far as to say it's cowardly.

In the long term we hope to see the realization of our dream to create The Empowerment Experiment Foundation Center, a place for research and education in Black economic empowerment. We'd probably base the Center in Atlanta, a city we love and have talked about moving to for a long time. The girls would get to spend more time with my side of the family, and now that Mima is gone, I need to take care of my father.

In our experiment we documented where our money went. The Center would do the same but on a much larger scale, incorporating thousands—maybe millions—of individual buy-Black experiments to track how the money consumers spent directly with Black businesses and indirectly via supplier, vendor, and franchisee diversity affects the quality of life in various neighborhoods around the country. Researchers would determine, as a result of consumers patronizing Black businesses, how many jobs were created; how many enterprises were created, rescued, and grown; how many new industries or markets were penetrated; how the incremental spending made an impact on mainstream organizations with supplier, vendor, and franchisee diversity; and how many new partnerships and franchises were developed and contracts were signed.

The Center would also explore the opportunity gaps for Black businesses in markets where Blacks represent a significant portion of the customer base; study the cultural and historical reasons why Black businesses are not, for the most part, competitive; and look at why Black consumers aren't supporting them. Based on the information we collect, we would develop practical solutions and programs that would increase self-help economics in those areas.

All of these activities will be research- and data-driven because we know the preaching and begging ain't gonna cut it. The Center will rely on hard evidence to facilitate what we always knew was possible: social change powered by consumer demand. Hey, did I just come up with our tagline?

I'm grateful for the wisdom we gained through the year, tough as it sometimes was to absorb. And yes, some of that wisdom came in the form of disappointment in my people. Clarence Jones, Martin Luther King Jr.'s attorney, may have said it best when he told me that Blacks must "rededicate themselves 24/7 to the pursuit of educational and business excellence. They have to assume greater personal responsibility for directly or indirectly encouraging conduct that creates adverse social and economic pathologies in our communities." These include all the common problems afflicting Blacks, according to Jones: "Rampant use of drugs," "lack of parental guidance to male children," "the cycle of young men going through life without a father," and, of course, violence. "The Black killing fields that take place in many of our urban areas is not because the White man did it," Jones said. "We did it to ourselves."

This reminds me of an episode of *Boondocks*, the comic strip and animated series by Aaron McGruder. In it Dr. King awakens from a coma and finds himself in modern-day Black America. He is astounded, angry, and deeply discouraged. At one point he gives a blistering sermon, saying

that all he sees are "a bunch of trifling, shiftless, good-for-nothing niggers"; that Black Entertainment Television "is the worst thing I've ever
seen in my life."

"Is this it?" he asks his stunned flock. "Is this what I got all those ass-
whippings for?"

Then he launches into a litany of character flaws possessed by "niggers"—a word that turns my stomach and should have a similar effect
on all African Americans. They are "living contradictions" who are "full
of unfulfilled ambitions," who "wax and wane, love to complain," who
"love being another man's judge and jury," and "procrastinate until it's
time to worry," who "love being late" and "hate to hurry."

McGruder's criticism—regarding my generation and the one after
it—is the frequent topic of discussion in Black forums and social settings. Although we acknowledge that we owe our freedom and our educational and economic opportunities to those who fought for equal
rights, we do nothing to continue that struggle. In my speeches I take
that point a step further—that we are, in effect, *negating* the impact of
their efforts by not being the proud, unified, culturally aware people we
used to be and that we shame our elders and defy their legacy by not focusing on our educational and economic empowerment.

On those days when I seem to have lost my way, I think about how—
and more important, why—we embarked on The Empowerment Experiment. The short answer is: We had to do it. I hope we made a
difference. I think we did, at least a little.

In the end I can't help admitting that I'm left with a fair amount of
bitterness I'm unable to shake—more so than John, who does not let the
failures and awful circumstances our people face get him down. He cares,
but he's become a little numb after all we've been through. And he's much
better than me at counting our blessings and continuing to work on making a difference where we can.

My worst fear is that Black people will always be the pitiable, ridiculed
underclass. We built nations and empires, invented industries and revolutionary products, and conquered slavery, rape, and genocide. We put a
Black man in the White House.

And we're still stuck at the bottom.

How will history view this generation of African Americans? Will they say that we had it all, that we made headway in corporate America and in the legal and educational arenas, but we earned our individual success and left our neighborhoods for disrespectful outsiders to raid? Will they say that we sold our history, potential, dreams, and destiny in exchange for the comforts of suburban life, shunning our own entrepreneurs and professionals, and treating them with condescension? Did we squander our chances? Fail to deliver on so much promise?

Or will history show that my generation—realists and dreamers, rich and poor—came together to empower those whose power had slipped away or was stolen, the masses who have yet to experience the American Dream? Will future generations say that the civil rights movement is alive because we realized that our liberty and political equality are moot if our economic power is disregarded and delegitimized? Will my generation usher in another era of pride and unity, which used to define our people, and once more express our greatness? Will we counter the enormity of the status quo, the fear of change, the ridiculous aversion we have to prosperity with common sense, creativity, and courage? Can we just try?

In November 2010 Cori was turning four and we wanted to get her a new bedroom set. My plan was to buy it from Seaway Furniture, a quality, Black-owned business on the South Side, about twenty miles from our house. Two big malls, a Target, Wal-Mart, Kmart, JCPenney, and a Sears are all within three miles of our place. Several furniture and mattress stores operate in my neighborhood. But we had our reasons for going to Seaway. The day before the expedition I called to check the store hours.

The line was disconnected—another quality Black business gone. When I hung up the phone, I stared at John and felt empty.

I know: It's tough. You're busy, weary, skeptical, and, yes, cynical and pessimistic. Trust me, I know. I am too. But I still believe.

Acknowledgments

John. I could just stop these acknowledgements here. With you. And that's all I ever want to be. With you. Thank you, my love, my buddy, my thought completer, my frame of reference, my soldier, savior, prince, and king—for balancing my crazy with your calm, believing in me, bettering me, and being there for me even when I could not return the favor. I love you. I love us.

Eduardo, my big brother, otherwise known as the "third leg in EE's three-legged table," we could not have done this without your faith, guidance, and visionary leadership. Thank you for being our counsel, confidant, and manifesting the magnificence of the Waite family. My whole life I depended on you and tried to be you. You made me read *Souls of Black Folk* when I was nine years old. Now we both know why.

Tom, my oldest brother, if I had one-tenth of your integrity, courage, and good ol' grit . . . Thank you for always protecting me. Thank you for preempting my sadness, shame, and suffering with your strong shoulders and soft heart. Thank you for keeping God first.

Papa, you will never know how much you mean to me and how deeply I appreciate the privilege of growing up with your love. Losing Mima was the only time you've ever needed me as much as I need you. And still, you never allowed me to give up or let up on this project—and not because you believe in the fight but simply and purely because you believe in me. Thank you for trusting me with your tears, sharing with me your sadness, and, still, even still, pushing me through all the pain so that we could make it through. Your smile is always my goal line.

Cara and Cori, my two ladies in making, I thank you for making my heavy sun rise every day, for amazing me, and for keeping me alive. You liberate me and enhance me. You stole so many tears, spoiled my worries, and seized so much pain. Squirt-burger (Cori), thank you for reluctantly but sweetly sharing your Momma, for making us laugh, and for wanting to be a part of my scary world. Long-legs (Cara), thank you for your endless questions, for trying to understand everything just so you can be with me and be like me. Thank you, my girls, for making life beautiful.

And for the rest of the family . . . Angela, Alan, Damon, Pam, Kim, Deidrea, Sheri, Tristen, Lyndon, Jordan, Little Damon, Dad (in West Bloomfield), and Debbie . . . thank you for being my home team—dependable, loving, supportive, unchanging, flawed in a fun way, and real. Aunt Patsy, thanks for the guidance, the truth telling, and finding a way to include EE in your life.

To Regina Byrd, Jennifer Fisher, Colette Savage—my dearest friends. Thank you for being there for me, each of you in your own way, while I try to shake up some minds instead of martinis. Know that although I have not been able to hang out with you guys, I live on the memories of our crazy times and hold on to our pure and perfect friendship.

To my new and growing EE family, I thank you for helping me find my purpose and for infusing your dreams into mine. Never for personal gain, your love, encouragement, assistance, and charity are pure and unconditional, and somehow you made me believe that I deserved that. I know I ask a lot of you, and though I hate needing you so much, I love depending on you . . .

- Don Goens, owner of FSH Communications, I thank God for sending you to us on our darkest day. You believed in us, in EE, when we couldn't. I love you for rescuing EE . . . really, for rescuing me and helping me stay true, focused, and motivated. Your generosity will never be forgotten.
- Michelle Flowers, owner of Flowers Communications Group, thank you for supporting a concept; a possibility; a delicate, daring, and,

for some, dangerous dream. I will always cherish you for not letting any of that stand in the way of our friendship and collaboration.

- Ted Gregory, you will never take the credit for bringing much-needed media attention to EE. You fought for us when so many wouldn't dare. Thank you for helping me present our story and our message—first in the media and then in this book. I love you, my Vanilla Fog, my soul brother from a White mother, for seeing beyond the racial BS, past the artificial, superficial barriers society throws our way, and straight through to my heart and my dream for a fairer America. Thank you for *seeing* me.

- To Steven Rogers, the proudest, boldest, most brilliant Black businessman in America, I say thank you for believing in this experiment from the very beginning and staking your reputation, career, and networks on it. Thank you, Professor, for being who you are and just by doing that, defying and denouncing all the horrible things "they" say and do to us. Thank you, my dear friend forever, for being "free."

- Dr. Dyson, my hero, my philosophical, ideological, spiritual, and lyrical twin . . . we did it, baby! You know we could not have made it out of the gate without you. Thank you for lending us your name, for the pep talks, for showing me my gifts and how to use them. Thank you, you intellectual warrior you, for inspiring me to write it out, not fight it out.

- Dr. Freddy Haynes, thank you for sharing your precious, powerful pulpit with me, for teaching me how to preach with passion and reason, and for showing me that my soul is just as important as my smarts. From the diagnosis to the death, you prayed Mima up and taught me how to convert my pain into power. I'm still trying to be you, Freddy—big ballin', shot callin', but never fallin' . . . for the hype.

- George Fraser, believe it or not, there are no words to describe how grateful I am for you and FraserNet. You found us during a tough time along our journey, and you lifted us up, carried us out, and nursed us through the hate, the apathy, the frustration, the ignorance, and the confusion. Thank you for showing me that the path will definitely be as prosperous as it is now painful. Looking forward to our Victory Party, my bad, brilliant brother.

- Brother Norm Bond! Or should I say, the Honorable Chairman of the National Alliance of Market Developers? You showed me that we all get what we deserve. Thank you for putting up with me. Thanks so much for all the advice, listening to my rants, keeping me close even when I pulled away, and for teaching me that everyone cannot make it to the Promised Land.

- Uncle Jim Clingman, professor, author, activist, loyal friend. You were my confidant, my teacher, and my truth compass. Thank you for showing me that being righteous is more important than being right. If—no—when we see the victory, it won't matter if you are not right there by my side.

- My dear Dr. Juliet Walker, there is no one who knows my heart and truly understands why I do this like you do. Thank you for representing the sisters like us—smart, sophisticated, strong, soulful, and not shutting up for no-damn-body! We both know that God brought us together to continue what Mima started. I adore you, cherish you, and wait for the chance to redeem all the limitless love.

- To Randy Fling, COO of Steed Media and *Rolling Out* magazine, the official media partner for EE's national tour, I offer my infinite gratitude, forever friendship, and heartfelt love for never asking me why, just when, where, and how much. Thank you for taking my mind away from how janky, broke-down, and bootleg it all is sometimes as well as showing me how glorious and victorious it will be.

- Karriem. Thank you for everything, every little and big thing you did and gave, and for doing, fighting, and giving out of love. Don't give up. We are one. I will always be here for you, my Knight in Shining EE Armor.

- My mentor and dear friend, Kevin Ross, you taught me how to be a leader, to believe in myself, to surround myself with quality people, and how to listen. You gave me my first break, my first chance to rumble with the big boys. Thank you for your love, friendship, and for preparing me for this journey. And thank you for joining the team and offering your wisdom, leadership, spirit of excellence, and judicious insights into this project.

I have been blessed to have the support of several other business and community leaders whom I've grown very accustomed to leaning on. My new friends, I promise you this: You will never feel like you wasted your time on me. I will give you my all and all I have is yours. I love you so very deeply and fully for living up to your duty as members of the Talented Tenth. Thank you for standing up for the rest . . .

Emmett Vaughn, director, Diverse Business Empowerment, Exelon Corporation, and 2008 recipient of the Lifetime Achievement Award for Contribution to Minority Economic Development by the US Department of Commerce; Jackie Mayfield, CEO and founder, Compro Tax; Peggy Morris, Lakei Forest Cosby, and every member of Sisters for Sisters Network, Inc.; Meagan and Darrius Peace, owners of Hayah Cosmetics and founders of the Magic City Black Expo; Tony Billinger, director of supplier diversity, Office Max; Michael Blake, White House liaison to the African American community and minority business; Vicky Hsi, supplier diversity lead, Kraft Foods; Carla Hunter Ramsey, director of supplier diversity, National Grid; Kenny Loyd, president and owner, South Coast Paper; Ron Busby, CEO and founder, US Black Chamber of Commerce; Don Bowen, chief program officer, National Urban League; Terry Clark, vice president, Entrepreneurship and Business Development, National Urban League; Paul and Sheena Jones, owners of JTE Spirits and founders of the Association of Black Alcoholic Beverage Companies; Marlon Hill, partner, Delancy Hill law firm; Marva Allen, CEO of Hue Man Bookstore and CEO of the Power of One (Harlem's "buy local" program); Dr. Pamela Jolly, CEO of Torch Enterprises; Regina Dyson, creator of Heritage Hues interiors and paints; Selena Cuffe, owner of Heritage Link Brands; Mike Hill, CEO and founder, the Atlanta Metro Black Chamber of Commerce; Devin Robinson, associate professor of economics, Oglethorpe University, author of *Rebuilding the Black Infrastructure*, and leader of the movement to reclaim the Black hair care industry; Mike Armstrong, SVP and GM, BET International; Lori Hall

Armstrong, chief activation officer, Verbify Consulting Firm; Michael Bowlds, CEO and founder, Mountaintop Marketing; Chuck Debow, director, National Black Chamber of Commerce; Andre Hughes, partner, Accenture, and CEO of Powered by Action; Ron Childs, vice president, Flowers Communications Group; Dr. Georgianne Thomas and Alvelyn Sanders, owners of Georgianne's Skin Treats; Dr. Moe Anderson, DDS, CEO and founder, Austin Black Newcomers Association; Pastor Otis Moss, senior pastor, Trinity United Church of Christ; Ed Swailes, president, The Syndicate; Derryl Reed, owner, Smokin' Joe Sauces; Chike Akua, CEO, Imani Enterprises, and author of *A Treasure Within: Stories of Remembrance and Rediscovery*; Tracye Dee Hinton, former owner, WineStyles South Loop; Nicole Jones, former owner, Sensual Steps Shoe Salon and now CEO, To The Nines; Grammy winner Kandi Burruss, owner, TAGS Boutique; Peaches Chin, co-owner, TAGS Boutique; Robin Douglass, CEO and founder, African American Chamber of Commerce of Westchester and Rockland Counties; Nickey Jefferson, professor of economics, Tuskegee University; the DeBriano family, founders, Tag Team Marketing and the Black Business Network; Mike Norman, CEO and founder, SoChange; Kenny Johnson, CEO and founder, The Richmond Group; Ian Robinson, director of marketing, Fort Washington River Tours; Farrah Gray, owner, Farrah Gray Publishing and author of *Reallionaire*; Michelle Goldsborough, CEO and founder, Parents Empowerment Group; Tionne "T-Boz" Watkins, member of world-famous girl group TLC; Mell and Angie Monroe, proprietors, Welcome Inn Manor; Yvette Moyo, founder, Real Men Cook and Real Men Cook Charities; Donna Bellinger, president, Chicago chapter of the National Alliance of Market Developers; Jonathan Swain, owner, Kimbark Liquors; Fred Zeno, owner, Compro Tax Central; Ken Smykle, CEO and founder, *Target Market News*; and Nicole and Andre Dandridge, owners, the Dandridge law firm.

Each and every one of you has a precious place in my heart and I look forward to working with you in furthering this movement.

I am indebted to all those organizations, universities, business owners, and community groups that invited me to speak, honored my family, hosted a fund-raiser, or otherwise enabled me to share EE in the community. You are the backbone of this new and important movement. Thank you for linking arms with us.

I cannot thank enough the team of researchers at the Kellogg Graduate School of Management. You all did a phenomenal job on the study. Trust me: That's a major compliment coming from an alum of the University of Chicago Booth Graduate School of Business. Sometimes people forget that EE was always about the study, the experiment, the knowledge, and the science, and that we were just the test subjects, the guinea pigs. Thane Gautier, Dwetri Addy, Ajamu Baker, Arielle Deane, Stephanie Dorsey, and Susan Edwards, I thank you for keeping EE pure and true. While here I want to express gratitude for Deborah Johnson Hall, owner of JAM Research, who worked on capturing the empowerment experiments of other families across the country. And I cannot forget Marrion Johnson and Aisha Kazeem of Northwestern University for volunteering your time and sharing your brilliant young minds with EE. You all represent the academic foundation of EE, and I look forward to your help measuring, monitoring, and tracking the progress of EE en masse.

I want to thank and send a huge hug to my entire book team. Sometimes I think getting this book done was tougher than conducting the experiment, so I am very fortunate and happy that I had such a talented, committed, professional, and caring team to help me through. Your respect, compassion, hard work, true understanding of, and genuine interest in this endeavor mean so much to me. Jessica, Mindy, Kirby, Julie, Susan, and Ted again, thank you for asking the tough questions, challenging me, exercising my brain, testing my talents, and really bringing out the best in me. I feel good putting our baby in your gifted hands.

I want to give a quick shout out to the mainstream media that covered EE. You didn't have to and may not have wanted to, but you made this happen, and you did it in a balanced, objective, open-minded way. Thank you for enabling the discussion we dreamed of and for presenting EE to the world.

To all those truth seekers and truth speakers in the Black media who reported on EE, I thank you for telling our story and keeping it alive even after the experiment. Thank you for converting our li'l project into a major movement. Maybe the revolution *should* be televised.

I am so very grateful for every one of you who took the time to visit our website, send an e-mail, read the newsletter, forward info about EE to your friends, join our Facebook Fan Group "Fans of The Empowerment Experiment," become a member of the EE nation by registering on the website at www.EEforTomorrow.com, donate to the EE Foundation, come out to our events, or to hear me speak. They may seem like little things to you, but they mean everything to me and my family. You are our fuel. EE is nothing without you. It's not about the Andersons anymore—it's about all of us. Thank you, and please stay involved and excited.

And finally, to all my soldiers and scholars, my fighters and dreamers, whether I know you or not, who are out there struggling for a better life for our kids, a better legacy for our community, and a better America for us all, I send strength, love, faith, and a fist in the air. I know you are giving your lives to this for the same reason I do . . . and that's because you know we can do more and we deserve more. We had it before and we will bring it all back. Y'all know what I mean.

From Ted Gregory:

Abiding gratitude to the Caramel Hurricane for her courage, integrity, passion, and grace; to Kirby Kim for his thoughtful initiative; to Mindy Werner and Lindsay Jones for their keen vision; to Jessica Campbell and all the folks at PublicAffairs for their important work; to my mom for her heart; to the kids for tolerating Distracted Dad Syndrome; and to Terri, my true love.

Appendix 1

Over the course of our adventure John and I discovered an enormous amount of illuminating information as well as numerous organizations that are working on issues related to Black economic empowerment. Here are some of the highlights.

Books

Behind the Dream: The Making of the Speech that Transformed a Nation, by Clarence B. Jones and Stuart Connelly (2011, Palgrave Macmillan)

Blackonomic$: The Way to Psychological and Economic Freedom for African Americans, by James Clingman (2000, Milligan Books)

Desegregating the Dollar: African American Consumerism in the Twentieth Century, by Robert E. Weems Jr. (1998, New York University Press)

Encyclopedia of African American Business, edited by Jessie Carney Smith (2006, Greenwood Press)

Encyclopedia of African American Business History, edited by Juliet E. K. Walker (1999, Greenwood Press)

The History of Black Business in America: Capitalism, Race, Entrepreneurship, by Juliet E. K. Walker (1998, Macmillan Library Reference USA; 2003, revised, St. Martin's Press)

The New Urban Renewal: The Economic Transformation of Harlem and Bronzeville, by Derek S. Hyra (2008, University of Chicago Press)

Race and Entrepreneurial Success: Black-, Asian-, and White-Owned Businesses in the United States, by Robert W. Fairlie and Alicia M. Robb (2010, The MIT Press)

Success Runs in Our Race: The Complete Guide to Effective Networking in the African-American Community, by George Fraser (1996, Quill)

Talking Dollars and Making Sense: A Wealth Building Guide for African-Americans, by Brooke Stephens (1997, McGraw-Hill)

Academic Institutions

Columbia University's Center on African American Politics and Society (http://iserp.co lumbia.edu/research-initiatives/centers/center-african-american-politics-and-society)

Morehouse College Entrepreneurship Center (http://www.morehouse.edu/centers
/entrepreneurship/index.html)

North Carolina A & T State University Center for Entrepreneurship and E-Business
(http://www.ncat.edu/~iceeb/)

Temple University's Center for African American Research and Public Policy
(http://www.temple.edu/caarpp/index.htm)

Tuskegee University's Cooperative Extension Program (http://www.tuskegee.edu
/about_us/outreach/cooperative_extension.aspx)

University of Texas's Center for Black Business History, Entrepreneurship and Technology (http://www.utexas.edu/research/centerblackbusiness/about_center.htm)

Ford Motor Company is partnering with Babson College, the leading academic institu-
tion for entrepreneurship, and a number of other historic Black colleges and universities
(HBCUs) to create programs for Black entrepreneurship. Known as the HBCU Entre-
preneurship Consortium, these institutions include Clark Atlanta University (Atlanta,
Georgia), Grambling State University (Grambling, Louisiana), Jackson State University
(Jackson, Mississippi), Morehouse College (Atlanta, Georgia), North Carolina A&T
(Greensboro, North Carolina), and Southern University (Baton Rouge, Louisiana).

Organizations

100 Black Men of America, Inc. (http://www.100blackmen.org/home.aspx)

Black Business Network (http://www.blackbusinessnetwork.com/)

Black Shopping Channel (http://www.blackshoppingchannel.com/)

FraserNet (http://www.frasernet.com/)

Houston Citizens Chamber of Commerce Economic Empowerment Initiative (http://
www.hccoc.org/index.html)

iZania (http://www.izania.com/)

Joint Center for Political and Economic Studies (http://www.jointcenter.org/about)

National Alliance of Market Developers (http://www.namdntl.org/)

National Association of Investment Companies (http://www.naicvc.com/)

National Black Chamber of Commerce (http://www.nationalbcc.org/)

National Black MBA Association (http://www.nbmbaa.org/home.aspx?PageID=637&)

National Council of Negro Women (http://www.ncnw.org/about/index.htm)

National Minority Supplier Development Council (http://www.nmsdc.org/nmsdc/)

National Urban League (http://www.nul.org/)

Powered by Action (http://www.poweredbyaction.org/)

Rainbow PUSH Coalition (http://www.rainbowpush.org/)

Recycling Black Dollars (www.rbdmedia.net)

United States Black Chamber of Commerce (http://usbci.org/)

Directories of Black-Owned Businesses

The Empowerment Experiment Foundation is in the process of building a national interactive directory of quality Black businesses to help facilitate our goal of proving the power of self-help economics. Stay tuned for that. Meanwhile, here are some other resources.

http://www.blackbusinesslist.com/
http://blackdoctor.org/ (doctors)
http://www.blackexperts.com/ (various professionals, experts, speakers)
http://www.blacknla.com/business.asp (Los Angeles area)
http://www.blackownednewyork.com/ (New York area)
http://blackpages.com/
http://www.bmoreblack.com/ (Baltimore area)
http://www.bmoreblack.com/ (Pittsburgh area)
http://www.gpsblack.com/
http://www.kcsoul.com/business-directory/ (Kansas City area)
http://www.myblacknetworks.com/
http://www.nabhood.net/ (hotels)
http://www.nareb.com/ (real estate agents)
http://reverse90.com/ (Philadelphia area)
http://shushmedeals.com/ (for women)
http://www.supportblackowned.org/
http://www.theblackbusinessdirectory.com/ (Philadelphia area)

Maggie's Tips for Buying Black the EE Way

1. *Begin with the "low hanging fruit."* Make it easy on yourself: Jump-start your new lifestyle by altering your spending habits on what is most convenient. Subscribe to a Black newspaper or magazine, support Black designers at the department stores, buy Black-made products at mass retailers and grocery stores, open an account at a Black-owned bank, buy gift cards at a Black-owned McDonald's or Burger King.
2. *Take baby steps.* Do this so you won't give up if your first attempt to "buy Black" does not go as planned. Start with some product, place, or person you know. That first good experience will be the impetus to start living differently. You cannot fly into flying.
3. *Use a Black company for a service you need on a regular basis.* Once you find a Black dry cleaner, mechanic, or bank, become a repeat customer. Now $1,200 is going to a Black business this year, just from making a simple switch. Have a portion or all of your paycheck deposited directly into a Black bank or credit

union. They're FDIC insured too! Now your money is helping to grow a Black investment or community bank.

4. *It's not a test—it's a relationship.* As with every major brand or company you support, from Wal-mart to your optometrist, there will be good and bad experiences with your new Black companies. Don't make those entrepreneurs overcome hurdles and maintain standards you do not impose on the big companies. Don't treat them with suspicion, expecting them to fail you. It's your new Black dry cleaner, a role model for your community that you choose to support because he helps sustain the neighborhood economically and is inclined to employ Black people. If the service or product costs a little more, pay it. Consider it an investment in the growth of a Black company. It speaks to your commitment and willingness to sacrifice.

5. *Buying Black at the mass retailers.* We have to support the Black manufacturers and distributors whose products are already in the stores. The mass retailers all have websites and 800 numbers. They also have diversity or supplier diversity executives. Ask them to stock Black-made products and to use Black vendors. We all have to do this. What if one such executive got twenty calls in one day?

6. *Shop online.* On websites like www.blackbusinessnetwork.com, www.izania.com, and www.blackshoppingchannel.com, you can find a wide range of goods and services. You will not find everything, but my guess is you will find something you assumed you could not. My detergent, NuWash, is better than Tide, but it's not in Publix or Kmart—yet. I found it at www.BlackBusinessNetwork.com. Compro Tax (www.Comprotax.net) does not have thousands of outlets like Jackson Hewitt and H & R Block, but the products and reward you get from supporting it are beyond compare. More resources can be found on our website, www.EEforTomorrow.com.

7. *Buy in bulk.* When you go to the one Black-owned dollar store in your city, buy five containers of lotion, ten bars of soap, three containers of dishwashing liquid, five boxes of pasta, and three bottles of veggie oil!

8. *Consult your local Black Chamber of Commerce and Urban League.* They know the best-quality local entrepreneurs, and they want to hear from you. (Go to http://usbci.org/, http://www.nationalbcc.org/, and http://www.nul.org/.) If they don't have the answer to your question, they know how to find it.

9. *Buy or Die.* When you buy Black, you are not just buying bananas, shoes, coffee, or a laptop; rather, you are making an investment in our collective well-being. So buy Black as if our future depends on it—because it does.

10. *Black businesses are not charities.* Do not think you are doing someone a favor by buying Black. Yes, it is our duty. But when you start thinking that this is an *extra* thing you *gotta* do, it transforms what should be a natural and voluntary act into a burden, which ultimately has an impact on your spending habits.

11. *Black is better.* You have to work from the paradigm that our businesses, entrepreneurs, goods, and services are the best. And they are the key to your community's future. That truth is priceless and better than anything else.

12. *Share your great finds with The Empowerment Experiment.* We are out there preaching about how Black businesses and professionals are the best in the world. We need to back that up. If you own a business, register it on the EE website (www.EEforTomorrow.com). If you find a great Black business, let us know so we can spread the word. Every time you do you make it easier for the next family or business to buy Black, and it improves the strength and credibility of our movement.

13. *Save your receipts.* Get a big envelope and put your receipt in it every time you make a purchase. Soon this action will become second nature. And when you look at these little pieces of paper at the end of the week or month, you will smile, recommit to this effort, and think about the future you're creating.

14. *Join with us.* We get asked all the time, "Have you been able to inspire others?" The movement will die if it's just the Andersons. From the start we envisioned a national campaign in which Americans would pledge to support Black businesses and the mainstream corporations that do business with Black businesses via substantive supplier, vendor, and franchisee diversity, and The Empowerment Experiment would facilitate and monitor the fulfillment of the pledges. We are building partnerships with several historic, activist, and professional organizations like Frasernet, civic groups, corporations, and academic institutions to do this. The money you spend is your EET (EE Total). This is what the EE Campaign—which we're calling the "What If?" Campaign—is all about. The cumulative spending will be tracked in real time and showcased on our website. So please make your purchases and investments really count by keeping track of your spending and passing that information along to us at www.EEforTomorrow.com.

The EE Foundation needs your support. Please send your donation to:

The Empowerment Experiment Foundation, Inc.
PO Box 464
Berwyn, IL 60402

Appendix 2

The Empowerment Experiment

The Findings and Potential Impact on Black-Owned Businesses

Dwetri Addy KSM '10,
Ajamu Baker KSM '11,
Arielle Deane KSM '11,
Stephanie Dorsey KSM '11,
Susan Edwards KSM '10

3/19/2010

This paper was completed by Kellogg students as an independent study project under the supervision of Steven Rogers, a Kellogg professor and director of the Levy Institute for Entrepreneurial Practice. Professor Rogers was an economic sponsor of The Empowerment Experiment and an advisor to John and Maggie Anderson as they complete this project.

Table of Contents

BACKGROUND

The Empowerment Experiment

The Empowerment Experiment (EE) is a creation of John and Maggie Anderson in which they, along with their two children, publicly committed to purchase solely from Black-owned businesses for one year beginning in 2009. The Andersons maintained a detailed account of the project by documenting the search for products and services, a log of purchases or investments made, and records of quality and pricing relative to a "typical" expenditure. The Empowerment Experiment researchers have used the data from the Andersons' reports and other supplementary sources to track the impact the study could have on black businesses if replicated in the United States.

The Andersons

John C. Anderson is cofounder and president of The Empowerment Experiment. John is currently president of In Sight Financial Management, a financial services firm that provides wealth protection strategies, asset management, and financial and estate planning to individuals and businesses. Prior to this role, John was a manager with Cap Gemini and Ernst & Young, and a finance director with Ameritech. John holds an AB in economics from Harvard University and an MBA from Northwestern University's Kellogg Graduate School of Management.

    Maggie Anderson is CEO and cofounder of The Empowerment Experiment. Maggie is an accomplished strategy professional with twelve years of legal, research, communications, and business strategy experience with a JD and an MBA from the University of Chicago.

    John and Maggie Anderson live in Oak Park, IL, with their two daughters.

ANALYSIS OF THE RESULTS

Businesses and Sectors

Over the course of 2009, the Andersons made 513 purchases and spent approximately $48,943. These purchases spanned approximately 23 sectors as described in Exhibit 1.[1] Child care, automotive, restaurants, and food merchandise expenses accounted for over 74% of the dollars spent with Black businesses or on Black products, which totals $36,373.71. While the Andersons were able to spend approximately 68% of their after-tax income with Black businesses, there were numerous products and industries that the Andersons were unable to find. As described in Exhibit 2, the luxury and higher-end clothing merchandise, food retail such as grocery stores (after the only Black-owned grocery store closed), and general home merchandise were some of the products the Andersons were unable to find in the Chicago metropolitan area. The Andersons often relied on Black-owned dollar stores to purchase products they would traditionally purchase at specialty retail stores.

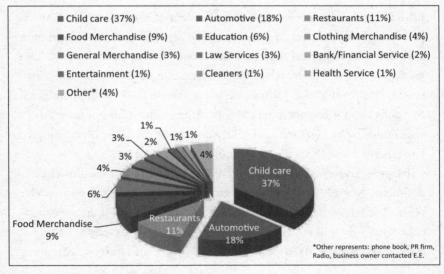

EXHIBIT 1 **Industry Sectors Represented**

---

[1]See Appendix 1 for full list.

Limited Available Products/Services	Sector
Sports magazine	Entertainment
Car seats	Automotive
Appliances	Appliances
Bath rugs	General Merchandise
Bed sheets	General Merchandise
Children pajamas	Clothing Merchandise
Children robes	Clothing Merchandise
Women undergarments	Clothing Merchandise
Women robes	Clothing Merchandise
Basketball shoes	Clothing Merchandise
Dietary vitamins (special)	General Merchandise
Depilatory	General Merchandise
Luxury housewares	General Merchandise
Treadmill	Fitness
Cellular phone service	Phone Service
Property Insurance	Property and Casualty Insurance
Utilities	Utilities
Brand-name cleaning products	General Merchandise
Hair clippers	General Merchandise
Men suits	Clothing Merchandise
Lawn treatment service	Property Maintenance Service
High end restaurants	Restaurants

EXHIBIT 2 Sector Gaps in The Empowerment Experiment

Quality and Service

The Andersons logged quality and service ratings for each of the businesses they patronized. The ratings were coded on a scale from 1 to 6, with the following qualitative ratings attributed: 1–Fair/Below Average; 2–Average/Satisfactory; 3–Good; 4–Great; 5–Excellent; 6–Outstanding. The top five sectors with consistently high quality and service were: Health Service, Appliance Repair Service, Security, Leisure/Hair/Spa, and Shipping Service (Exhibit 3). These services on average ranked 5.6 out of 6. In contrast, the sectors with the lowest ratings for both quality and service were Banking/Financial, Dry Cleaning, Real Estate, and Transportation (Exhibit 4). In aggregate, 45% of the industries represented scored a 5 or above. Other sectors, such as Restaurants, were widely utilized, but represented only average ratings for both quality and service.

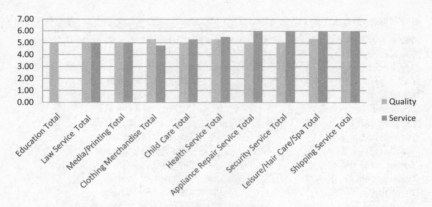

EXHIBIT 3 Highest Quality and Service Ratings by Sector

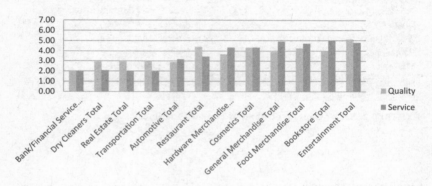

EXHIBIT 4 Lowest Quality and Service Ratings by Sector

Marketing and Sources

Finding Black-owned businesses that could meet the Andersons' product and service needs was a challenge. The main channels utilized were web research, personal referrals, and organizational referrals (Exhibit 5). These three channels accounted for a purchase total of $37,530.62 (~77% of the purchases). Black-owned business web directories FindmeChicago.com and Blackpages.com were significant web research sources for the Andersons, while the Chicago Urban League was the dominant source for organizational referrals.

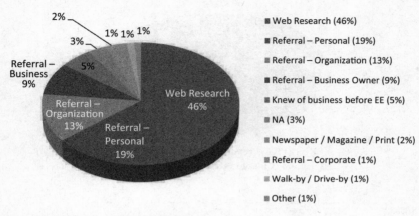

Web Research (46%)

Referral – Personal (19%)

Referral – Organization (13%)

Referral – Business Owner (9%)

Knew of business before EE (5%)

NA (3%)

Newspaper / Magazine / Print (2%)

Referral – Corporate (1%)

Walk-by / Drive-by (1%)

Other (1%)

EXHIBIT 5 Sources as % of Dollars Spent

Geography

Assumptions

Over the course of the experiment, the Andersons' purchases were made primarily but not exclusively in the Chicago metropolitan area. In this paper, we focused on purchases made from Black-owned businesses within the Chicago metropolitan area. Additionally, products that were manufactured by Black-owned firms but not purchased in Black-owned establishments were not included (example: Sean John shirt purchased at Carson Pirie Scott).

Analysis

The majority of Black-owned businesses from which the Andersons purchased were located in the city of Chicago versus its surrounding suburbs (Exhibit 6). The majority of the businesses (73%) were located in the city and 27% in the suburbs. Also, a large portion of the purchases were from businesses located on the city's South Side and Chicago's western suburbs (Exhibit 7). This observation is consistent with the fact that the Andersons live in a western Chicago suburb (Exhibit 7).

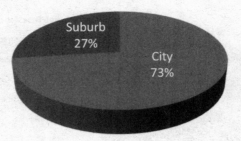

EXHIBIT 6 Proportion of Businesses by Location (Chicago vs. Suburbs)

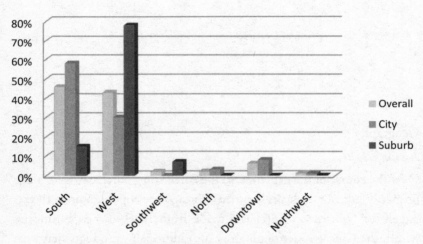

EXHIBIT 7 Number of Black-Owned Businesses per Region

In terms of the frequency of purchases, the purchases were more likely to be made in the city rather than the suburbs (see Exhibit 8), however the total dollars spent were significantly higher in the suburbs.

	Area	Quantity		Amount	
EXHIBIT 8 Number of Purchases Made at Black-Owned Businesses and Dollars Spent (Chicago vs. Suburbs)	City	288	57%	$ 13,391.99	32.6%
	Suburb	213	43%	$ 27,673.32	67.4%
	Total	501	100%	$ 41,065.31	100.0%

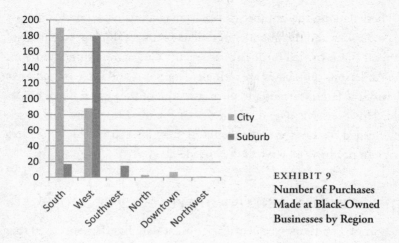

EXHIBIT 9
Number of Purchases
Made at Black-Owned
Businesses by Region

Following the city vs. suburbs analysis was an exploration of purchase locations within Chicago (i.e. north, south, west, downtown, northwest, and southwest). Per Exhibit 9, the majority of purchases made in the city were made in communities on the South and West sides of the city (65% and 31%), which are predominantly African American.

In contrast to number of purchases, Exhibit 10 shows that the highest amount of dollars spent was on the city's South Side rather than the West Side ($9,199.78 versus $3,651). For purchases made in the suburbs, the highest quantity of dollars spent was in the western suburbs ($21,725).

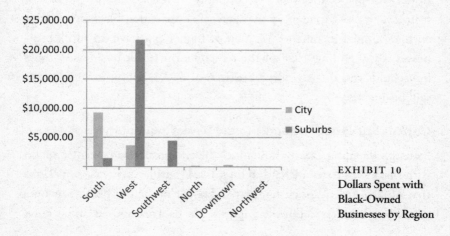

EXHIBIT 10
Dollars Spent with
Black-Owned
Businesses by Region

These data on the number of Black-owned businesses patronized by the Andersons and the quantity of dollars spent are not representative of the total Black-owned businesses across the Chicago metropolitan area. The Andersons' purchases are a single data point and are representative solely of the family's needs and purchases, not of the typical Black household. However, this data does show that for the Andersons' purchases, they needed to travel extensively across the Chicago metropolitan area to obtain products or services they needed.

THE POTENTIAL BENEFITS OF SELF-HELP ECONOMICS

Analysis of The Empowerment Experiment data has demonstrated that in a metropolitan area, namely Chicago, Black families have the power to impact Black businesses by purposefully spending their disposable income. It is important to note that as a one-family sample, the findings cannot be perfectly statistically generalized to the US population as a whole. However, the experiment provides an illustration of what may be possible.

While the Andersons directed approximately 68% of their after-tax income to Black businesses, this large percentage may not be attainable for many Black families who cannot or will not devote an extraordinary amount of time searching for, traveling to, and repeatedly purchasing from Black-owned businesses. Accordingly, we ran a number of scenarios, from 2% to 68%, to identify the aggregate impact that Black households with an annual income of $75,000 or higher can have on Black businesses. By spending 10% of their income on Black businesses, these households can theoretically transfer over $17.5 billion in revenue for said businesses.

Current Self-Help Economics in the Black Community

Statistics detailing exactly how much Black consumers currently spend with Black businesses are hard to find. Black-business-owners.com claims that African Americans currently spend 6–8% of their disposable income with Black businesses, but the origins of the data are unclear. In his book

	2008	2013
Black Buying Power	$ 913,076,570.00	$ 1,239,492,591.00
5% Remaining in Black Communities	$ 45,653,828.50	$ 61,974,629.55
2% Captured by Black-Owned Businesses	$ 18,261,531.40	$ 24,789,851.82

EXHIBIT 11 Current Dollars Recycled in Black Community (assuming after-tax income percentages)

PowerNomics, Claud Anderson cites: "We spend approximately 95% of our income outside of our communities. Only two percent remains in Black hands inside the Black community."[2] Based on these two sources, we will assume Black consumers recycle between 2% (conservatively) and 5% of their after-tax income within the Black community.

With these assumptions, it is clear that the Black community is forgoing potential benefits of group economics by not spending and/or reinvesting more money within the Black community. The numbers are striking: In 2008, Black buying power was estimated to be approximately $913 billion; in 2013, it is expected to reach $1.2 trillion.[3] Unfortunately, even with liberal estimates, only pennies on the Black dollar are staying within the Black community (Exhibit 11).

This demonstrates that as much as $894 billion are being left on the table. While 100% of those dollars may not enter the Black community, a larger percentage than 2–5% should be feasible.

Expanding The Empowerment Experiment: Quantifying the Impact

The Andersons' expenditures (to both Black and non-Black owned businesses) totaled approximately $135,000 in 2009. Based on that figure, they are in the top 6% of all Black households in terms of disposable

---

[2]Claud Anderson, *Powernomics: The National Plan to Empower Black America* (Bethesda, MD: PowerNomics Corporation of America, 2001), p. 143.

[3]Selig Center for Economic Growth, *The Multicultural Economy* (Terry College of Business, University of Georgia, Athens: Selig Center for Economic Growth, 2008).

	Current (Conservative)	Current (Aggressive)	Potential			
% of After-tax Income Spent with Black Businesses	2%	5%	10%	25%	50%	68%
Dollars into Black Businesses/Community (in millions)	$3,558	$8,895	$17,789	$44,472	$88,946	$120,967

EXHIBIT 12 Financial Impact of Self-Help Economics Based on Black Households with After-Tax Income of $75,000 or More

income.[4] Under the assumption that higher income individuals have more resources to devote to methodically patronizing Black businesses, we found that the aggregate of Black households with at least $75,000 of after-tax income reveals incredible potential for "Black" dollars, even with small increases (Exhibit 12).

While the 68% mark is ambitious, if Black households with substantial disposable income increased their spending from the conservative estimate of 2% ($3.6B) to 10% ($17.8B) with Black businesses, more than $14 billion[5] would be contributed to Black entrepreneurs or owner/operators' revenues. If this logic were simply applied to all income levels, the impact would be substantial (Exhibit 13).

As previously mentioned, the analysis focused on families that are economically similar to the Andersons because they are more likely to have the financial means and overall capacity to divert their resources to Black businesses. Accordingly, in order to scale The Empowerment Experiment,

---

[4]US Census Bureau, 2008.
See complete calculations in Appendix 6.
In the calculations, the percentage spent for Black households with $100,000 or more were calculated based on a ceiling of $100,000, so the potential dollar amount is larger than depicted here.

[5]$14B was calculated based on 2008 Census projections, taking into account income bands and population of Black households with after-tax income of more than $75,000.

	Current (Conservative)	Current (Aggressive)	Potential			
% of After-tax Income Spent with Black Businesses	2%	5%	10%	25%	50%	68%
Dollars into Black Businesses/Community (in millions)	$12,900	$32,250	$64,450	$161,250	$322,500	$438,600

EXHIBIT 13 Financial Impact of Self-Help Economics Based on All Black Households

we suggest that the movement start with higher-income individuals who can attract and patronize a diverse set of businesses in Black communities, followed closely by middle- and lower-income individuals. The added dollars from Black consumers should encourage would-be entrepreneurs to enter the market and capture the value of the Black consumer.

Expanding The Empowerment Experiment: Impact on Black Business Owners

Black Business Owner Realities

One of the challenges Black consumers face is that there simply are not enough Black-owned businesses that would make it convenient for local residents to "buy Black." According to the US Census Bureau, while African Americans comprise 12.8% of the total population (2008 projections), 2002 data demonstrated that only 5.2% of all firms were Black-owned. This is a striking comparison to Asians who, in the same years, comprised 4.5% of the population but owned a proportionate 4.8% of firms.

If Black entrepreneurs saw more viable, sustainable opportunities for launching businesses in the Black community, these numbers could change drastically. Right now, there seems to be a vicious cycle that discourages potential entrepreneurs from realizing the revenue opportunity in Black communities (Exhibit 14).

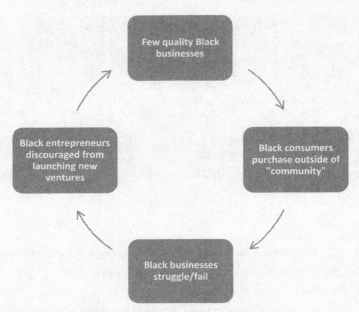

EXHIBIT 14 Vicious Cycle for Black Entrepreneurs

Black Business Owner Potential

Notwithstanding this cycle that Black entrepreneurs face, $14 billion, even as a conservative estimate, is a considerable value that is left on the table. To illustrate the power of the $14B, we calculated the number of Subway franchises that could be opened in Black communities if that revenue was generated for Black businesses. In the realm of entrepreneurship, franchises are often simpler and less risky to launch than a start-up; additionally the costs are known, which provides for a straightforward analysis. While Subway is not intended to represent the need for quality Black-owned businesses in all industries (as discovered by the Andersons), it will serve as a proxy for potential opportunity.[6]

_____

[6]We used Subway because it is one of the easiest and most economical franchises to start. See http://www.subway.com/StudentGuide/facts_figures.htm.

	Franchise Costs	Impact of $14 Billion
Lower bound	81,300	172,201 stores
Upper bound	203,000	68,965 stores

EXHIBIT 15 Potential Impact on Black Business Owners

It costs between $81,300 and $203,000 to start a Subway franchise.[7] Using the upward bound of the Subway cost structure, the added $14 billion is enough to fund the creation of approximately 68,965 new franchises or more than two times the number of existing Subway restaurants all over the world.[8]

Further, each Subway store employs 8 to 13 people. Using the model we have created, the conservative estimate of 68,965 stores can create 551,724 to 896,551 new jobs (Exhibit 15).[9]

This model can be replicated for different franchises, across different industries, and for different business models. This model illustrates that with very small changes in consumption spending, the impact can be potentially far-reaching. Admittedly, Black entrepreneurs will have to make the first move and create quality businesses for Black consumers to patronize *and* find a way to capture the value of the Black consumer, which has yet to be done at scale. Despite this hurdle, it is clear that buying Black can create wealth and jobs for both the Black community and the community at large.

THE POWER OF THE BLACK CONSUMER

As previously discussed, the 2008 buying power of the Black consumer was estimated at $913 billion.[10] To contextualize this impact, this buying

---

[7]Id.

[8]See http://www.subway.com/subwayroot/index.aspx.

[9]Each Subway store employs 2–3 full-time employees and 6–10 part-time employees. See http://www.subway.com/StudentGuide/facts_figures.htm.

[10]Selig Center for Economic Growth. (2008). *The Multicultural Economy.* Terry College of Business, University of Georgia. Athens: Selig Center for Economic Growth.

Ranking	Economy	Millions of International Dollars
1	United States	14,204,322
2	China	7,903,235
3	Japan	4,354,550
4	India	3,388,473
5	Germany	2,925,220
6	Russian Federation	2,288,446
7	United Kingdom	2,176,263
8	France	2,112,426
9	Brazil	1,976,632
10	Italy	1,840,902
11	Mexico	1,541,584
12	Spain	1,456,103
13	Korea, Rep.	1,358,037
14	Canada	1,213,991
15	Turkey	1,028,897
	US Black Population's Buying Power	913,076
16	Indonesia	907,264
17	Iran, Islamic Rep.	839,438
18	Australia	762,559
19	Poland	671,927
20	Netherlands	671,693

EXHIBIT 16 Gross domestic product 2008, PPP

power can be compared to GDP purchase power parity for some major world economies. If the US Black population were considered an economy unto itself, it would rank as having the sixteenth highest GDP compared with other countries.[11]

---

[11]World Bank Statistics, 2008. See http://siteresources.worldbank.org/DATASTATISTICS /Resources/GDP_PPP.pdf.

The estimated Black buying power in 2013, over $1.2 billion, is more than the current GDP of Canada. Given the extraordinary buying power of the US Black consumer, Black businesses should make a concerted effort to understand how to attract and engage Black consumers. This consumer base is growing, young, and eager to purchase consumer products and services.[12] Additionally, this kind of information may be successfully leveraged in making a case for the market potential for new business launches.

CAPTURING THE VALUE OF THE BLACK CONSUMER

Historical data illustrate that capturing the value of Black consumers has been difficult for Black entrepreneurs.[13] Therefore, we would be remiss to ignore this obstacle in encouraging consumers to "buy Black" and Black entrepreneurs to launch more sustainable businesses. There are three key areas on which Black business owners and entrepreneurs can focus in order to capture meaningful value: awareness, accessibility, and absence (gaps in sectors served).

Awareness

Business awareness was a significant hurdle for the Andersons as they specifically searched for Black businesses. It is not a stretch to assume that this would significantly hinder a broader population of Black households from supporting Black businesses. As previously detailed, the Andersons used web research, personal referrals, and organization referrals to identify Black businesses. As illustrated in Exhibit 5, web research is a powerful tool for business owners to reach potential consumers. Businesses should leverage online Black business search engines and ensure that their business websites clearly highlight Black ownership. This will allow them to more easily reach a large Black customer base that is

---

[12]Selig Center for Economic Growth. (2008). *The Multicultural Economy.* Terry College of Business, University of Georgia. Athens: Selig Center for Economic Growth.

[13]See Appendix 7 regarding number of black retail businesses.

increasingly utilizing the web. The combination of a web presence and referrals provides consumers with a method of validating the service and
quality of a business. This is essential for Black businesses to attract and
enable potential customers to feel more confident about supporting them
on a regular basis.

Once awareness has been developed, Black businesses must maintain
high levels of quality and service in order to capture value and maintain
it, which generates positive referrals. With the prevalence of social networking and consumer reliance on word of mouth, there is an incredible
weight put on the quality of each individual experience. One negative
review by a leader in an influential organization or a trusted community
member can be detrimental to the long-term success of a Black business.
In this study, 72 percent of the industries represented scored above average in their overall quality and service ratings, which means that there
are Black businesses that are delivering at a level on par with or better
than some of their nonminority business counterparts. However, building a sustainable Black business may mean reaching levels well above average. Ensuring high levels of quality and service will help break the
vicious cycle with regard to Black business empowerment. High-quality
products and services will help to pave the way for customers to become
supporters and vocal champions of these businesses instead of averters.

Accessibility

A major issue encountered by the Andersons was the accessibility of Black-
owned businesses. Exhibit 17 on the next page shows the locations of the
Black-owned businesses against the location of the Andersons' household.
The Andersons sometimes had to travel at most 52 miles in order to purchase products/services from Black-owned businesses. This travel re-
quirement would be difficult for the average family and signifies the
opportunity entrepreneurs have in terms of serving the needs of minority
communities. If entrepreneurs focused on establishing their businesses in
primarily African American communities, they would receive a higher frequency of purchases and also capitalize on local residents who are unable
or unwilling to travel long distances for their basic consumer needs.

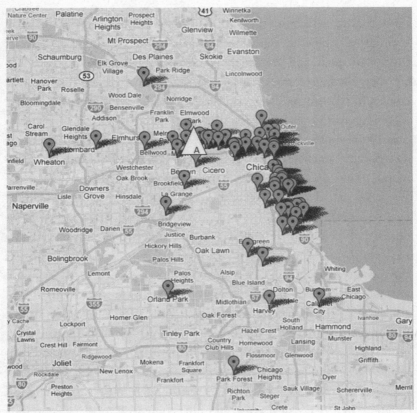

EXHIBIT 17 Map of Andersons' Home and Black-Owned Businesses
Note: Anderson home is denoted by the triangle.

Absence

There were a significant number of gaps in availability of consumer products/services provided by some of the identified Black-owned businesses in the Chicago metropolitan area. As shown in Exhibit 2, product sectors where the Andersons were most noticeably affected were Clothing Merchandise, General Merchandise, and Restaurants. This means that dollars were likely left on the table during this Empowerment Experiment, and this represents a market for businesses to meet. Understanding the target market by utilizing tools such as surveys to assess their product/service needs is critical to identifying these gaps. Doing this enables growing businesses to determine the optimal mix of products/services to serve their target, which ultimately helps maximize the consumer experience, the dollars spent, and the likelihood of repeat business.

Many of the recommendations identified speak to existing business owners in terms of growing and developing their businesses. However, there is a great opportunity for Black entrepreneurs to capitalize on industries where few or no Black businesses currently exist. For example, The Empowerment Experiment illuminated a lack of Black-owned businesses within the Chicago metropolitan area in core industries such as Grocery/Produce, Insurance, and Luxury Retail. Increasing Black business representation in all industries is positive. However, targeting industries where there is severe Black owner underrepresentation provides entrepreneurs a significant value-capture opportunity. Industries where there is already a proliferation of accessible, well-advertised competitors will be harder for entrepreneurs to penetrate than industries in which a major need is going unfulfilled within the Black community. Entrepreneurs need only research the dynamics of their specific community to determine the gaps that need to be addressed and find convenient and unique ways to deliver to customers. Taking advantage of these opportunities will begin to lay the foundation for sustainable and differentiated Black businesses and ultimately lead to Black economic empowerment.

CASE STUDY WITHIN THE EMPOWERMENT EXPERIMENT

In-Depth Absence Analysis: Grocery Stores

The Andersons' Experience

During The Empowerment Experiment, the Andersons struggled to find a Black-owned grocery store. Farmers Best Market, the sole grocery store they found, which was started by Karriem Beyah in 2008, has since closed due to high mortgage costs. Per Karriem, an individual needs "seven figures or more" to establish a grocery retail operation in the Black community.[14] Prior to Farmers Best Market, Chatham Grocery was the only Black-owned grocery store in Chicago serving African American residents for 25 years. However, it was sold to a Lebanese investor despite efforts to find a Black buyer. The country has seen a decline in Black-owned businesses after desegregation; the predominantly African American Garfield Park neighborhood in Chicago has seen a decline in retail stores from 900 businesses in the 1960s to only 89 in 2007.[15] Neighborhoods that were once solely serviced by Black-owned grocery retailers are now food deserts—isolated geographic areas, typically inhabited by minorities, where there is no access to fresh foods.

The History

On a macro level, there was a time when Black-owned grocery stores were plentiful. According to the *Encyclopedia of African-American Business*, 6,339 Blacks were identified as being owner/operators of grocery stores.[16] "In the early 1930s, grocery stores were considered the largest category of Black-owned enterprises."[17] An unfortunate by-product of the civil rights movement and the end of segregation, however, was the dispersion of the Black consumer. "The numbers and strong economic base in [B]lack communities, unified out of necessity during segregation, were diluted into mainstream."[18]

At the beginning of the twenty-first century, there were only 19 Black-owned grocery stores in the United States.[19] This number included the then successful Community Pride grocery stores of Richmond, VA,

---

[14]Mitchell, Chip. "Storm Gathers Over Chicago Retail Property." *Chicago Public Radio* 17 Aug. 2009.

[15]Sarmah, Satta. "Business Matters: Sustaining Growth in Pilsen, Garfield Park." *Medill Reports* 14 Nov. 2007.

[16] Jessie Carney Smith, Millicent Lownes Jackson, Linda T. Wynn, "The Encyclopedia of African-American Business" 353-54, Greenwood Press 2006.

[17] Id. at 354.

[18] Id.

[19] Id. at 354 (quoting James Clingman).

which were ranked number 44 on the Black Enterprise Top 100 Indus-
trial/Service Listing for 2003.[20] In 2004, Community Pride was forced to
close its doors due to problems with its supplier.[21]

The Current Reality

Today, it is extremely difficult to locate Black-owned grocery stores. Our
online search yielded three Black-owned grocery stores; however, we later
learned that the telephone number listed for Food World (Southfield,
MI) was wrong, and the Bravo supermarket in Harlem is actually Hispanic-owned and not Black-owned. The only Black-owned grocery store
that is relatively easily found is Leon's Thriftway in Kansas City, MO.
This store was founded in 1968 by Leon Stapleton. He stated that when
he started Leon's Thriftway there were several Black-owned grocers in
Kansas City, but now he is the only one left.[22]

According to the 2002 Census Economic Report, there are 9,016 Black-
owned food and beverage retail businesses.[23] This number may be misleading, as it includes businesses such as liquor retail stores and specialty
food stores in addition to grocery stores. Even so, when compared to the
total number of food and beverage stores in the United States, 148,901,
Black-owned businesses only represent 6 percent.[24] This is disheartening
considering Blacks comprised 13 percent of the US population in 2002.[25]
This is also interesting given that Black consumers overindex in grocery

[20] Hocker, Cliff, "A $16 Million Win for the Little Guy: Grocery Store Owner Defeats
Major Wholesaler." Black Enterprise, September 2007. http://findarticles.com/p/arti-
cles/mi_m1365/is_2_38/ai_n20511343/.

[21] Community Pride was eventually awarded a $16 M jury verdict against its supplier for
forcing Community Pride into bad deals and failing to appropriately supply Community Pride with sellable merchandise. Id.

[22] Reported by Lisa Benson, "Woman Vows to Only Shop at Black-owned Stores."
2/28/2010. http://www.nbcactionnews.com/news/local/story/Woman-Vows-to-Only-
Shop-at-Black-Owned-Stores/iIPO-DBzu0-0hEA_9SJHwQ.cspx.

[23] "Black-Owned Business Firms: 2002." 2002 *Economic Census* August 2006.

[24] "Food and Beverage Stores: 2002." 2002 *Economic Census* September 2004.

[25] McKinnon, Jesse. "The Black Population in the United States: March 2002." April
2003.

purchases as compared with the rest of the population.[26] These numbers demonstrate why the Andersons had a difficult time finding Black-owned grocery retailers. In order to reflect the percentage of Blacks within the United States, nearly 10,341 additional Black-owned grocery stores need to be opened. This demonstrates a significant opportunity for Black entrepreneurs to capture, as this is a market that is not being served by mainstream retailers such as Safeway. However, capital requirements need to be lessened by assistance from the Small Business Administration to allow Black entrepreneurs to open these retail operations as illuminated by Karriem Beyah's unsuccessful efforts.

Implications

According to a report that discussed the successful creation of Minority Owned Businesses, "viable small businesses capable of expanding their operations and generating jobs commonly possess three traits: (1) involvement of skilled and capable entrepreneurs who have (2) access to financial capital to invest in their business ventures and (3) access to markets for the products of their enterprises."[27] By the expansion of certain Empowerment Experiment principles, with a larger, more geographically diverse sample, Black entrepreneurs may be able to make the case to themselves and investors that they will have access to the right markets and therefore acquire the needed capital.

Health crises within the Black community are often attributed to the lack of fresh food grocery stores in minority communities. For example, "In 2006 [...] only 41% of stores in South L.A. sold fresh produce compared with 71% of stores that sold fresh produce in L.A. County."[28] With

---

[26] Selig Center for Economic Growth. (2008). *The Multicultural Economy.* Terry College of Business, University of Georgia. Athens: Selig Center for Economic Growth.

[27] Timothy Bates. (2006). The Urban Development Potential of Black-Owned Businesses. American Planning Association. Journal of the American Planning Association, 72(2), 227-237. Retrieved March 18, 2010, from ABI/INFORM Global.

[28] Racial and Ethnic Approaches to Community Health (REACH U.S.): Finding Solutions to Health Disparities: At A Glance 2009. http://www.cdc.gov/chronicdisease/resources/publications/AAG/reach.htm

adequate marketing, appropriate pricing, and consumer-convenient lo-cations, this is an opportunity for Black entrepreneurs to not only gen-erate capital, but provide a more far-reaching community benefit.

CONCLUSION

The Empowerment Experiment has laid the foundation for leveraging the economic power of the Black American consumer. Although the breadth and depth of the experiment were limited, it reinforces key issues and opportunities within this large consumer base that have direct im-plications for the growth of Black entrepreneurs and ultimately for "self-help" economics. The research identifies the immense impact that can be implemented if Black consumers make a small change in their cur-rent shopping and purchasing habits and if Black entrepreneurs imple-ment some of the lessons learned from the experiment. Ultimately, successful execution of The Empowerment Experiment on a larger scale, consistently, throughout the nation will create generations of financial stability and wealth in the Black population that have yet to be achieved.

APPENDIX 1 Full List of Industries Represented, Dollars Spent, and % of Total
Dollars Spent

Sectors	Dollars Spent	%
Appliance Repair Service	$465.00	0.95%
Automotive	$8,903.23	18.19%
Bank/Financial Service	$1,100.00	2.25%
Bookstore	$58.74	0.12%
Child Care	$17,857.50	36.49%
Cleaners	$584.75	1.19%
Clothing Merchandise	$1,955.55	4.00%
Cosmetics	$111.94	0.23%
Education	$2,700.00	5.52%
Entertainment	$700.24	1.43%
Food Merchandise	$4,379.47	8.95%
General Merchandise	$1,601.49	3.27%
Hardware Merchandise	$169.51	0.35%
Health Service	$511.49	1.05%
Law Service	$1,250.00	2.55%
Leisure/Hair Care/Spa	$283.25	0.58%
Media/Printing	$91.00	0.19%
Miscellaneous	$300.00	0.61%
Real Estate	$250.00	0.51%
Restaurants	$5,233.51	10.69%
Security Service	$359.00	0.73%
Shipping Service	$13.22	0.03%
Transportation	$65.00	0.13%
Grand Total	**$48,943.89**	

APPENDIX 2 Full List of Industries Not Represented

Limited Available Products/Services	Sector
Sports magazine	Entertainment
Carseats	Automotive
Appliances	Appliances
Bath rugs	General Merchandise
Bedsheets	General Merchandise
Children pajamas	Clothing Merchandise
Children robes	Clothing Merchandise
Women undergarments	Clothing Merchandise
Women robes	Clothing Merchandise
Basketball shoes	Clothing Merchandise
Dietary vitamins (special)	General Merchandise
Depilatory	General Merchandise
Luxury housewares	General Merchandise
Treadmill	Fitness
Cellular phone service	Phone Service
Property Insurance	Property and Casualty Insurance
Utilities	Utilities
Brand-name cleaning products	General Merchandise
Hair clippers	General Merchandise
Men suits	Clothing Merchandise
Lawn treatment service	Property Maintenance Service
High-end restaurants	Restaurants
Groceries	Food Merchandise

APPENDIX 3 Full List of Sources Used to Find Businesses

Finding Business Source	Dollars Spent	%
Business owner reached out to EE	$332.94	0.68%
Knew of business before EE	$2,696.50	5.51%
NA	$1,496.49	3.06%
Newspaper / Magazine / Print	$1,130.79	2.31%
Phonebook / Cold call	$21.63	0.04%
PR firm	$70.42	0.14%
Radio	$130.00	0.27%
Referral – Business Owner	$4,185.46	8.55%
Referral – Corporate	$696.54	1.42%
Referral – Organization	$6,167.32	12.60%
Referral – Personal	$9,087.92	18.57%
Walk-by / Drive-by	$652.50	1.33%
Web research	$22,275.38	45.51%
Grand Total	**$48,943.89**	

APPENDIX 4 Complete Breakout of Rankings by Industry

Rank	Quality Rating	Score
1	Shipping Service Total	6.00
2	Leisure/Hair Care/Spa Total	5.33
3	Clothing Merchandise Total	5.31
4	Health Service Total	5.29
5	Entertainment Total	5.11
6	Appliance Repair Service Total	5.00
7	Child Care Total	5.00
8	Education Total	5.00
9	Law Service Total	5.00
10	Media/Printing Total	5.00
11	Security Service Total	5.00
12	Restaurant Total	4.40
13	Cosmetics Total	4.33
14	Food Merchandise Total	4.26
15	Bookstore Total	4.00
16	General Merchandise Total	3.92
17	Hardware Merchandise Total	3.67
18	Real Estate Total	3.00
19	Transportation Total	3.00
20	Dry Cleaners Total	2.93
21	Automotive Total	2.875
22	Bank/Financial Service Total	2.00

Rank	Service Rating	Score
1	Appliance Repair Service Total	6.00
2	Leisure/Hair Care/Spa Total	6.00
3	Security Service Total	6.00
4	Shipping Service Total	6.00
5	Health Service Total	5.50
6	Child Care Total	5.29
7	Bookstore Total	5.00
8	Law Services Total	5.00
9	Media/Printing Total	5.00
10	General Merchandise Total	4.92
11	Entertainment Total	4.80
12	Clothing Merchandise Total	4.76
13	Food Merchandise Total	4.72
14	Cosmetics Total	4.33
15	Hardware Merchandise Total	4.33
16	Restaurant Total	3.45
17	Automotive Total	3.18
18	Dry Cleaners Total	2.07
19	Bank/Financial Service Total	2.00
20	Education Total	2.00
21	Real Estate Total	2.00
22	Transportation Total	2.00

APPENDIX 5   Black Purchases in 2008 (www.targetmarketnewst.com)

Products/Services	($Billion)	%
Housing and Related Charges	$166.30	33.21%
Education	$71.00	14.18%
Food	$65.30	13.04%
Cars and Trucks – New and Used	$31.50	6.29%
Apparel Products and Services	$26.90	5.37%
Health Care	$23.90	4.77%
Insurance	$19.00	3.79%
Telephone Services	$17.20	3.44%
Household Furnishings and Equipment	$12.90	2.58%
Contributions	$11.00	2.20%
Media	$8.30	1.66%
Personal Care Products and Services	$6.60	1.32%
Travel, Transportation, and Lodging	$6.40	1.28%
Consumer Electronics	$4.50	0.90%
Miscellaneous	$4.40	0.88%
Computers	$3.50	0.70%
Gifts	$3.50	0.70%
Beverages (Nonalcoholic)	$3.10	0.62%
Tobacco Products and Smoking Supplies	$3.10	0.62%
Beverages (Alcoholic)	$2.80	0.56%
Entertainment and Leisure	$2.80	0.56%
Toys, Games, and Pets	$2.40	0.48%
Appliances	$2.20	0.44%
Sports and Recreational Equipment	$1.00	0.20%
Housewares	$0.80	0.17%
Books	$0.30	0.06%
Total	$500.70	

APPENDIX 6 Calculation of Impact Potential of After-tax Spending in the Black Community

Financial Impact of Self-Help Economics Based on Black Households with After-Tax Income of $75,000 or More

After-tax Income	$75,000 to $77,499	$77,500 to $79,999	$80,000 to $82,499	$82,500 to $84,999	$85,000 to $87,499	$87,500 to $89,999	$90,000 to $92,499	$92,500 to $94,999	$95,000 to $97,499	$97,500 to $99,999	$100,000 and over	Total
Number of Black Households	15000	11600	13400	10800	12300	10500	7800	10100	8300	8000	847000	1,929,000
Mean of Income Bracket	$ 76,250	$ 78,750	$ 81,250	$ 83,750	$ 86,250	$ 88,750	$ 91,250	$ 93,750	$ 96,250	$ 98,750	$ 100,000	
Spend in Black Community												
2%	$ 236,373,450	$ 182,698,840	$ 217,748,660	$ 180,898,920	$ 212,173,770	$ 186,373,950	$ 142,949,220	$ 189,373,990	$ 157,849,180	$ 157,999,200	$ 1,694,000,000	$ 3,357,839,180
5%	$ 590,933,625	$ 456,747,100	$ 544,371,650	$ 452,247,300	$ 530,434,425	$ 465,934,875	$ 355,873,050	$ 473,434,975	$ 394,622,950	$ 394,998,000	$ 4,235,000,000	$ 8,894,597,950
10%	$ 1,181,867,250	$ 913,494,200	$ 1,088,743,300	$ 904,494,600	$ 1,060,868,850	$ 931,869,750	$ 711,746,100	$ 946,889,950	$ 789,245,900	$ 789,996,000	$ 8,470,000,000	$ 17,789,195,500
25%	$ 2,954,668,125	$ 2,283,735,500	$ 2,721,858,250	$ 2,261,236,500	$ 2,652,172,125	$ 2,329,674,375	$ 1,779,365,250	$ 2,367,174,875	$ 1,973,114,750	$ 1,974,990,000	$ 21,175,000,000	$ 44,472,989,750
50%	$ 5,909,336,250	$ 4,567,471,000	$ 5,443,716,500	$ 4,522,473,000	$ 5,304,344,250	$ 4,659,348,750	$ 3,558,730,500	$ 4,734,349,750	$ 3,946,229,500	$ 3,949,980,000	$ 42,350,000,000	$ 88,945,979,500
68%	$ 8,036,697,300	$ 6,211,760,560	$ 7,403,454,440	$ 6,150,563,280	$ 7,213,908,180	$ 6,336,714,300	$ 4,839,873,480	$ 6,438,715,660	$ 5,366,872,120	$ 5,371,972,800	$ 57,596,000,000	$ 120,966,532,120

Note: Used after-tax income definition 8; see http://www.census.gov/hhes/www/cpstables/032009/rdcall/1_012.htm.

After-tax income (mean of all Black households)		$ 42,840
Number of Black Households		15,056,000
Spend in Black Community	2%	$ 12,899,980,800
	5%	$ 32,249,952,000
	10%	$ 64,499,904,000
	25%	$ 161,249,760,000
	50%	$ 322,499,520,000
	68%	$ 438,599,347,200

APPENDIX 7 Black-Owned Retail Businesses, 2002

Includes firms with paid employees and firms with no paid employees. The U.S. totals are based on the 2002 Economic Census, whereas the gender, Hispanic or Latino origin, and race estimates are based on the 2002 Survey of Business Owners (see Appendix C for information on survey methodology and sampling error). Detail may not add to total because a Hispanic or Latino firm may be of any race. Moreover, each owner had the option of selecting more than one race and therefore is included in each race selected. Firms with more than one domestic establishment are counted in each industry in which they operate, but only once in the U.S. total. This table is based on the 2002 North American Industry Classification System (NAICS).

2002 NAICS code	Kind of business	All firms[1]		Firms with paid employees				Relative standard error of estimate (percent)[2] for column—					
		Firms (number) A	Sales and receipts ($1,000) B	Firms (number) C	Sales and receipts ($1,000) D	Employees (number) E	Annual payroll ($1,000) F	A	B	C	D	E	F
44-45	**Retail trade**	102 098	13 586 551	8 824	11 550 216	44 618	981 842	1	3	3	3	2	4
441	Motor vehicle and parts dealers	6 332	7 283 839	756	6 959 709	14 297	525 027	2	6	8	6	6	7
442	Furniture and home furnishings stores	1 509	261 835	301	228 135	1 368	30 253	9	14	18	16	16	11
443	Electronics and appliance stores	1 709	206 603	318	166 061	925	17 777	5	22	16	25	18	22
444	Building material and garden equipment and supplies dealers	1 044	190 171	273	169 823	1 157	26 536	5	17	13	19	21	23
445	Food and beverage stores	9 016	1 857 351	2 445	1 381 216	9 695	127 820	5	5	5	6	7	5
446	Health and personal care stores	11 584	566 766	779	448 174	2 570	58 567	6	10	8	12	10	13
447	Gasoline stations	1 080	1 105 606	771	1 063 994	3 412	46 650	8	17	10	18	15	16
448	Clothing and clothing accessories stores	10 166	441 714	839	221 138	3 123	30 096	5	9	12	17	13	15
451	Sporting goods, hobby, book, and music stores	4 677	205 449	378	122 603	1 122	15 933	4	13	12	22	17	17
452	General merchandise stores	S	S	S	S	S	S	S	S	S	S	S	S
453	Miscellaneous store retailers	12 337	498 602	995	263 102	3 123	38 485	3	5	8	5	16	13
454	Nonstore retailers	40 558	749 529	693	345 244	2 542	45 071	3	10	9	19	20	16

Source: Survey of Business Owners, U.S. Census Bureau, 2002 Economic Census.

APPENDIX 8 Black Spending by Category

U.S. Average Annual Spending and Item Share for Black and Non-Black Consumers, 2006

Item	Black Consumers		Non-Black Consumers		Difference in Share of Total (percentage points)
	Average Spending Per Consumer Unit (dollars)	Share of Total (percent)	Average Spending Per Consumer Unit (dollars)	Share of Total (percent)	
TOTAL ANNUAL EXPENDITURES	34,583	100.0	50,287	100.0	0.0
FOOD AT HOME	2,796	8.1	3,503	7.0	1.1
FOOD AWAY FROM HOME	1,735	5.0	2,826	5.6	-0.6
ALCOHOLIC BEVERAGES	210	0.6	537	1.1	-0.5
HOUSING	12,754	36.9	16,859	33.5	3.4
Shelter	7,378	21.3	9,986	19.9	1.5
Utilities, fuels, and public services	3,461	10.0	3,388	6.7	3.3
Natural gas	593	1.7	497	1.0	0.7
Electricity	1,333	3.9	1,257	2.5	1.4
Fuel oil and other fuels	39	0.1	152	0.3	-0.2
Telephone services	1,154	3.3	1,078	2.1	1.2
Water and other public services	342	1.0	405	0.8	0.2
Household operations	545	1.6	1,003	2.0	-0.4
Housekeeping supplies	482	1.4	661	1.3	0.1
Household furnishings and equipment	888	2.6	1,820	3.6	-1.1
Household textiles	87	0.3	163	0.3	-0.1
Furniture	300	0.9	485	1.0	-0.1
Floor coverings	10	0.0	53	0.1	-0.1
Major appliances	119	0.3	258	0.5	-0.2
Small appliances & misc. housewares	52	0.2	117	0.2	-0.1
Miscellaneous household equipment	319	0.9	745	1.5	-0.6
APPAREL & SERVICES	1,762	5.1	1,889	3.8	1.3
Men and boys	385	1.1	452	0.9	0.2
Women and girls	636	1.8	767	1.5	0.3
Children under 2	108	0.3	94	0.2	0.1
Footwear	391	1.1	292	0.6	0.5
Other apparel products and services	241	0.7	285	0.6	0.1
TRANSPORTATION	6,130	17.7	8,832	17.6	0.2
Vehicle purchases (net outlay)	2,362	6.8	3,565	7.1	-0.3
Gasoline and motor oil	1,740	5.0	2,294	4.6	0.5
Other vehicle expenses	1,742	5.0	2,439	4.9	0.2
Public transportation	286	0.8	535	1.1	-0.2
HEALTH CARE	1,497	4.3	2,940	5.8	-1.5
Health insurance	927	2.7	1,538	3.1	-0.4
Medical services	248	0.7	728	1.4	-0.7
Drugs	272	0.8	547	1.1	-0.3
Medical supplies	49	0.1	127	0.3	-0.1
ENTERTAINMENT	1,172	3.4	2,540	5.1	-1.7
Fees and admissions	192	0.6	663	1.3	-0.8
Television, radios, sound equipment	747	2.2	928	1.8	0.3
Pets, toys, and playground equipment	143	0.4	450	0.9	-0.5
Other	91	0.3	500	1.0	-0.7
PERSONAL CARE PRODUCTS & SERVICES	519	1.5	594	1.2	0.3
READING	46	0.1	127	0.3	-0.1
EDUCATION	495	1.4	941	1.9	-0.4
TOBACCO PRODUCTS & SMOKING SUPPLIES	187	0.5	346	0.7	-0.1
MISCELLANEOUS	544	1.6	887	1.8	-0.2
CASH CONTRIBUTIONS	1,384	4.0	1,935	3.8	0.2
PERSONAL INSURANCE & PENSIONS	3,354	9.7	5,531	11.0	-1.3
Life and other personal insurance	245	0.7	333	0.7	0.0
Pensions and Social Security	3,109	9.0	5,198	10.3	-1.3

Source: Shares were calculated by the Selig Center for Economic Growth, based on data obtained from the U.S. Department of Labor, Bureau of Labor Statistics, Consumer Expenditure Survey, 2006.

Notes

Introduction

xii   *it is in African American neighborhoods? Six hours.* . . . Brooke Stephens, *Talking Dollars and Making Sense: A Wealth-Building Guide for African-Americans* (New York: McGraw-Hill, 1997), 18.

xii   *in this country goes to Black-owned businesses.* . . . Michael H. Shuman, "Community Entrepreneurship: To Turn Communities Around, Training Programs Must Teach a Double Bottom Line," National Housing Institute Shelterforce Online, September/October 1999.

xii   *only 7.5 percent of Latinos and 5.1 percent of Blacks.* . . . Robert W. Fairlie and Alicia M. Robb, *Race and Entrepreneurial Success: Black-, Asian-, and White-Owned Businesses in the United States* (Cambridge, MA: MIT Press, 2008).

xii   *Black-owned firms? $74,018.* . . . Ibid.

xii   *which generated 2 percent of the nation's business revenues.* . . . Shuman, "Community Entrepreneurship."

xii   *groceries, footwear, clothing, and shoes than the overall population* . . . Jeffrey M. Humphreys, "The Multicultural Economy 2008," Terry College of Business/Selig Center for Economic Growth, University of Georgia, http://www.terry.uga.edu/selig/docs/buying_power_2008.pdf, 7–8.

xii   *categories of apparel, video game hardware, and PC software.* . . . "African-American/Black Market Profile," Magazine Publishers of America, 2007, http://www.magazine.org/ASSETS/2457647D5D0A45F7B1735B8ABCFA3C26/market_profile_black.pdf, 11.

xvii   *within a year 80 percent of the people diagnosed with the disease.* . . . Hirshberg Foundation for Pancreatic Cancer Research, "Prognosis of Pancreatic Cancer," http://www.pancreatic.org/site/c.htJYJ8MPIwE/b.891917/k.5123/Prognosis_of_Pancreatic_Cancer.htm.

Chapter 1

1   *and some of the highest murder rates in the city.* . . . "Austin," Great Cities Institute Neighborhoods at the University of Illinois at Chicago, http://www.uicni.org/page.php?section=neighborhoods&subsection=austin, 1.

2   *Bulldozers cleared away most of the charred ruins.* . . . Stevenson Swanson, Chicago Tribune, *Chicago Days: 150 Defining Moments in the Life of a Great City* (Chicago: Contemporary Books, 1997), 210–11.

6   *neighborhoods with high need for grocery stores and supermarkets."* . . . "Going to Market: New York City's Neighborhood Grocery Store and Supermarket Shortage," New York City Department of City Planning, http://www.nyc.gov/html/dcp/html/supermarket/index.shtml, 2.

7   *in the* American Journal of Public Health *told a similar story.* . . . Carol R. Horowitz, Kathryn A. Colson, Paul L. Hebert, and Kristie Lancaster, "Barriers to Buying Healthy Foods for People with Diabetes: Evidence of Environmental Disparities," *American Journal of Public Health* 94, no. 9 (September 2004): 1549–54, http://www.ncbi.nlm.nih.gov/pmc/articles/PMC1448492/.

11   *the last couple of decades have exacerbated the problem.* . . . William J. Wilson, *The Declining Significance of Race: Blacks and Changing American Institutions*, 2d ed. (Chicago: University of Chicago Press, 1980).

11   *and they are falling further and further behind."* . . . "The Two Nations of Black America," *Frontline*, 1997, http://www.pbs.org/wgbh/pages/frontline/shows/race/interviews/wilson.html.

16   *Basically, their numbers dwindled.* . . . Jessie Carney Smith, Millicent Lownes Jackson, and Linda T. Wynn, eds., *Encyclopedia of African American Business* (Westport, CT: Greenwood Press, 2006), 353–54.

16   *grocery stores existed in the United States.* . . . Dwetri Addy, Ajamu Baker, Arielle Deane, Stephanie Dorsey, and Susan Edwards, "The Empowerment Experiment: The Findings and Potential Impact on Black-Owned Businesses," March 19, 2010, appendix 2 of this volume, 253.

16   *provide the stores with satisfactory material for sale.* . . . Cliff Hocker, "A $16 Million Win for the Little Guy: Grocery Store Owner Defeats Major Wholesaler," *Black Enterprise*, September 2007, http://www.blackenterprise.com/2007/09/01/a-16-million-win-for-the-little-guy/.

16   *Since 1968, the rest of them have all closed.* . . . Addy et al., "The Empowerment Experiment," 254.

17   *the 148,901 food and beverage stores in the United States.* . . . Ibid.

17   *nearly 10,341 additional Black-owned grocery stores need to be opened."* . . . Ibid., 255.

Chapter 2

24 *world" and had the highest land values in the city.* . . . Harold M. Mayer and Richard C. Wade, *Chicago: Growth of a Metropolis* (Chicago: University of Chicago Press, 1969), 24.

24 *West Side's population quadrupled, from 57,000 to 214,000,* . . . Ibid., 64.

24 the riots that erupted after King's assassination. . . . "East Garfield Park," Encyclopedia of Chicago, http://www.encyclopedia.chicagohistory.org /pages/404.html; "West Garfield Park," Encyclopedia of Chicago, http:// www.encyclopedia.chicagohistory.org/pages/1338.html; "Near West Side," Encyclopedia of Chicago, http://www.encyclopedia.chicagohistory.org/pages /878.html; and "Austin," Encyclopedia of Chicago http://www.encyclopedia .chicagohistory.org/pages/93.html.

Chapter 3

39 *"outsiders" or at businesses outside the community.* . . . "CITIworks 'City of Excellence' Economic Development through Dollar Circulation YOUR CITY & Surrounding Counties," Hudson Strategic Group, Inc., 2004, http://gsaabo.net/CITIworks-Generic.ppt, 4.

40 *the few hours it now remains in a Black neighborhood.* . . . Stephens, *Talking Dollars and Making Sense,* 18.

40 *outside of their own South Side communities."* . . . Natalie Moore, "South Siders Spend Billions Each Year Outside of Their Neighborhoods," WBEZ-FM, September 1, 2009.

40 *all households there was $370 million a year.* . . . Michael Shuman, *Going Local: Creating Self-Reliant Communities in a Global Age* (New York: Free Press, 1998), 106.

40 *is not the absence of money, but its systematic exit."* . . . Ibid., 107.

40 Black Enterprise *published the article in 1983.* . . . Udayan Gupta, "From Other Shores—Recent Wave of Asian, Latin American and Caribbean Immigrants Is Stirring Fears of Displacement in the Black Community," *Black Enterprise* 13, no. 8 (March 1983): 51–56.

42 *from $318 billion in 1990 to $845 billion in 2007.* . . . "African-American/ Black Market Profile," Magazine Publishers of America, 2008, http://www .magazine.org/ASSETS/2457647D5D0A45F7B1735B8ABCFA3C26/market _profile_black.pdf, 6.

42 *jumped by nearly 73 percent to $791 million.* . . . Ibid., 18.

42 *at least $75,000 has increased 47 percent since 2005.* . . . Todd Wasserman, "Report Shows a Shifting African-American Population," *Brandweek,* January 12, 2010, 1.

42 terms as 'mammy,' 'pickaninny,' 'coon,' and 'nigger.'" . . . Robert E. Weems Jr., *Desegregating the Dollar: African-American Consumerism in the Twentieth Century* (New York: New York University Press, 1998), 1.

43 war-related industries and other manufacturing. . . . "Great Migration," Encyclopedia of Chicago, http://www.encyclopedia.chicagohistory.org/pages /545.html.

43 services that African American companies produced. . . . Weems, *Desegregating the Dollar*, 10.

43 to take business away from Black companies. . . . Ibid., 18.

43 Blacks' lingering social and psychological hangups." . . . Ibid., 27.

43 African American pioneers in corporate America." . . . Ibid., 3.

43 "buxom, broad-faced, grinning mammies." . . . Ibid., 33.

43 "darky," and "Pickaninny" in advertising. . . . Ibid.

44 $1.5 billion more than the national income of Canada. . . . Ibid., 34.

44 Dodgers owner Branch Rickey, Professor Weems writes. . . . Ibid., 3.

45 and a degree of glamour for the same dollar." . . . Ibid., 74.

46 in a culture that was angry at its powerlessness. . . . Ibid., 80–90.

46 African Americans spent about $750 million in 1977. . . . Ibid., 93.

46 substance, to place similar warnings on their labels. . . . Ibid., 94–95.

47 insurance carrier meant one was "moving up." . . . Ibid., 95–96.

47 without the corporations returning the favor. . . . Robert E. Weems Jr., "African American Consumerism Since the 1960s: Spending Power or Spending Weakness?" paper presented at annual meeting of Association for the Study of African American Life and History, 2010, 8.

47 was the downright paltry sum of $512,193. . . . Weems, *Desegregating the Dollar*, 112.

47 causes in African American and Hispanic communities. . . . Ibid.

48 Estée Lauder decided to pay attention to it. . . . Grayson Mitchell, "Battle of the Rouge," *Black Enterprise* (August 1978): 23–29.

48 in the United States were Black-owned is shocking. . . . Weems, *Desegregating the Dollar*, 122, 125.

49 phenomenon have been white businessmen." . . . Weems, "African American Consumerism Since the 1960s," 5–6.

50 the power to produce, as well as to consume. . . . Weems, *Desegregating the Dollar*, 131.

Chapter 4

66 racism—however nuanced—they experience. . . . Myra Croasdale, "Racial Fatigue: Minority Doctors Feeling the Pressure," *American Medical News*, July 23–30, 2007, http://www.ama-assn.org/amednews/2007/07/23/prsa0723.htm;

material also obtained from abstract of Marcella Nunez-Smith, Leslie A. Curry, JudyAnn Bigby, David Berg, Harlan M. Krumholz, and Elizabeth H. Bradley, "Impact of Race on the Professional Lives of Physicians of African Descent," *Annals of Internal Medicine* 146, no. 1 (January 2, 2007): 45–51, http://www.annals.org/content/146/1/45.abstract.

66   *This drives Black physicians from the profession.* . . . Nunez-Smith et al., "Impact of Race on the Professional Lives of Physicians of African Descent."

66   *13,000 below the number of Hispanic physicians.* . . . "The Black Physician Workforce," National Medical Association, October 2009, http://www.nmanet.org/index.php?option=com_content&view=article&id=2&Itemid=3.

67   *the current ratio is 73 per 100,000 people.* . . . V. Rao and G. Flores, "Why Aren't There More African-American Physicians? A Qualitative Study and Exploratory Inquiry of African-American Students' Perspective on Careers in Medicine," *Journal of the National Medical Association* 99, no. 9 (September 2007): 986–93, http://www.nmanet.org/images/uploads/Journal/OC986.pdf, 986.

67   *only 4.2 percent of medical school faculties."* . . . "Missing Persons: Minorities in the Health Professions: A Report of the Sullivan Commission on Diversity in the Healthcare Workforce" (Durham, NC: Sullivan Commission, September 2004), 2, http://www.aacn.nche.edu/media/pdf/sullivanreport.pdf.

67   *health care, the quality of which is not improving.* . . . "2009 National Healthcare Disparities Report," US Department of Health and Human Services, http://www.ahrq.gov/qual/nhdr09/nhdr09.pdf, 3, 4, 6, 7.

67   *eighty-three thousand African Americans every year.* . . . David Satcher, "What If We Were Equal," *Health Affairs* (March 2005), http://content.healthaffairs.org/content/24/2/459.full.

Chapter 5

71   *nonsense to do what building we should want."* . . . Quintard Taylor, "Maria W. Stewart Advocates Education for African-American Women," Blackpast.org, http://www.blackpast.org/?q=1832-maria-w-stewart-advocates-education-african-american-women, 1.

72   *Walker, who became Maria's mentor.* . . . Cheryl R. Jorgensen-Earp, "Maria W. Miller Stewart, Lecture Delivered at Franklin Hall," *Voices of Democracy* (September 2006), http://umvod.files.wordpress.com/2010/07/jorgensen-earp-stewart.pdf, 15, 18, 19.

72   *whispers of something more diabolical persisted.* . . . Ibid., 20.

72   *W. E. B. Du Bois later gave broader exposure.* . . . Ibid., 21, 15.

72 *She died in 1879.* . . . Ibid., 34–35.

72 *her 2006 piece for the journal* Voices of Democracy. . . . Ibid., 36.

73 *the Free African Society, founded in 1787 in Philadelphia.* . . . Juliet E. K. Walker, *The History of Black Business in America: Capitalism, Race, Entrepreneurship* (New York: Macmillan Library Reference USA, 1998), 85–86.

73 *that had not been produced from slave labor."* . . . Juliet E. K. Walker, ed., *Encyclopedia of African American Business History* (Westport, CT: Greenwood Press, 1998), 90.

73 *began in the mid-1820s.* . . . Ruth Ketring Nueremberger, "The Free Produce Movement: A Quaker Protest Against Slavery," PhD diss., 1942, Duke University Press (abstract).

73 *cheerfully recommended to her store."* . . . Walker, *The History of Black Business in America*, 149.

73 *kind among the colored people of this city."* . . . Ibid.

74 *racial pride and keep money in Black communities.* . . . Walker, *Encyclopedia of African American Business History*, 180–81.

74 *and means, are all given to the white man."* . . . Ibid., 181.

74 *in response to the lack of capital available to them.* . . . Walker, *The History of Black Business in America*, 151.

74 *conducted by their own race, even at some disadvantage."* . . . Ibid., 183.

74 *to promote African American–owned businesses.* . . . Ibid., 184.

74 *the world is long in any degree ostracized."* . . . Walker, *Encyclopedia of African American Business History*, 589.

74 *called "the Golden Age of Black Business."* . . . Walker, *The History of Black Business in America*, 182.

75 *the most powerful Black organizations in the world.* . . . Walker, *Encyclopedia of African American Business History*, 76.

75 *without inconvenience or inefficiency."* . . . Ibid., 186.

75 *Negro Business Leagues were functioning in thirty states.* . . . Ibid., 590.

75 *"Buy Something From a Negro Merchant!"* . . . Weems, *Desegregating the Dollar*, 17.

75 *promoting National Negro Trade Weeks.* . . . Walker, *Encyclopedia of African American Business History*, 526.

75 *gets vision enough to use its strength."* . . . Weems, *Desegregating the Dollar*, 57.

76 *People's Cooperative supermarket at the Tuskegee Institute.* . . . Walker, *The History of Black Business in America*, 231–32.

76 *hospitals and churches in the late nineteenth century."* . . . Walker, *Encyclopedia of African American Business History*, 451.

76 *forty hospitals, all supported by African Americans.* . . . Ibid.

76 *only nineteen hundred "Negro-owned" businesses;* . . . Ibid., 430.

76 *white-collar jobs, many of which were in Black businesses.* . . . Ibid.

76 *professionals as well as financing and insurance companies.* . . . Ibid., 82.

76 *enterprise," sociologist E. F. Frazier wrote in 1923.* . . . Ibid., 202.

77 *a tradition of industry, reliability, and integrity."* . . . William Kenneth Boyd, *The Story of Durham, City of the New South,* 2d ed. (Durham, NC: Duke University Press, 1927), 278–79.

77 *there were only two airports in the entire state.* . . . Walker, *Encyclopedia of African American Business History,* 81–82.

77 *A gunshot was fired, and a race riot ignited.* . . . 2001 report by the Oklahoma Commission to Study the Tulsa Race Riot of 1921, http://www.okhistory .org/trrc/file1.pdf, iv–v.

77 *an Oklahoma state commission's 2001 report on the riot.* . . . Ibid.

77 *Thousands of occupations were lost."* . . . Walker, *Encyclopedia of African American Business History,* 204.

78 *aggregate retail sales drop was only 13 percent.* . . . Walker, *The History of Black Business in America,* 225–26.

78 *leading them to patronize local, Black-owned businesses.* . . . Weems, *Desegregating the Dollar,* 62.

78 *that led to the demise of the family's business.* . . . Ibid., 63.

78 *There is GREAT POWER in 15 BILLION DOLLARS!"* . . . Ibid., 54 (emphasis original).

79 *movie theaters, workplaces, hotels, and other public services.* . . . Walker, *Encyclopedia of African American Business History,* 262.

79 *businesses that sold primarily to the Black community.* . . . "Operation Breadbasket," Stanford University's Martin Luther King, Jr. Research and Education Institute Encyclopedia, http://www.kinginstitute.info/.

79 *"negotiate a more equitable employment practice."* . . . Ibid.

79 *$25 million a year going to Black neighborhoods.* . . . Ibid.

79 *two thousand jobs, worth about $15 million.* . . . Ibid.

79 *sustained black consumer economic retribution."* . . . Weems, *Desegregating the Dollar,* 69.

80 *in the* Encyclopedia of African American Business History. . . . Walker, *Encyclopedia of African American Business History,* 75.

80 *enough to lift African Americans up economically.* . . . Ibid., 77.

80 *nearly 13 percent of Americans who were Black.* . . . Ibid.

80 *which has sometimes contradicted earlier rulings.* . . . "The Adarand Case: Affirmative Action and Equal Protection," Constitutional Rights Foundation, http://www.crf-usa.org/index2.php?option=com_content&task=view&id =221&pop=1&page=0&Itemid=49, 1–2.

81 *traditionally the hardest hit in economic declines.* . . . Walker, *Encyclopedia of African American Business History,* 150.

81   *who studies racial inequality and public policy.* . . . Ibid., 481.

81   in communities with large minority populations." . . . Ibid., 480–81 (emphasis added).

81   *communities, both of which can be very unstable.* . . . Ibid., 150.

82   *white corporate America and demand employment.".* . . . Walker, *The History of Black Business in America,* 273.

82   *by gaining jobs and using their consumer muscle.* . . . Dr. Juliet Walker, interview with author, January 23, 2011.

82   *specific goals to achieve black economic parity.".* . . . Dr. Juliet Walker, interview with author, January 24, 2011.

83   *"black capitalism" of the 1960s and '70s,* . . . Walker, *The History of Black Business in America,* 271.

83   *positive outcomes for the Virtual Black Community."* . . . iZania, http://www.izania.com/info/about/about-izania/.

83   *$100.5 billion in purchases from minority-owned businesses.* . . . NMSDC, http://www.nmsdc.org/nmsdc/app/template/contentMgmt%2CContentPage.vm/contentid/1319;jsessionid=9FADD104329DE83648411E2BB9B491C2.

84   *a way to build a community that is self-sustaining.* . . . Harvest Institute, http://www.harvestinstitute.org/.

84   *was estimated at about $913 billion in 2008,* . . . Addy et al., "The Empowerment Experiment," 243.

84   *Canada and Turkey, and above Australia and Poland.* . . . Ibid., 248.

84   *African American buying power equal to that of Canada.* . . . Ibid., 249.

84   *pennies on the Black dollar" to the Black community.* . . . Ibid., 243.

85   *after-tax income of $75,000, or roughly 2.65 million families* . . . "Annual Social and Economic (ASEC) Supplement," US Census Bureau, http://www.census.gov/hhes/www/cpstables/032010/hhinc/new01_006.htm.

85   *twice the number of existing Subways in the world.)* . . . Addy et al., "The Empowerment Experiment," 247.

85   *can create 551,724 to 896,551 new jobs."* . . . Ibid., 247.

86   *The answer: $32.2 billion.* . . . Ibid., 243.

Chapter 6

96   *Baby Phat Line, and Sean "Diddy" Combs' Sean John line.* . . . "Blacks in the Fashion Industry," Maxizip.com, January 29, 2010, http://maxizip.com/2010/11/blacks-in-the-fashion-industry/.

96   *few big players because that business is challenging."* . . . Gary Lampley, interview with author, February 4, 2011.

96   *has a great deal of talent but lacks access to capital."* . . . Ibid.

97   *amassing of capital comes from generations.*"... Steven Rogers, interview with author, January 31, 2011.

97   *the chance for that intergenerational wealth.*"... Ibid.

97   *wealth among Whites and Asians is eleven times higher.*... Fairlie and Robb, *Race and Entrepreneurial Success*, 3.

98   *1 to 1.7 percent higher than what White-owned firms paid.*... David G. Blanchflower, Phillip B. Levine, and David J. Zimmerman, *Discrimination in the Small Business Credit Market* (Cambridge, MA: National Bureau of Economic Research, 2002).

Chapter 7

119   *of the White community and the Black community.*"... Clarence B. Jones, interview with author, October 8, 2010.

119   *and the capital assets in the White community.*"... Ibid.

120   *who were always economically disadvantaged,*" Jones said.... Ibid.

Chapter 8

130   *only comfort we should expect will be in an afterlife.*"... Stephens, *Talking Dollars and Making Sense*, 20.

131   *it is time to claim it as being long past due.*"... Ibid., 22.

131   *financial problems that exist in the Black community.*"... Ibid., 16.

131   *anything that can be considered racially divisive.*"... Dr. Juliet Walker, interview with author, October 6, 2010.

132   *what they've acquired than some of the older ones.*"... Jones interview, October 8, 2010.

134   *What people chose to do with that remains to be seen.*"... Ted Gregory, "Adding Up Family's Year Buying Black," *Chicago Tribune*, January 11, 2010.

139   *benefits of reforms can further compound resistance.*"... Raghuram Rajan, "Crabs in a Bucket: Why Constituencies Are as Important as Constitutions in Battling Underdevelopment," *Finance & Development* 43, no. 2 (June 2006): 4.

139   *and I'll never have anything, so why try?*"... Stephens, *Talking Dollars and Making Sense*, 22.

139   *whites drove blacks out of their trades.*"... Jessie Carney Smith, ed., *The Encyclopedia of African American Business* (Westport, CT: Greenwood Press, 2006), xxviii.

140   *highly suspicious charges of raping White women.*... Walker interview, October 6, 2010.

140 *as punishment for those dubious allegations of rape.* . . . Arthur F. Raper, "Lynchings and What They Mean," Southern Commission on the Study of Lynching, 1931.

140 *political competition from their poorer Black neighbors.* . . . Raper, "Lynchings and What They Mean."

140 *White tension over economic competition from Blacks.* . . . Gregory Mixon and Clifford Kuhn, "Atlanta Race Riot of 1906," The New Georgia Encyclopedia, http://www.georgiaencyclopedia.org/nge/Article.jsp?id=h-3033; Steven Essig, "Race Riots," Encyclopedia of Chicago, http://encyclopedia.chicago history.org/pages/1032.html.

141 *beauty supply industry, which generates over $9 billion a year.* . . . Jeff Stilson, *Good Hair*, Roadside Attractions, Los Angeles, CA, 2009.

141 *people who are inflicted with their own sense of inferiority."* . . . Jones interview, October 8, 2010.

Chapter 10

170 *of the average sales for White-owned businesses.* . . . Robert W. Fairlie and Alicia M. Robb "Why Are Black-Owned Businesses Less Successful than White-Owned Businesses? The Role of Families, Inheritances, and Business Human Capital," *Journal of Labor Economics* 25, no. 2 (2007): 293.

170 *compared to 30.4 percent for White-owned firms.* . . . Ibid.

170 *40 percent of all Black-owned firms had negative profits.* . . . Ibid.

170 *Black firms were one-half that of white firms.* . . . Ibid.

171 *a family member's business before starting their own.* . . . Ibid., 290.

171 *For White households, that figure was nearly $98,000.* . . . Lynnette Khalfani-Cox, "The State of Wealth in Black America," *Ebony* (August 2011), http://stage.ebonyjet.com/CurrentIssue/Aug2011_The_State_of_Black_Wealth_in_America.aspx.

171 *27.4 percent of non-minority-owned businesses.* . . . Ying Lowrey, "Dynamics of Minority-Owned Employer Establishments 1997–2001" US Small Business Administration, Office of Advocacy, February 2005, http://archive.sba.gov/advo/research/rs251tot.pdf, 1.

171 *access to capital and less management and technical training.* . . . Alicia M. Robb and Robert W. Fairlie, "Access to Financial Capital Among U.S. Businesses: The Case of African-American Firms," *The Annals of the American Academy of Political and Social Sciences* 613, no. 1 (September 2007): 47–72; Steve Bergsman, "Accounting for Small Businesses," *Black Enterprise* (November 1992): 37, http://books.google.com/books?id=0Qx9M76jn7gC&pg=PA37&lpg=PA37&dq=lack+of+managerial+skills+in+Black-owned+businesses&source=bl&ots=Ey2TXv-Syc&sig=V8gZAI4IX4OuVycFcdK3LahiJ1Y&hl=en&ei=aO

oeTo3lLuzLsQKSwOC1Bw&sa=X&oi=book_result&ct=result&resnum=2&v
ed=0CCEQ6AEwAQ#v=onepage&q=lack%20of%20managerial%20skills%
20in%20Black-owned%20businesses&f=false.

172   *black-owned firms are associated with less successful businesses."* . . . Fairlie and
      Robb, "Why Are Black-Owned Businesses Less Successful than White-
      Owned Businesses?" 309.

172   *the rate for White business owners was 23.3 percent.* . . . Ibid., 296.

172   *general and specific business human capital."* . . . Ibid., 312.

178   *Foster, founder of the Negro National Baseball League.* . . . "History of
      Bronzeville," Bronzeville Area Residents and Commerce Council, http://
      www.thebarcc.org/history.php.

178   *accumulated real estate holdings totaling $100 million.* . . . John McWhorter,
      "Toward a Usable Black History," *City Journal* (Summer 2001), http://
      www.city-journal.org/html/11_3_toward_a_usable.html.

178   *Bronzeville, rose 67 and 192 percent, respectively."* . . . Derek S. Hyra, *The
      New Urban Renewal: The Economic Transformation of Harlem and Bronzeville*
      (Chicago: University of Chicago Press, 2008), 43.

178   *the White population grew to 4 percent.* . . . Ibid., 167.

178   *the White population is now closer to 6.6 percent.* . . . "Douglas Neighbor-
      hood," Great Cities Institute Neighborhoods at the University of Illinois at
      Chicago, http://www.uicni.org/page.php?section=neighborhoods&subsection
      =douglas.

179   *individuals who have lived in these communities."* . . . Kelly Virella, "Beyond
      Burnham: Black and White, Seeing Red All Over," *The Chicago Reporter*,
      August 31, 2009, 5, http://www.chicagoreporter.com/index.php/c/Cover
      _Stories/d/Black_And_White,_Seeing_Red_All_Over.

179   *that those merchants are following the money.* . . . Ibid., 3.

179   *once-impoverished neighborhoods like Bronzeville.* . . . Hyra, *The New Urban
      Renewal,* 130.

179   *Sheryll Cashin calls "integration exhaustion."* . . . Sheryll Cashin, *The Failures
      of Integration: How Race and Class Are Undermining the American Dream*
      (New York: PublicAffairs, 2004), 5.

179   *also influence the changes that occur in a neighborhood.* . . . Hyra, *The New
      Urban Renewal,* 147.

179   *property values and the displacement of the poor."* . . . Ibid., 149.

180   *the neediest to other high-poverty neighborhoods.* . . . Ibid., 146.

180   *"historic preservation and racial heritage tourism."* . . . Michelle Boyd, "The
      Downside of Racial Uplift: The Meaning of Gentrification in an African
      American Neighborhood," *City & Society* 17, no. 2 (2005): 271.

180   *a version of the "rising tide lifts all boats" aphorism.* . . . Ibid., 274, 276.

181   *cost of neighborhood goods and services," Boyd notes.* . . . Ibid., 281–83.

181 *Whites and neighborhoods looking to catch a break. . . .* Mary Pattillo, "Introduction," *Black on the Block: The Politics of Race and Class in the City* (Chicago: University of Chicago Press, 2007).

181 *simultaneously debates over what it means to be black." . . .* Ibid.

182 *higher-end stores in Bronzeville were somewhat scarce. . . .* Joslyn Slaughter, interview with author, October 8, 2010.

182 *learn that we deserve to live in a different environment." . . .* Ibid.

183 *nice amenities like everybody else." . . .* Ibid.

186 *only serve to strengthen the whites in power." . . .* Sudhir Alladi Venkatesh, "Urban Puzzle," *Boston Globe*, March 31, 2007, 4.

Chapter 11

188 *She definitely made an impact." . . .* Joyce King, e-mail to Chike Akua, November 4, 2009.

191 *in the United States, six of which are in Chicago. . . .* "Mexican Grocery Stores in the United States," http://www.fyple.com/category/food-drink/food-retailer/grocery-store/mexican-grocery-store/.

191 *other areas of the country with large numbers of Hispanics. . . .* Steve Raabe, "Latino-Grocery Boom Likely to Slow as Second-Generation Shoppers Surge," *Denver Post*, March 11, 2010, http://www.denverpost.com/business/ci_14651611.

Epilogue

204 *African American businesses that we otherwise wouldn't have. . . .* Addy et al., "The Empowerment Experiment," 235.

205 *something with which Karriem might take issue. . . .* Ibid., 249.

205 *their diversity can be seen as valuable and appealing. . . .* Ibid., 252.

205 *in the Black population that have yet to be achieved." . . .* Ibid., 256.

206 *traditional investments by mainstream venture capitalists." . . .* Timothy Bates and William Bradford, "Minorities and Venture Capital: A New Wave in American Business," Kansas City, MO, Kauffman Foundation, 2003, http://www.kauffman.org/uploadedFiles/minorities_vc_report.pdf.

206 *an economic argument that says this is good for business." . . .* Steven Rogers, interview with author, January 31, 2011.

207 *nationwide, including 126 owned by African Americans. . . .* Information provided by Donna Meacham Blackman, CPA, Vice President, Finance, Global Lodging Services FBP, Marriott International Inc.

208 *"to be wealth creators, instead of wealth spenders." . . .* New York Life agent promotional material for The $50 Billion Empowerment Plan.

209　*sense of community in neighborhood after neighborhood.* . . . . "Starbucks Acquires Remaining Interest in Magic Johnson Enterprises' Urban Coffee Opportunities," Starbucks Newsroom, October 21, 2010, http://news.starbucks .com/article_display.cfm?article_id=452.

211　*needed," I felt my heart drop into my stomach.* . . . Slaughter interview, October 8, 2010.

212　*who are not comfortable with the status quo."* . . . Corey Tabor, interview with author, February 28, 2011.

216　*social and economic pathologies in our communities."* . . . Jones interview, October 12, 2010.

Index

CREDIT: RANDY FLING

Maggie Anderson is CEO and cofounder, along with her husband, of The Empowerment Experiment and The Empowerment Experiment Foundation. Since the completion of the Andersons' landmark experiment, Maggie has become the leader of a self-help economics movement that brings together business owners, consumers, corporations, and professional and activist groups to make sure more quality Black-owned businesses get supported—as stand-alone entities and as suppliers, vendors, and franchises. A sought-after speaker, she is the new voice of "conscious consumerism," representing American consumers of all backgrounds who want to make sure their buying power positively impacts struggling communities. She has appeared on CNN, MSNBC, Fox News, and *CBS Morning News* as well as many other national television and radio shows. She received her BA from Emory University and her JD and MBA from the University of Chicago. She lives in Oak Park, Illinois, with her husband, John, and their two daughters.

Ted Gregory is a Pulitzer Prize–winning reporter for the *Chicago Tribune*.

For more information, visit http://eefortomorrow.com.

PublicAffairs is a publishing house founded in 1997. It is a tribute to the standards, values, and flair of three persons who have served as mentors to countless reporters, writers, editors, and book people of all kinds, including me.

I. F. STONE, proprietor of *I. F. Stone's Weekly*, combined a commitment to the First Amendment with entrepreneurial zeal and reporting skill and became one of the great independent journalists in American history. At the age of eighty, Izzy published *The Trial of Socrates*, which was a national bestseller. He wrote the book after he taught himself ancient Greek.

BENJAMIN C. BRADLEE was for nearly thirty years the charismatic editorial leader of *The Washington Post*. It was Ben who gave the *Post* the range and courage to pursue such historic issues as Watergate. He supported his reporters with a tenacity that made them fearless and it is no accident that so many became authors of influential, best-selling books.

ROBERT L. BERNSTEIN, the chief executive of Random House for more than a quarter century, guided one of the nation's premier publishing houses. Bob was personally responsible for many books of political dissent and argument that challenged tyranny around the globe. He is also the founder and longtime chair of Human Rights Watch, one of the most respected human rights organizations in the world.

. . .

For fifty years, the banner of Public Affairs Press was carried by its owner Morris B. Schnapper, who published Gandhi, Nasser, Toynbee, Truman, and about 1,500 other authors. In 1983, Schnapper was described by *The Washington Post* as "a redoubtable gadfly." His legacy will endure in the books to come.

Peter Osnos, *Founder and Editor-at-Large*